PERSONAL DEVELOPMENT IN COUNSELLING AND PSYCHOTHERAPY

SOFIE BAGER-CHARLESON

Learning Matters
An imprint of SAGE Publications Ltd
1 Oliver's Yard
55 City Road
London EC1Y 1SP

SAGE Publications Inc.
2455 Teller Road
Thousand Oaks, California 91320

SAGE Publications India Pvt Ltd
B 1/I 1 Mohan Cooperative Industrial Area
Mathura Road
New Delhi 110 044

SAGE Publications Asia-Pacific Pte Ltd
3 Church Street
#10–04 Samsung Hub
Singapore 049483

Editor: Luke Block
Development editor: Lauren Simpson
Production controller: Chris Marke
Project management: Diana Chambers
Marketing manager: Tamara Navaratnam
Cover design: Wendy Scott
Typeset by: Kelly Winter
Copy editor: Sue Edwards
Printed by: Ashford Colour Press Ltd.

Library of Congress Control Number:
2012938959

British Library Cataloguing in Publication Data

A catalogue record for this book is available from the British Library

ISBN 978 14462 5 711 1
ISBN 978 08572 5 935 6 (pbk)

Contents

Foreword

Many theorists claim that therapy is an interpretive activity in which the therapist seeks to understand the client's world. However, therapists' interpretations are influenced by their personal mode of being and, therefore, understanding the therapist's self is as important as understanding the client's self. If therapists want to understand their clients better, then they need to understand themselves better.

Sofie Bager-Charleson is firmly established as a commentator on the role that reflective practice and personal development play in both the training and evolving professional lives of counsellors and psychotherapists, and that is why this book is so valuable. Both trainee therapists and experienced practitioners can benefit from regularly attending to their own personal development and the pages within offer a step-by-step guide to that process.

It is important that personal and professional development for counsellors and psychotherapists is a planned, purposeful, monitored and, most importantly, lifelong process. Sofie eloquently tells us how this works in theory and in practice. Sofie also reminds us that Freud called therapy 'an impossible profession' but she doesn't let that show-stopping pronounce-ment defeat her. Instead, she shows us how to use reflective learning and practice to become increasingly self-aware and aware of the impact our 'therapist selves' has on our clients.

A core strength of this book is the way in which Sofie explores the idea of a therapist's personal development as an ever-evolving process and she provides some very practical guidance for promoting and monitoring this process for ourselves. Sofie also examines the concept of being a 'good enough' practitioner. This does not mean that therapists can 'get by' with a minimal level of professional expertise; it means being good enough for the task in hand while acknowledging that personal development is a fundamental professional responsibility. This developmental need is not essential to just counsellor and psychotherapist training; it is a vital factor in the higher educational process generally because criticality, including self-criticality, is central to post-graduate study. That is why the learning outcomes of this series are targeted to meet the requirements of an educationally sophisticated readership.

Personal development is a challenging process and not for the faint-hearted. For therapists the process is not even a private one: supervisors and trainers are also involved in an interactive, two-way procedure. Helpfully, Sofie examines the central issues that impact on these vital developmental tasks and shows us how to manage them. If, as therapists, we can face the fears that self-exploration can sometimes engender, then we will be better equipped to empathetically travel with our clients as they too embark on a journey to face their own fears.

All therapists, from trainee to advanced practitioner, are constantly researching their clients. As they do this they cannot avoid researching themselves; it is an unavoidable consequence of the nature of the therapeutic relationship. This is why Marie Adams' chapter, in which she discusses the value of research as part of the ongoing therapist's personal development process, is especially valuable. She places reflective research firmly at the boundary between therapists' personal and professional lives. Inevitably, this is a potential source of intrapersonal conflict. Marie explores how resolving such conflict is a vital part of being able to meet clients' needs.

Beverley Costa's chapter is an excellent example of 'praxis' – the application of learning to action. She helps us to place our learning from this book into a practical context and bravely tells us about how her own experiences and reflective learning made her the advanced practitioner that she is today.

By the end of the book Sofie shows us how to become a 'listener with a voice' and offers us practical tips on how to manage the practicalities of attending to our individual developmental needs. She tells us how to plan our own developmental journeys, and how to find the balances and checks that are right for our individual circumstances.

Finally, while therapy might have been called an 'impossible profession', we certainly don't have to be 'impossible professionals'. The guidance, advice, activities, case studies and reflection points within these pages show us exactly how focusing on our personal development can make us into some very 'possible' practitioners indeed.

Dr Norman Claringbull
Series Editor
www.normanclaringbull.com

About the author and contributors

Sofie Bager-Charleson is a psychotherapist, supervisor and writer. She draws from psychoanalytic, existential and cognitive behavioural theory with a particular interest in postmodern influences on therapy. She holds a PhD from Lund University in Sweden, where she specialised in attachment issues within families and reflective practice among teachers. She writes both fiction and non-fiction. She works as an academic adviser for psychotherapists on the work-based doctorate programme, DPsych, at Metanoia/ Middlesex University. She runs workshops and courses in therapeutic practice, and on reflective and creative writing, in both Sweden and England.

Dr Marie Adams is a psychotherapist and writer. Along with her private practice in Exeter, she is also associated with the Metanoia Institute in London and the Iron Mill Institute in Devon. She is a consultant psychotherapist with the BBC, where she gives workshops on Understanding Trauma and Mental Health to journalists and production staff. Marie's academic research has focused particularly on the private lives of therapists and how this impacts on their work with clients and patients. Her book on the subject is scheduled for publication in 2013.

Dr Beverley Costa is trained as a group and individual psychotherapist and psychodramatist, with a doctorate in Psychotherapy from Metanoia/ Middlesex University. She has worked in multicultural educational organisations, and is the founder and Director of Mothertongue – a culturally sensitive therapeutic support service for people from black and minority ethnic communities. Mothertongue was founded in 2007 and has won numerous awards, such as the award of Excellence in the Practice of Counselling and Psychotherapy from the BACP in 2008 and the Queen's Award for Voluntary Service.

Acknowledgements

I should like to thank the many colleagues, students and clients who, directly and indirectly, have contributed material to this book. I am particularly grateful to Marie Adams and Beverley Costa: thank you for sharing ideas, visions and for each contributing a chapter.

There are innumerable others who have made important contributions such as Maxine Daniels, with her insightful research about victim empathy programs for sex offenders. In addition, my colleagues, students and supervisees at Metanoia have all been instrumental. Our doctorate, DPsych at Metanoia, is an exciting environment in which to work. Our students are experienced practitioners and bring new perspectives to both clinical practice and research. I have redrafted many chapters after our exciting discussions and would like to express my gratitude for your input. My friends and writing buddies Francesca Thorpe, Susan McGrath, Sheila Lauchlan, Pam Critchley and Sherna Ghyara Chatterjee are also valued contributors. Our regular chats provide me with an invaluable sense of direction and meaning in clinical practice as well as life in general. A special thanks to you, Francesca.

I would also like to thank my supportive editors Lauren Simpson, Luke Block and Norman Claringbull for their patience, knowledge and enthusiasm.

Thank you too, to my mother Anna-Lena for reminding me regularly about the joys of creative writing, and for showing such an interest in my work. That is much appreciated.

Finally, I'd like to take this opportunity to express my love to Dermot and Fina, Finbar and Leo. I should have liked to indulge in the subject of how much you mean to me and how wonderful I think you are – each and every one of you. But to save you the embarrassment I limit myself to saying thank you for being and for bringing purpose and meaning to everything I do.

Introduction

All training involves changes, but therapy training involves particularly deep shifts in its students. Trainee therapists are not only altering their thinking and developing new skills, but will also, as Folkes-Skinner et al. (2010, p19) put it, *adapt their personality*. Some therapists may be prepared for this. Others, like myself, are taken by surprise. I have written this book with my own initial confusion and with the subsequent experiences of supervisees, students and numerous colleagues and friends in mind.

Chapter 1 examines how to integrate personal development in our professional learning and vice versa. An essential part of therapy training is *the task of learning how to creatively and effectively use oneself in the treatment process* (Klein et al., 2011, p297). This raises questions around what skills are taught and what personal assets must already be there, from the start. What might separate a lay helper from a professional helper? What might be considered as common themes with regard to therapists' development across the entire spans of their careers?

Chapter 2 looks at the concept of 'good enough' therapists. Who chooses to become a therapist in the first place, and why? The ACCTT model is introduced as a way of conceptualising transformative learning where mistakes and critical incidents on a personal as well as professional level can become something we learn from – 're-use' or 'recycle' into constructive learning experiences. The ACCTT model is introduced in the context of 'reflexive awareness' and reflective, double-loop learning.

Chapter 3 focuses on trust and support for personal and professional growth. Therapists are, ironically, often good at hiding their own weaknesses. We will explore obstacles such as shame, lack of trust and other factors that can prevent helpers from receiving support.

In Chapter 4, we will look at modalities. As therapists, we are requested to choose between different theoretical orientations. How do we do that? On what basis do we arrive at knowledge and 'truths' within therapy? Are there any real rights or wrongs, true or false, when it comes to the kinds of wounding and healing with which we are faced? Research shows that the development of an orientation is 'emotionally daunting' and the novice stage has been compared to 'trekking with a crude map'. We will look closely at some of the core modalities, and will explore therapy in the context of what critical hermeneutics refers to as a dialectic process, where we move between a 'narrative' and an 'explanatory commitment', to understand both 'with' and 'about' our clients.

In Chapter 5 we approach the idea of a therapist's explanatory commitment in more detail. We will explore different types of motifs behind theoretical orientations, ranging from a postmodern focus on power to considering therapists' potential unique and personal motivations. We also return to the idea of double looping, and will look at different therapists' own under-standing of their theoretical framework. We shall meet therapists with different personal and professional backgrounds, and will follow their attempts to make sense of personal and socio-cultural experiences in the context of their choice of modality and way of working. We shall look at reflective writing as a form of research – a way of 're-searching' or critically reviewing experiences with new perspectives in mind.

Chapter 6 focuses on practice-based research. We will explore the link between everyday practice and research. We will look at the rationale for practice-based research, and explore some of the stages in terms of problem formulation, literature review, choice of method, etc. Practice-based research is illustrated further, in Chapter 7, where Dr Marie Adams presents her research into the field of how therapists' personal crises may impact on their work. What happens when a therapist experiences a crisis in her own life? When should we work and when is it best not to, as problems surface in our own lives? Marie reflects on these questions after interviewing 40 therapists from three different countries about their ways of handling the boundaries between their personal and professional selves.

In Chapter 8, transformative learning is examined with reference to Beverley Costa's decision to provide a new therapy service. What happens if we cannot find our niche within existing services? In this chapter, Beverley, the founder of the multilingual therapy agency Mothertongue, reflects on how cultural tensions have impacted upon her life and her subsequent choice of orientation as a therapist. Beverley offers a personal account of some of the complexities involved in finding a mode of training that reflects the complexities of being from an ethnic minority. She shares some of the practical, theoretical and emotional learning as part of this process.

Chapter 9 turns the focus back on to the reader. Therapists are, as Kottler (2011) suggests, often separated from the outside world 'ensconced in a soundproof chamber'. How does this 'compartmentalised isolation' affect the therapist? This chapter looks at the balance between hearing and being heard. Do you experience 'flow' at work? Have you got the right support and inspiration to experience a balanced life? Writing and drawing/painting are suggested as valuable additions for the listener with a voice.

CHAPTER 1

What is personal development?

CORE KNOWLEDGE

- Personal development and personal development planning are incorporated in most forms of training today. Personal development involves a deliberate attempt to review, plan and take responsibility for our own learning.
- What constitutes a 'skilled' counsellor and psychotherapist? What skills are taught and what personal assets must already be in place?

LISTENING TO OTHERS

We are listeners. We relate to people. Can that really be a profession? What does this listening and relating actually mean? This book shares psychoanalyst Donnel Stern's idea that therapy responds to a deep-seated need for relatedness.

There are many different ways of construing the aims and objectives of psychotherapy. The assumption guiding my view of therapy is that we provide people with a place where they can listen to themselves. We can think for ourselves but might only *really listen to ourselves through the other's ears*, as Stern puts it:

> If we are to know our own experience in reflective terms, if we are to be able not only to construct narratives, but to be aware of the narrative we construct, we do need to feel that we are known by the other . . . Our witness is our partner in thought.

> (2010, p111)

Relatedness is the nexus from which experiences emerges, writes Stern (2010, p4). From babyhood onwards, we need witnesses to 'make experience coherent and real'. The therapeutic relationship is approached in this book as a response to this need for 'partners in thoughts' as 'part of the process of self-formation'.

Carl Rogers, the founder of person-centred therapy, refers to this kind of understanding in terms of understanding *with* the person, not *about*:

> [U]nderstanding with a person, not about him, is such an effective approach that it can bring about major changes. [I]t means to see the expressed ideas and attitudes from the other person's point of view, to sense how it feels to him, achieve his frame of reference to the things he is talking about.
>
> (1961, p226)

My experience of therapy both as a client and as a therapist, as both Stern and Rogers propose, is that something happens to us when we are being really heard. Rogers describes this beautifully:

> I have often noticed that the more deeply I hear the meanings of [the other] person, the more there is that happens. Almost always when a person realises he has been deeply heard, his eyes moisten . . . It is as though he [has been] tapping out a message in Morse code . . . 'Does anybody hear me? Is anybody there?' And finally one day he hears some faint tapping which spells out 'Yes'. By that simple response he is released from his loneliness; he has become a human being again.
>
> (1995, p10)

'Real' understanding is a very rare form of understanding. It is something unusual in today's society. We do not normally permit ourselves to hear from another person's perspective, continues Rogers: *Our first reaction to most statements which we hear from other people is an immediate evaluation, or judgement, rather than an understanding of [them]* (1961, p18).

In order to 'understand precisely' where another person is coming from, we need to 'enter thoroughly and completely and empathically' into another person's 'frame of reference'. Rogers reflects on how this kind of hearing invariably brings changes in both parties. 'Real' hearing is 'risky':

> When someone expresses a feeling or attitude or belief, our tendency is, almost immediately to feel 'That's right'; 'That's stupid' . . . I believe this is because understanding is risky. If I let myself really understand another person, I might be changed by that understanding [myself].
>
> (1961, p18)

PHENOMENOLOGY

Modalities often overlap. The underpinning theories of the psychoanalytic Stern and the person-centred Rogers merge, for instance, in their attempt to share the client's lived experience. One aspect of a 'good therapy' is here addressed in terms of a willingness and ability to understand 'the phenom-enological experience' of the client. Therapy involves an exploration of the world as it appears to the client, i.e. a phenomenological inquiry. The concept of phenomenology derives from the Greek words *phainómenon* ('that which appears') and *lógos* ('study') and concerns itself thus with things, phenomena, as they appear to us in light of our particular lived experiences. The philosopher Maurice Merleau-Ponty specialised in the 'phenomenology of perception' and asserted, like all existentialists, that there is no one 'fixed' meaning with life to be 'found':

> *Phenomenology . . . does not believe that man and the world can be understood on the basis of their state of fact . . . We must not wonder if we really perceive the world. Rather we must say that the world is that which I perceive . . .*
>
> (Merleau-Ponty, in Friedman, 1999, p86)

Most therapeutic models agree on the value of a phenomenological under-standing. It is when it comes to communicating back our understanding, and assisting clients in their attempts to interpret and reconstruct the significance of events, that differences in opinion between therapists can emerge. One important aspect of therapeutic mastery is, as Klein et al. (2011, p289) assert, *to learn how to organise, evaluate, and convey information that is gathered.* There comes a point when we have to revert to our own under-standing as a point of reference, and learning to reflect over this is, as suggested earlier, an essential skill in therapy. As Rogers implies, 'real' hearing usually involves allowing ourselves to change with the client. Stern stresses, in turn, how the therapist invariably brings his or her own lived experiences and pre-understandings into the relationship. This can create both opportunities and potential problems.

PERSONAL DEVELOPMENT

Personal development encourages us to consider 'the engine' that drives us. It requires a third-person perspective on one's professional life and raises questions about how we integrate our personal experiences and develop-ment in our professional planning. What drives us and why? What are our weaknesses and where lie our strengths? And how do different training and career options respond to these? What impact do we have on clients? How does a certain client affect us? Personal development addresses questions ranging from our emotional responses to situations and people, and our basic beliefs surrounding knowledge, to trustworthiness and truth. How do we think therapy works, and why? On what basis do we generate our knowledge and reach conclusions that we regard as 'true'?

Personal development is incorporated into most areas of study today – it can be taught as a core subject or as part of career-planning modules. It encourages us to review, plan and take responsibility for our own learning and professional development, often in the form of personal development planning (PDP). The Quality Assurance Agency (QAA) defines PDP as follows:

> *Personal development planning is a structured and supported process undertaken by an individual to reflect upon their own learning, performance and/or achievement and to plan for their personal, educational and career development.*
>
> (QAA, 2004, p4)

Personal development is, admittedly, an ambiguous concept. As Spencer (2006, p109) puts it: *There are surprisingly few guidelines on personal development training, other than that courses should devote time to it.* A significant feature in all references to personal development is the image of individuals as lifelong and self-directed learners.

There is also a slightly darker side to the emphasis on our personal responsibility for our professional development. Personal development has developed in the context of limited or unpredictable employment opportunities. For good or for bad, lifelong employment can no longer be expected within any field of work and the responsibility for a prosperous career rests increasingly on the shoulders of the individual. Young people are being advised to prepare to change career more than once during their working life. Flexibility and being prepared to adapt are key concepts in any type of career planning today. This uncertainty holds, at the same time, great opportunities. It encourages us to consider our options both carefully and creatively, rather than entering into professional life routinely, habitually or without much prior thought.

Personal development brings important questions into our career planning. It synthesises and draws from:

- **reflective practice theory** with its focus on the underlying values of the practitioner;
- **evidence-based theory** with its emphasis on transparency and accountability; and
- **critical psychology**, which highlights how *psychological health or ill-health will depend on past philosophical traditions, current socioeconomic and political climates and battles over power* (Youngson, 2009, p15).

ACTIVITY 1.1

Dorothea Brande, who coined the concept of 'creative writing' in the 1930s, contends that writing is about turning ourselves and our experiences into objects of attention. This activity is intended to be what Brande calls *a primer lesson in considering oneself objectively.* Brande (1934/1996, p55) writes:

You are near a door . . . put the book aside, get up, and go through that door. From the moment you stand on the threshold turn yourself into your own object of attention. What do you look like, standing there? How do you walk? What, if you knew nothing about yourself, could be gathered of you, your character, your background, your purpose just there at just that minute? If there are people in the room whom you must greet, how do you greet them? How do your attitudes to them vary? Do you give any overt sign that you are fonder of one, or more aware of one, than the rest?

• Try to capture your impressions of yourself in the doorway. Write down as much as you can and put it aside until later.

PERSONAL DEVELOPMENT IN MENTAL HEALTH

The idea of ongoing career planning involves continuous reassessment of goals and aims. Clinical staff within the NHS are, for example, required to produce a PDP on an annual basis. Personal development is one of the *essential shared capabilities*, which require keeping *up-to-date with changes in practice and participating in life-long learning, personal and professional development for one's self and colleagues through supervision, appraisal and reflective practice* (ESC, Department of Health, 2004, p3).

Knowledge, skills and awareness are, as Johns (2002, p4) puts it, the tenets of our *traditional trinity revered in adult education*; and it is the *awareness* that specifically *underpins purposeful personal development*. People within the helping professions are seldom, if ever, engaged in solely technical tasks. The knowledge required for our kind of work is, as Johns (2002, p5) puts it, *more than sterile theory and skills [and] not merely a mechanistic means to an end.* Scaife agrees and concludes that: *the term personal and professional development acknowledges that I carry out my work as an expression of who I am* (2010, p49).

Our principal tool is our self. It ought to, as Johns puts it:

be unarguable that personal development – a consistent and continual striving for self and other awareness, knowledge, understanding and

acceptance – should be an essential and indeed pre-eminent element in
counselling training at any level, in any theoretical orientation.

(2002, p3)

DEVELOPING WITHIN AN 'IMPOSSIBLE PROFESSION'

Sigmund Freud (1900/1976) described therapy as an 'impossible' profession. His reference is likely to revolve around the idea of 'transference', and his ideas about clients revisiting early relationships with their therapist. When clients like us too much, said Freud, we should watch out for idealisations and displaced emotions; and when they dislike us intensely we have to 'sit with' the experience and welcome it as part of what the client tried to communicate as his or her problem. Freud's comparison with politics and parenting offers us also an opportunity to go beyond the issue of transference and consider the role of the therapist in the context of the complexity involved in all forms of 'carer' and helper roles:

> *It almost looks like analysis is the third of those 'impossible' professions*
> *in which one can be quite sure of unsatisfying results. The other two, much*
> *older-established, are the bringing up of children and the government of*
> *nations.*

(1900/1976, p45)

There is an inherent ambivalence in all strands of helping. A relationship based on caring for others is riddled with ambiguities; it is open to a range of misunderstandings with regard to giving and receiving, closeness and independency. The 'cycle of caring' involves, as Skovholt and Trotter-Mathison affirm:

> *making positive attachments, being engaged and making positive*
> *separations . . . It is this endless cycle of caring, with distinct phases, that*
> *makes up the life of the practitioner . . . It is not easy to be skilled at each*
> *phase, because they are distinct and call for different practitioner attributes.*

(2011, pp21–2)

The cycle of caring involves attachments and separations, openings and closures, over and over again. We are close, we merge and hear as 'partners in thought' (Stern, 2010) and will then need to step away to make sense in light of who we are, where we come from and where we want to be in the near future – as persons and as professionals. Skovholt and Trotter-Mathison (2011, p21) assert that: *as with good parenting, the challenge is to be good at both attachment (roots) and separation (wings).*

What separates a lay helper, such as a friend or family member, from a professional helper is, stress Skovholt and Trotter-Mathison (2011, p56), the need for *self-consciousness or reflectivity about the helping process*. In Case study 1.1, Zack Eleftheriadou (2010, pp180, 176) reflects on her experiences from her work with torture victims. Her account illustrates how a day's work for a therapist often involves great tragedies to which both the client and the therapist react strongly, and how it is the therapist's role to contain them both.

Case study 1.1

The task of tackling the perverse experience of torture and being able to experience a healing relationship is a long and difficult one. The therapist may struggle to encourage the person to reclaim a sense of space, self, body and mind as they hear from the client how they have been abused by the persecutor. Similarly, the therapist can experience a fear that, like the client who feels they will never be rid of the oppressor, they cannot get rid of the client's stories. It becomes vital to tune into the individual level of tolerance of such experiences and, subsequently, the ability to experience them again in therapy. Ambiguous feelings towards the torturers may have to be explored, which may also be unconsciously transferred to the therapist [. . .] Countertransference of the therapist can include feelings of hopelessness and helplessness, a sense of paralysis and impotence . . . Countertransference is a complicated process and it consists of not only what is evoked by the client's material, but how it makes an individual therapist react, linked to their personal story.

COMMENT

Eleftheriadou refers to the psychoanalytically inspired concepts of trans-ference and countertransference. However, regardless of the theoretical orientation, the therapist needs to be prepared for different types of trauma and strong emotions on many levels. Some of these feelings are invoked in the therapist by the client. The example below shows a common situation in which the therapist aims to contain a client who struggles with her sense of self worth. Cashdan (1988, p130) recounts an experience with a client who projects her feelings of being unlovable upon the therapist:

> Beth: *'Does it pay for me to keep coming?'*
> Therapist: *'I'll be here next week . . . same time, same place.'*
> Beth: *'I'm not sure I'll be coming.'*
> Therapist: *'You decide what's best. Just remember, this time is yours; I'll be here no matter what you decide.'*

Sometimes, the feelings evoked are linked to the therapist's personal story. Eleftheriadou (2010, p184) continues:

> *Understanding our part in the relationship can free the client to explore and understand their emotional world . . . [P]ersonal development and supervision . . . is not only desirable and useful, but of absolute necessity. It is a way of constantly monitoring and ensuring that we do not get too involved in the client's emotional experience.*

THE 'EVOLUTION' OF THE HELPER

During the last decade, some significant research has emerged in the field of personal development for counselling and psychotherapy. Orlinsky, Ronnestad, Skovholt and Trotter-Mathison are examples of therapists who have generated much research about *essential characteristics and development of the psychotherapist* (Orlinsky and Ronnestad, 2005, p16). Their findings are based on interviews, story-writing and large-scale surveys covering the experiences of nearly 5,000 therapists from over 20 countries. Trotter-Mathison et al. conclude:

> *The willingness of clients to address their vulnerability and weaknesses, while also recognising their strengths and resources, is an essential ingredient of optimal counselling and therapy. Similarly, practitioners' recognition of their own limitations, whilst also seeing the potential for transcending them, characterises professional development.*
>
> (2010, pix)

With reference to their large qualitative, interview-based research, Ronnestad and Skovholt (cited in Trotter-Mathison et al., 2010, p6) offer a model of counsellor/therapist development that is interesting to consider in light of the complexity involved in the therapeutic process. The model aims to describe the *evolution of therapists' development across the entire spans of their careers*.

1. The **lay helper** phase. A lay helper is *a novice who helps others in a non-professional setting [without] any formal training in counselling.* Ronnestad and Skovholt (cited in Trotter-Mathison et al., 2010, p6) assert that the lay helper can be prone to problem identification, advice giving and boundary issues. Trotter-Mathison et al. continue:

> *[In lay helping] there is a projection of one's own experiences and one's own solution to the life of the other. The lay helper often gives answers and these can have a base in the notion of common sense. There will usually not be a self-consciousness or reflectivity about the helping process.*
>
> (2010, p56)

2. The **beginning student** phase. This first stage of the training *signals a time of high dependency, vulnerability and anxiety in trainees as they seek out the 'right way' . . . [often] modelled by expert clinicians.* Trotter-Mathison et al. (2010, p59) highlight the temptation to elevate the anxiety either by retreating, or through 'clinging on to' one way of understanding the complex reality:

   There has been an increase in understanding the complexity of the professional world . . . If the anxiety is too strong the student may retreat. Leaving the field, or rigidly clinging on to one way of understanding reality (one theoretical approach), are two retreat styles that reduce the anxiety but, unfortunately, also reduce the capacity for cognitive complexity, a long-term key to senior expertise . . .

3. The **advanced student** phase. This stage involves an increased focus on the reactions of the therapist. Trotter-Mathison et al. (2010, p6) suggest that students at this stage typically *value time not only to discuss skill development, but also to process how they are feeling about their experiences, supervision, and their own development.* It is usually a rather 'raw' stage of the development.

4. The **novice professional** phase. This is a phase when *therapists learn to increasingly incorporate their own personalities into treatment,* as Trotter-Mathison et al. (2010, p173) put it. This can be an unsettling experience. The ambiguity of emotions and meaning-making processes returns as an inevitable dimension of our work. The constraints of the training institute are left behind *but in their wake, therapists often discover that graduate school has not prepared them as well as hoped [for an] independent practice.* To develop, as Klein et al. (2011, p278) put it, *skilful use of self* characterised by self-awareness and the 'know-thyself' principle, personal therapy, supervision, readings and peers become essential means of support.

5. The **experienced professional** phase. This is a phase when Ronnestad and Skovholt (cited in Trotter-Mathison et al., 2010, p6) note *a focus on establishing authenticity.* They continue:

   Experienced professionals nearly universally recognise the centrality of the therapeutic relationship in contributing to client change. They also become increasingly comfortable with the necessary ambiguity in counselling interactions.

6. The **senior professional** phase. At this stage, *self-confidence is often tempered by acknowledgement of the real limitations of their impact on*

client change with an increased focus on the client as hero (Ronnestad and Skovholt, cited in Trotter-Mathison et al., 2010, p6). The senior therapist has typically worked for 20 years or more and often builds *a practice on their own authenticity and idiosyncratic approaches to the field.*

ACTIVITY 1.2

Writing is an essential way of providing you with your own 'spaces' for reflection.

- As you read this book you are encouraged to underline, scribble in the margins and use a separate notebook to record your thoughts, reactions and ideas.
- Take some time to consider each of the stages of the development addressed above. What issues resonate particularly with you? In which phase of the therapist's journey would you position yourself today? Write down three or four things relating to your personal and professional life that capture the stage that you are at right now.

EMOTIONAL RESILIENCE AND PSYCHOLOGICAL MINDEDNESS

Klein et al. explore the meaning of psychological mindedness with the following abilities in mind:

> *[Psychological mindedness involves] an interest in discovering the meaning of things, a curiosity about human motivation, a capacity for introspection, an interest in latent as well as manifest content, and a fundamental curiosity about what makes people tick.*

> (2011, p273)

The ability to mobilise inner resources and develop adaptive coping strategies is referred to by Skovholt and Trotter-Mathison (2011) and Klein et al. (2011, p274) as a form of *emotional resilience*. O'Leary (in Klein et al., 2011, p38) asserts that *resilience is a vital component of psychological-mindedness and a critical attribute of the effective therapist.* Another side of psychological mindedness is, as suggested, openness for learning. Therapists typically want to 'find out' and explore. Klein et al. (2011, p273) write that the *passion for learning, marked by new learning and curiosity* is something that, for therapists, *generally appears early in life, propelling children towards growth and discovery.* Therapists report having been curious from an early stage in life and Klein et al. assert that:

[therapists often have a] passion that results in a relentless quest for new knowledge, both objective, externally-based knowledge and subjective, internally-based knowledge.

(2011, p273)

Carl Rogers captures this level of curiosity when he writes about the *obsession with communication* as the foundation for his work:

I can see perhaps one overriding theme in my professional life. It is my caring about communication. From my very earliest years it has, for some reason, been a passionate concern of mine. I have been pained when I have seen others communicating past one another. I have wanted to communicate myself so that I could not be misunderstood. I have wanted to understand, as profoundly as possible, the communication of the other, be it a client or friend or family member ... This obsession with communication has had its own unexpected rewards.

(1995, p65)

REFLECTION POINT

- How would you describe your curiosity? Are there any themes, which you recognise as long-lasting interests, reflected in your professional life?

CHAPTER SUMMARY

- This chapter looked at personal development as a purposeful attempt to review, plan and integrate your own personal and professional learning. Personal development imposes a dynamic and holistic perspective on to the therapist. It involves focusing on prior learning with an interest in how experiences directly and indirectly can affect our thoughts, feelings and behaviour with our clients.
- Personal development is about awareness; it invites us to learn about the 'engine that drives us' and encourages us to examine how our own personal histories, our underlying cultural values and theoretical models may impact on the way we feel, think and act, both at and outside our work today. Personal development addresses questions ranging from our emotional responses to situations and persons, to our basic beliefs and our relationship to knowledge, trustworthiness and truth.
- The idea of 'mastery' within therapy was explored with reference to a significant difference between a lay helper and a professional helper in terms of knowledge of the actual 'helping' process. It was suggested that a lay helper is *a novice who can be prone to problem*

identification, advice giving, and boundary issues (Trotter-Mathison et al., 2010, p6).

- An important aspect of professional involvement is, as Klein et al. (2011, p279) suggest, the *capacity to accurately monitor moment-to-moment shifts in the process of treatment.* Maintaining ongoing introspection and self-monitoring activities are part of this ability to 'master the basics'.

CHAPTER 2

The 'good enough' therapist

CORE KNOWLEDGE

- This chapter introduces the concept of being 'good enough' for someone willing to engage in what the psychoanalyst Donald Winnicott (1963) referred to as a caring relationship geared towards containing strong emotions as evoked in two imperfect people.
- This chapter looks at ways of using problems, critical incidents and mistakes as openings for further learning, rather than ignoring, enacting or displacing issues on to our clients.
- We will look at the research into motivations for becoming a therapist. Who chooses to become a therapist? What, if any, are the common themes among people who choose therapy as a career?
- The ACCTT model is introduced as a way of conceptualising and assessing professional development based on transformative learning, where mistakes and critical incidents can be 're-used' or 'recycled' into something useful or constructive. The ACCTT model is introduced in the context of 'reflexive awareness' and reflective, double-loop learning.

The idea of a 'good enough' therapist is a running theme rather than a separate issue in this book. An underpinning belief of the book is that 'perfect' therapists are neither desired nor possible for a therapeutic relationship based on mutual trust. The phrase 'good enough' is borrowed from the paediatrician and child therapist Donald Winnicott (1963), who coined the phrase 'good enough mother' for an 'ordinary' mother who engages with her baby on the basis of a loving relationship between two imperfect people. This chapter explores ways of using critical incidents and mistakes as openings for further learning, rather than ignoring, enacting or displacing issues on to our clients.

THE IMPACT OF THE THERAPIST AS A PERSON

There appears to be a shift within most modalities today towards a greater recognition of the impact that therapists' own behaviour, thoughts and emotions will have on therapeutic relationships and the overall outcome of their work. While therapeutic models inspired by psychoanalytic and humanistic theory usually emphasise the role of the therapeutic relationship, cognitive behavioural therapy (CBT) and other evidence-based approaches have historically regarded therapeutic relationships as 'secondary' to the technical, skill-based aspects of treatment. The family of evidence-based approaches can be seen as, as the CBT therapist Neuhaus (2011, p220) puts it, *actively re-evaluation itself with regard to the therapist's role*. Spencer writes:

> *The purpose of personal development training is to help trainees increase their awareness of how their personality, behaviour, personal and cultural beliefs might impact on, and influence, their clients.*
>
> (2006, p109)

Neuhaus (2011, p224) concludes: *I define personal development to include present and past*. Personal development involves a dynamic and holistic perspective from the therapist. It involves focusing on prior learning with an interest in how experiences can directly and indirectly affect our thoughts, feelings and behaviour with our clients. Neuhaus continues:

> *Present refers to the developmental process of learning how to become a therapist who reacts as a person with emotions, thoughts and behaviour both inside and outside the hour. Past refers to one's personal history (e.g. life span development, identity development and family relationships) that may have a significant influence on the ways in which the therapist reacts.*
>
> (2011, p224)

Case study 2.1

Julie is in her second year of diploma training in integrative counselling. She is married to Paul, an accountant, with one daughter who is in her second year at university. Julie has previously worked in childcare. 'I have always liked looking after people,' says Julie. Both her parents are dead. She is close to her younger brother who is a GP and who, as Julie puts it, has always been the 'golden boy' of the family. She has recently started her clinical placement at a local GP's surgery. Yesterday she was advised about a new client enquiry from a woman, Alice, with bereavement as her presented problem. Julie felt both nervous and excited about seeing her new client. She felt sorry for her – Julie knew only too well what it was like to lose someone you love.

However, during their first session Julie is struck by Alice's confidence and neat appearance. Alice is a psychologist, who asks 'probing' questions about Julie's qualifications. Halfway through the session, she asks if there is someone else whom she can see – she is concerned whether Julie is experienced enough to deal with her issues. Julie leaves the session feeling deskilled, angry and sad. She tells her supervisor afterwards that the client seems unreasonable and would be too difficult for her to work with. When the supervisor encourages Julie to describe her feelings, she answers that she feels 'bullied':

Supervisor: 'What's it like for you to be bullied?'
Julie: 'Well, you're made to feel rubbish, aren't you; useless, like you can't do anything right and like no one really cares about you.'
Supervisor: 'Is this the first time you've experienced that kind of feeling?'
Julie: 'No! I used to feel like this a lot. I wasn't exactly bullied, but my brother was bossy . . . he always thought he knew best, it used to really get up my nose!'

COMMENT

Julie and her supervisor are able to explore how Julie's fears about not being good enough might have come into play during her session with Alice. Julie returns to the moment when she started to feel uncomfortable and recognises feeling deskilled at quite an early stage of their conversation. Perhaps, muses her supervisor, there had been a collusion taking place? Maybe both Julie *and* Alice had a fear of failure? Or maybe Julie's fears triggered something in Alice; perhaps a sense of dread of being 'too much' for people? Julie and her supervisor explore how Alice might feel in seeking help, being a 'helper' herself.

ACTIVITY 2.1

- Think about particularly significant times in your life. Can you identify separate incidents or recognise particular themes that have affected you, such as bereavement, illness, separation or divorce, depression, or upheavals such as moving house or to a new country?
- How might these experiences impact on the way that you react to (certain) clients, either in a good or bad way, as strengths or weaknesses; or perhaps both?

PERSONAL DEVELOPMENT IN THERAPY TRAINING

For counsellors and psychotherapists, the boundary between our professional and our personal selves is often fluid. Folkes-Skinner et al. (2010, p91) stress that *all education demands change*, but therapy training usually involves particularly deep changes. Folkes-Skinner et al. (2010, p91) remind us that *trainee therapists are required not only to change their thinking and to develop new skills, but also adapt aspects of their personality.* Furthermore, Folkes-Skinner et al. assert that:

> *[Therapy training] is a potentially disturbing personal journey that requires a deconstruction of the self to meet the needs of clients. This change process appears to be influenced and supported by experiential learning exercises such as role-play and group supervision, but may be fundamentally driven by experiences working with real clients.*
>
> (2010, p91)

Skovholt and Trotter-Mathison (2011, p80) conclude that *at work, counsellors, therapists, teachers and health professions live in an ocean of emotional distress.* They found that many novice practitioners experienced an acute level of stress that they often felt ashamed to talk about.

As a supervisor, teacher, friend and colleague I have learnt that the 'always coping on one's own' approach is far from uncommon among people within the helping professions. In his reflections on therapy as a profession, Kottler captures for many of us an underlying dichotomy in our work:

> *Being a therapist is truly a lifelong journey, one in which we accompany others on a road towards enlightenment or peace or salvation. [However] our journey to become therapists began for most of us, not with the urge to save the world or help people, but rather to save ourselves.*
>
> (2011, p1)

Many studies (Miller, 1997; Page, 1999; Sedgwick, 2005; Bager-Charleson, 2010a) highlight the asymmetry involved in helping relationships. When working with vulnerable people it is important to consider the 'darker' sides of the motivations behind choosing a philanthropic career. The Jungian analyst Adolf Guggenbuhl-Craig writes:

> *People are most cruel when they can use cruelty to enforce the 'good'. We must refrain from playing the part of someone who never falls into the shadows and must be prepared to admit our mistakes with this regard . . . An honest analyst will realise with horror from time to time that in his daily work he has been acting exactly like an unconscious quack and false prophet.*
>
> (1991, pp73, 113)

RECYCLING NEGATIVE EXPERIENCES AS A MEANS OF TRANSFORMATIVE LEARNING

Sussman (1992) has conducted one of the most detailed studies of therapists' motivations. He suggests that *an important determinant of the desire to practice psychotherapy involves the attempt to come to terms with one's own psychological conflicts* (1992, p180). In all of his 14 interview cases, Sussman found signs of disturbance in one form or another. Some of them are reflected in the following categories and quotations.

- Narcissistic needs: *I was not allowed to be competent at home.*
- Aggrandisement of ego-ideal: *[I was thinking about becoming a priest.] Within [our] catholic church, to become a priest is the highest achievement. Priests are the most grand, powerful, important figures. They get to wear beautiful vestments, smell of incense and hear confessions, conduct masses and offer communion. [Therapists are also important figures who people turn to with their confessions.]*
- Exhibitionism: *I think that I have a frustrated actress in me at this point.*
- Masochistic tendencies: *[I am being] used as an instrument which is smashed against the wall, thrown out of the window, kicked . . . [laughs] made to feel enormously sad. Just the enormous range of emotions I get subjected to on a daily basis in my body, mind and soul has the accumulative effect over the years of being a container for all that intense emotion.*
- Problems with family members: *I think my mother was full of loss and self-absorbed.*
- Voyeurism: *I thought that might be a very interesting part of the work, a sort of private, secret chamber of therapist and patient that really wasn't so different from sharing your secrets with a priest.*

GOOD OR BAD?

The motives for becoming a therapist can sound sinister. Reik (1948, cited in Sussman, 1992, p149) went as far using the phrase *psychological canni-balism* for what he regarded as a therapist's sublimated *wish for incorporation.* In our own inquiry (Bager-Charleson, 2010b) we found a peculiar split between 'good and bad' in the literature about therapists. There were the beautiful accounts of therapeutic practice offered by humanistic and some analytical therapists on the one hand. Buber (1947), Rogers (1995) and Jung (cited in Sedgwick, 2005) refer to sparkling encounters and 'I–thou' moments *without which we are not really living as human beings* (Rogers, 1995, p14). Jung (cited in Sedgwick, 2005) speaks about the 'alchemic bath' where therapist and client are able to create gold together. Psychoanalytic writers and certain other analytic therapists, such as Guggenbuhl-Craig (1991) and Miller (1997), support, on the other hand, Sussman's emphasis on the dark sides of therapists' motivations. Here the motivations revolve predominantly around the therapist being caught in the only role he or she knows, that is the helper role. The career becomes a matter of escaping, displacing and sublimating one's own wishes and unmet needs.

When approaching a large group of therapists with a questionnaire about their motivations for practice, this dichotomy between 'good' and 'bad' motivations was at the back of our minds (Bager-Charleson, 2010a). We distributed a questionnaire to 280 therapists and received 238 replies. The survey involved the following question: 'Why did you choose to be a therapist?' There were six answers to choose from.

1. I have always been *interested in people*.
2. I enjoy the *analytical, investigative element* of therapy most.
3. The *flexible working hours* were essential when considering a career.
4. I believe that my *own childhood* influenced my choice of career.
5. A *crisis in later life* brought me into therapy and raised my interest in working as a therapist myself.
6. None of the above resonates with me; instead I chose to work as a therapist for the following reason(s) . . .

There was an overwhelming number of references to personal crisis in the responses. Some 70 per cent of respondents cited either a childhood or later-life 'crisis' as the trigger for becoming a therapist (Figure 2.1).

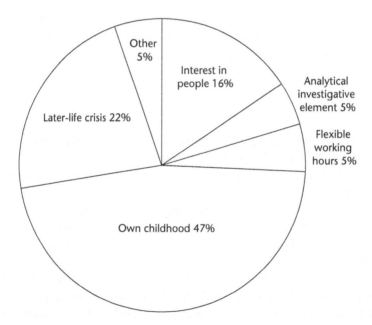

Figure 2.1: Responses to a survey from 238 counsellors and psychotherapists, arranged over six categories (Bager-Charleson, 2010b)

ACTIVITY 2.2

- Why have you chosen to become a therapist? Which of the themes in the questionnaire resonates most with you?

Some therapists recounted both childhood and adult crises in their question-naire responses. References were made to how negative childhood experi-ences often affect the way we are equipped to deal with further adult crises. One therapist felt that this experience had made her extra sensitive to clients who struggle with their own strong emotions:

We never ever spoke about feelings when I grew up. This left me feeling very inadequate for many years. I felt odd for having emotions which, of course, made the death of my partner extra difficult to deal with. I find again and again that clients have this kind of problem; it is as if they think they are going mad for having strong feelings. My own experience of that has made me extra sensitive to that, I think.

Several therapists referred to how their own personal therapy has helped them to challenge old, narrow constructs about themselves and others. One therapist wrote about how he 'realised in therapy just how abusive my upbringing had been':

I came from a very angry household . . . Without really knowing why at the time I decided to never have children myself. My partner at the time really wanted children and it was this that brought us into couple therapy. Our marriage ended in spite of it, and I see that as mainly my problem . . . To cut a long story short, I realised in therapy just how abusive my upbringing had been. I have been in therapy for six years, and I feel ready to move on. I'd like to give something back, and I feel that I can do that through my own work with kids now.

One therapist elaborates on the combination of an interest in people and an adult crisis:

Mine is a mixture of 1 and 5. An initial general curiosity, about how people ticked, and human behaviour. This was intensified when I found I was unable to have children.

A curiosity for relationships and in 'how people tick' was referred to by several therapists. One therapist wrote about how her interest in relation-ships was nourished by witnessing her sisters becoming mothers:

I became increasingly interested in my sisters' different styles of parenting, their parent/child interactions and the children's behaviour. As an observer, supporter and, often, agony aunt to my sisters, I felt a need to understand child behaviour and parent interaction and wanted to know how things went wrong and what parents could do.

For some, more factors than two were included in the questionnaire response. The therapist below refers to a combination of an interest in people, personal childhood experiences and an adult event/crisis:

I have marked three criteria (1, 4, 5) . . . It was important in my family to have an 'interesting' career. Something that seemed worthwhile . . . I have always been interested in people and psychology . . . A careers assessment that I underwent at a time when I had dropped out and was entirely uninterested in any career suggested psychology and social work. It was a crisis – the breakdown of my first marriage – that got me to therapy in the first place. I found it exciting and fascinating; I've been passionate about therapy ever since.

Common features

Our personal inquiry does not qualify for any grand conclusion regarding the total population of psychotherapists. It does, however, contribute with an insight into how often therapists used the term 'crisis' in a positive sense. In most cases 'crisis' is referred to in terms of something of an 'eye opener':

When I lost my job my world turned upside down. I am glad now that it made me look at the world differently. I value other things now. My own personal therapy changed my outlook on life. I would have answered (1) if you asked me at the beginning of my training! I see now that it was more about vigilance . . . in the beginning I just felt I was cut out for this kind of job. I would take in everything in the room and my supervisor would tell me that I was being so very emotionally sensitive and astute. But really, I was frightened. My own therapy helped me to recognise that.

The bereavement counselling opened my eyes to a completely different way of being. I was used to sales and that sort of thing. Counselling opened up a whole new world for me, very different from sales. But it was also through my own counselling that I realised what a secondary place emotions used to have in our household.

I was fortunate enough to adopt . . . As each year passed things seemed to get worse and the strain of caring for one of the children was having a negative effect on the whole family. I was determined not to allow the placement to break down but the strain of holding things together had become overwhelming and I became stressed. This is when I sought counselling. I found it an immensely enlightening and enriching experience and from the very first session I wanted to be a counsellor too.

There is, perhaps not surprisingly, a mixture of reasons in the therapists' accounts of why they chose to become therapists. It seems difficult, if not inappropriate, to imply a split between 'good' versus 'bad' motives. The uniting theme seems instead to be the 'eye-opening' factor. Whether linked to a childhood event or an adult crisis, the personal experience of therapy had an impact not only on the therapists' choice of career but also on their relationships, family and/or general outlook on life.

The previously mentioned Jungian analyst David Sedgwick (2005) stresses that the therapist's wound or 'pathology' is neither altogether good nor altogether bad. It is not so much a question about *what* has happened as *how* the event and experience is being *known and utilised*. Michael Sussman's study supports this thinking. He highlights how the success a wounded therapist may achieve is linked to his or her ability to reflect, having learnt from one's own suffering:

> *Not everyone who has suffered and can identify with emotional suffering in others will be an effective therapist. These characteristics must be coupled with the following features: the capacity to control such identifications; the experience of having learned from one's own suffering, and thereby having matured; and the capacity for synthesising pleasurable, as well as painful, life experiences.*
>
> (1992, p249)

TRANSFORMING EXPERIENCES

The idea of transforming experiences into something 'useful' thus becomes in this sense the crucial factor. The question 'why practise as a therapist?' cannot be explained only with reference to what has happened to the therapist, but requires additional references to how the experiences may have been transformed. The ACCTT model (see page 32) is intended as a tool for conceptualising such a transformative experience.

Acknowledging, connecting and transforming are examples of 'phases' that may help us to travel from simply noticing a problem to putting it into context and eventually reaching some kind of transformation.

Lehmann (2008, p208) highlights how transformation involves *the develop-ment of awareness of what . . . pushes us to feel and act in the way we do*. As part of this growing awareness, old beliefs and previously held values become tested and challenged. Lehman continues:

> [W]e develop a sense of ownership for what lies within our repertoire of
> professional actions. The transformation process includes the realisation
> of multiple truths and perspectives for every situation and brings into
> consciousness the choices that are made in the process of interpreting lived
> experiences.
>
> (2008, p298)

Transformative learning is not just about positive experience; it highlights
the value of bringing negative experiences to the forefront.

REFLECTION POINT

- Can you think of a personal crisis or problem that has become an asset in your
  work as a therapist?

PERSONAL EXPERIENCES OF TRANSFORMATIVE LEARNING

Case study 2.2 illustrates some learning experiences from my own training,
at a stage when I was practising as a couple counsellor. I am referring to my
clients as Andy and Janet, although in reality the case draws on a couple of
difficult case experiences from the first year of my career. It highlights my
own abrupt confrontation with some underlying motivations for wanting
to retrain as a therapist.

Case study 2.2

Janet and Andy have been married for five years and have two children aged two
and four. Andy wants to 'break up before it's too late' as he is worried about
upsetting their children, as he himself used to get when his parents argued. 'But
we never argue,' says Janet. 'It's just a question of time,' answers Andy. Andy is a
bricklayer and Janet works as a dinner lady. Andy smiles often and has confident
body language. He often mocks my 'psychobabble'. 'Look love, I know you're just
trying to be helpful, but this touchy feely stuff just doesn't work on guys like me,'
says Andy at the end of their first session, through which Janet has cried. They
continue to attend the sessions, in spite of Andy's cynicism.

    Ever since our first session, I have worked with a psychodynamically informed
hypothesis that Andy approached his own marriage with a blueprint from his
parents' unhappy relationship. He often compares Janet with his mother who, by
the sound of it, was cruel and vindictive. Janet, however, seems benign. She spends
most of the sessions crying in a corner. I wonder why Andy is so keen to perceive

his relationship as 'doomed'. I hope to get him to explore his idea of himself as so ill-suited for relationships. Janet clearly loves him, and frequently reminds him that their relationship is nothing like his parents'. I too could see that he was a good man, underneath. Why couldn't Andy see that for himself?

One supervision session in particular stands out in my memory. I attended it prepared to discuss a paper by Donald Winnicott about 'clinical fear of break-down'. My supervisor was surprised. I found her reaction strange. Why shouldn't I come prepared? I begin to wonder if I will be able to trust my supervisor. Has she really got anything to contribute; should I perhaps start looking for another? I am at the beginning of my career, and need to learn as much as possible; I feel burdened by the responsibility of my role and feel that my supervisor does little to meet my needs. Perhaps I have come to the wrong place?

I decide to give it another go and hope to discuss my hypothesis about what Winnicott (1963) refers to as a compulsive need to repeat a past experience in the hope of reconnecting and repairing the 'original failure in the facilitating environment'. My understanding of this is guided by the psychoanalytically inspired focus on projective identifications of 'split off' and denied feelings. I believe that Andy projects split-off emotions and fears, based on an early object relationship, on to Janet. There is, to my mind, a kind of cause and effect. I believe that, if old fears and fantasies about relationships are revealed, the relationship between Andy and Janet will improve (see Figure 2.2).

'You always call Janet "Andy's wife"', reflects my supervisor during another session. I leave feeling misunderstood. I so desperately want to learn. I feel so lost. Does she not realise that the direct focus on Andy would help Janet enormously? Maybe I should begin to look for another supervisor?

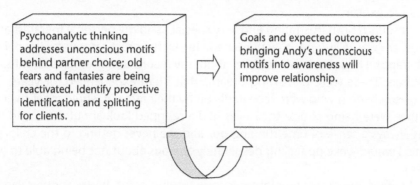

Figure 2.2: Single-loop, cause-and-effect thinking around the problem

COMMENT

As therapists we are not engaged in a 'solely technical task'. How we carry out our work is also an expression of who we are. Working with Andy and Janet highlighted to me how important the combination of supervision and personal therapy was in order to move on.

DOUBLE-LOOP LEARNING

Case study 2.3

I sensed that something was wrong. I felt 'jet-lagged' after each session of couple counselling. I often returned home feeling disconnected and detached from my surroundings; revved up, somehow, and experiencing feelings that I could not begin to explain.

'It sounds both frustrating and very special,' said my personal therapist at one stage, as I was telling her how burdened I felt by the great responsibilities of being a therapist. I had previously told her about my recurring nightmares about saving children. These were harrowing dreams that I had experienced for years. They involved children who were repeatedly hit by their father. I would meet their eyes as they were being struck; their eyes had a resigned look about them and there was always a sense of time running out and me never getting to the children in time. I would wake up feeling desperately anxious about not being able to 'save' them.

I regard one particular nightmare as a turning point. It was another variation on the theme of helplessness. Janet had her leg in a cast and was in a wheelchair being pushed, erratically, by Andy. I could see her being hurt, but was unable to get to her, to help. As we explored the dream in therapy, it occurred to me how mad and unreliable I had perceived Andy to be up to now, and how responsible I felt for everyone around me. I recall a kind of 'point of no return' after this moment, as if something fell into place. There was almost a physical sensation that the penny had dropped. I could see – and perhaps more importantly feel – some of the deep-seated effects of having cared for my parents as a child. But I also had to face my own destructive forces; my own pent-up anger as well as a fear of being unreliable. I knew that I needed help but, more importantly, I was finally able to experience, on a deeper level, that help was possible to get. It became the beginning of a powerful experience of therapeutic healing for me, which lasted for seven years.

COMMENT

I have tried to illustrate the new angle to my work with Janet and Andy with what Schön refers to as 'double-loop' learning (see Figure 2.3). Double-loop learning involves moving beyond one's obvious line of vision. Hawkins and Shohet refer to the difference between single- and double-loop learning as follows: *[T]he second loop reflects on the first loop in a way that explores its attitudes, values and assumptions* (2005, p78).

This means that we revisit our strategies with a new perspective. We have to, as Carter and Gradin (2001, p4) assert, *try on the perspective, the world view of an 'other' for long enough to look back critically at ourselves, our ideas, our assumptions, our values.*

Double-loop learning thus involves a reflexive approach to our old ways of understanding things, in the sense that we arrive back at our personal frameworks with new 'lenses'.

Personal looping

For me, double-loop learning was like taking off a pair of too-dark sunglasses; it helped me to see possibilities that contrasted with the gloomy outcomes I had expected based on prior experiences. I was reminded that the situation I grew up in (with a bipolar father and, as a result, an exhausted mother, with myself in the middle as the imagined responsible party) did not reflect the way the rest of the world worked. My childhood world might have revolved around keeping my father from spiralling out of control; but neither my own adult world, nor that of others, had to follow this restricted format. Sometimes, double-loop learning highlights cultural or gender-related pre-understandings and prejudices; sometimes we are restricted by theoretical models and at other times it is our own personal history that blurs our vision or obscures our understanding of the events we are faced with.

Theoretical looping

The events described above prompted me to learn more about how therapists react. Countertransference and projective identification were important new concepts, which highlighted not only how the client's images of themselves and relationships can be transferred and projected on to the therapist, but also how the therapist's reaction can impact upon the therapeutic relationship.

I felt surprised and relieved at seeing Janet as a person in her own right. The collusion in putting Janet's needs to one side had been possible partly because of her own experiences from growing up in a household with a schizophrenic brother. There had been an underlying similarity between our childhood experiences that had captured us in the 'selfless' focus on Andy. This had, in turn, restricted Andy's learning experiences and exaggerated his fears of being damaging to others, prompting his desire to run away and 'hide in a bedsit'.

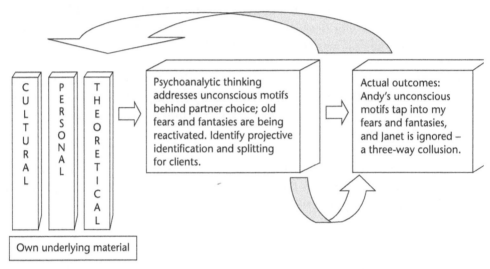

Figure 2.3: Double-loop learning illustrates how our own personal, cultural and/or theoretical beliefs and underlying assumptions influence our strategies in the workplace

ACTIVITY 2.4

- Think of a moment when you felt anxious or stressed in connection with a client encounter (in role play or in real life). How did that make you feel? Did the feeling last? Did you, for instance, react through dreams, sadness or hyperactivity? Did you indulge in, for example, overeating, or other means of displacement or enactment?
- Was this kind of reaction 'typical' or 'atypical' for you when under stress?

Looping back on to my 'espoused' theory, which I was committed to working with, I was surprised to see how much the theory had resonated with my own personal wounding. Winnicott's (1963) idea about an urge to repeat past experiences in the hope of reconnecting and repairing the 'original failure in the facilitating environment', was now something that explained my own rationale for working as a couple counsellor in the first place. In supervision, I was gradually able to become less fixated with a theory. We joked about the theory as a comfort blanket, something that I had drawn comfort from at a time when I felt catastrophe looming. To remain tolerant to ambiguity we need to feel contained and safe enough to examine a problem from many angles. I initially regarded my supervisor as a threat rather than as a support. My own general trust in others needed first to be restored through personal therapy. Not trusting prevented me from taking on board new perspectives.

Argyris and Schön (1974) suggest that people often *think* of themselves as adhering to a certain theory, while their actual 'theory-in-use' can sometimes be quite different. We do not, in other words, always practise what we preach. Argyris and Schön coined the phrase *espoused theory* for the theory to which we officially commit ourselves:

> *When someone is asked how he would behave under certain circumstances, the answer he usually gives is his espoused theory of action for that situation. This is the theory of action to which he gives allegiance, and which, upon request, he communicates to others.*
>
> (1974, p6)

However, Argyris and Schön found that people often worked according to quite contrasting sets of values, without really recognising it: *However, the theory that actually governs his actions is this theory-in-use [with implicit values and assumptions, often taken for granted]* (1974, p7).

Reflective practice theory encourages us, as suggested, to challenge our frameworks of understanding, rather than rigidly defending them. The case study with Janet and Andy illustrates how I *felt* faithful to a psycho-analytically inspired framework for an understanding of our work, until I needed to reconsider the model. My own input in terms of implicit and unaddressed values and beliefs, such as that 'all family fathers are likely to suffer from potential psychotic breakdown', made the actual theory-in-use very different from the one I had committed to.

Cultural looping

As I examined the work with Andy and Janet from new angles, I recognised how I had chosen to interpret Andy's comments as banter while he had, in fact, tried to put across some of his own confusion around 'psychobabble'.

It reflected, partly, my own uncertainty and felt like a way of 'covering up' my own insecurities. But it also highlighted how I was able to hide behind grand words and how there was an educational difference in the room. Perhaps a saving grace was that I would often mispronounce my words – being a foreigner sometimes takes the edge off things. Janet said that she had felt it helpful that I was Swedish; to her I had been more of a Swedish chef – someone who had been quaint and sometimes mispronounced things. Andy, however, said that 'his friends had joked about Swedish massage'. When gradually seeking to explore the potential implications of having a Swedish therapist, my supervisor helped me to recognise how there had been an erotic transference in the room. My supervisor encouraged me to explore the issue further with more direct reference to Andy, and with the potential indirect impact on Janet in mind. However, that was too much for me at the time. Erotic transference is, for many of us, a difficult, albeit often essential, issue to explore with clients and it became something that was put on my already long list for further learning.

THE 'GOOD' COMPLAISANT WIFE

Of particular significance for my further training was, however, the experience of having failed to recognise the needs of Janet. When exploring how this had happened, there was a sense of collusion between us on the basis of our background, with Janet having had a schizophrenic brother. The recognition of having attempted to 'save' Janet's and Andy's marriage at all costs, including keeping Janet invisible and silent, was disturbing. It prompted me to explore the role of therapy and therapists in a socio-cultural perspective. My own childhood desire to save families was indeed, as suggested, confronted by my supervisor. But it also felt as if I had colluded with where and how I worked at the time in terms of a typical white, middle-class agency staffed predominantly with housewives like myself – financially secure enough to work unpaid. Although great changes were about to take place within the agency, there were still some traces of general Surrey affluence and, in some cases, self-righteous intentions to hide behind, which helped me to avoid examining why divorce was such a scary thing for me. This experience fuelled an interest in further training, which combined intrapersonal aspects with interpersonal interests within a socio-cultural framework. I felt that the integrative training at Roehampton University offered this, with its MSc in humanistic, psychoanalytic and postmodern theory.

Milner and O'Byrne (2004) argue that therapy is a political concern; our practice conveys norms and values that can be linked to a bigger cultural, political context. We contribute to make society 'work' and run smoothly. An underlying cultural assumption for our work is, for instance, that a child should attend school and that an employee should return to work each day.

Do we ultimately, ask Milner and O'Byrne, assess 'needs' with the interests of our client or with society in mind? They contend that: *[The counsellors] are political agents, however much they may disavow this* . . . (2004, p17).

REFLECTION POINT

• Can you think of any situations in which your power in the therapeutic relationship has been influenced by factors such as gender, ethnicity or social class?

REFLEXIVE AWARENESS

The term 'reflexive awareness' is an underpinning concept for transformative learning. Like the concept of personal development, reflexivity is an ambiguous yet frequently used concept today. It is often used in the context of research as a means of conceptualising the impact the researcher may have on the research process. Here, reflexivity is used with reference to how our own cultural, theoretical, personal and linguistic assumptions might impact upon our work. Technically, we can distinguish between different kinds of reflexivity, for example reflexive self-awareness and critical reflexivity.

Reflexive self-awareness involves reflecting on one's thoughts and reactions in the sense that personal blind spots and potential new and different angles are brought to the forefront when problem solving. As suggested in Chapter 1, countertransference is an example of an attempt to explore our own reactions and responses to clients. Transference is a concept coined in classic psychoanalysis to conceptualise ways *in which the feelings, wishes and actions of the patient in relation to the therapist may be unconsciously influenced, coloured and distorted by earlier childhood experiences* (Holmes and Lindley, 1998, p126). While the term 'transference' has been reserved for the client's reaction to the therapeutic relationship, 'countertransference' revolves around the way the therapist reacts to the client. Holmes and Lindley refer to the concept as follows:

> *Countertransference . . . comprises both the therapist's 'blind-spots' – her unconscious and childhood-derived wishes and fantasies in relation to the patient – and affective responses of which she is aware, which can be put to good use in helping her to understand the patient.*
>
> (1998, p126)

Critical reflexivity is about looking at our work with cultural and theoretical values and biases in mind. It concerns the link between ourselves and our social structure, for instance, in terms of what Youngson (2009, p15) refers to as how *psychology has its own repressive history stemming from societal norms.* Gardner writes:

> *Being 'critical' adds an expectation of exploring practice in the context of the social system in which it operates, looking, for example, at the influence of social expectations about such issues as gender or age, class or ethnicity.*
>
> (2006, p145)

ACCTT SMART

Reflexivity requires us to engage in different and sometimes foreign perspectives, and through this to expand our original framework of understanding. The ACCTT SMART model (Figure 2.4) is, as suggested, intended as an aid to conceptualise and discuss this process.

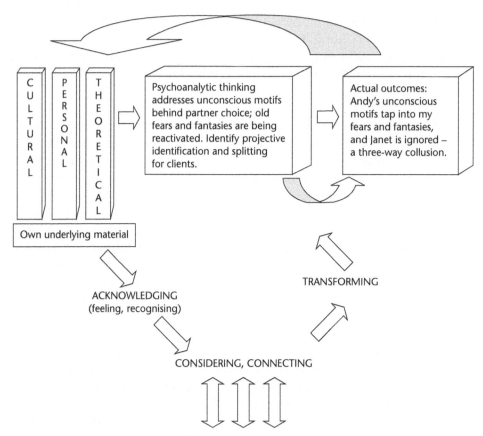

Figure 2.4: ACCTT SMART model for tranformational learning

The value of recycling

ACCTT always starts with a problem and refers to the way in which we may 'recycle' our experiences into useful, transformative learning. To avoid going around in circles, it is important to connect with and consider a problem and open up the exploration for new input. It is important to reach out for nourishment, inspiration and new knowledge from the following sources:

- personal therapy;
- supervision;
- clinical experience and client contact;
- reflective writing;
- training, research and general continuing professional development (CPD);
- resting and relaxing;
- creative activities.

Each of these activities and learning points is explored in this book, with reference to research as well as personal experiences. Two colleagues have, in addition, contributed generously with their different experiences and accounts of their transformative learning. You are encouraged throughout the book to weave in your own experiences, negative as well as positive.

Constructivism

Reflective practice invites us to approach 'truth(s)' and 'knowledge' as being constructed from the client's interaction with his or her environment rather than as being 'revealed' by the expert. Schön says:

> In the constructionist view, our perceptions, appreciations and beliefs are rooted in the worlds of our own making that we come to accept as reality.
> (Schön, cited in Winter et al., 1999, p184)

There are different constructivist models. They hold in common, as Rosen and Kuehlwein (1996, p5) put it, *[that] they reject the postulation that our mental representations mirror an objective reality*. To varying degrees the constructivist models argue that meaning and reality are created and not discovered.

The issue of how we arrive at knowledge – about our clients, ourselves and our work – will be explored from different angles, for instance, as part of your own ACCTT SMART model, which is discussed in Chapter 9. The model focuses on using a critical incident as a trigger for generating new knowledge.

There are, of course, many ways of conceptualising a learning process. The main focus in this book revolves around how personal experiences can develop into learning experiences with a transformational value and impact on our practice.

ACCTT SMART in more detail

The ACCTT model builds on many different approaches to learning as conceptualised by, for instance, Biggs and Collis's (1982) SOLO taxonomy (which stands for Structure of Learning Outcomes) and the way Moon (2004), Atherton (2009) and Roffey-Barentsen and Malthouse (2009) have developed this thinking. The ACCTT model is also influenced by Kolb's (1984) and Gibbs' (1988) models for experiential learning. My purpose, at this stage, is to introduce the model and invite you to keep it in mind when considering your own personal and professional development. ACCTT stands for:

- **Acknowledging** a problem in terms of recognising it, sensing it, feeling it and reflecting on your usual way of responding to these 'rattling' noises in your engine. Fight or flight? Ignore, suppress or enact? How do we react when a problem occurs with our client and why do we react in the way we do? When is our behaviour in the present linked to experiences from the past? How do anticipations based on prior experiences come into our work? When are they useful and when do they obscure, blur or even sabotage our understanding of what happens in the present? What do we need to help us understand our reactions? Are, for instance, supportive supervision, good training and personal therapy in place? If not, why is that?
- **Considering** the situation on a 'unistructural' level involves exploring the 'rattling' sound of the engine through simple and obvious connections, in an environment where it feels safe to associate freely, perhaps brainstorm or 'pour' out events as they occur to us in the moment. It is a phase when 'sitting with' or 'staying with' the sensation is appropriate, and when we must feel free to express that something has gone wrong. We need someone whom we feel is on our side, at this stage – a so-called critical friend, who can see where we are coming from and respect how we feel, but who will help us to establish new and different perspectives.
- **Connecting** on a 'multistructural' level involves a phase where a number of connections can be made, both through discussion and personal reading and thinking. Why have I, for instance, not addressed lateness with my clients? How can I understand this with regard to my own personal history? And how can the impact of a therapist's personal history be understood as a whole; what else have others experienced and concluded within the same field? What is there to learn; how can I take my experience forward and learn from both my own and others' experiences in the field? And why do certain explanations and frameworks for the new understanding work

better than others for me? How do I see therapy working? What do I expect a therapist to achieve, and why? This can be an extrovert phase, when we read a lot, discuss with others and compare different theories and ways of looking at the problem.

- **Transforming on a 'relational' level.** This involves putting new learning into practice, for instance seizing an opportunity to address lateness in the context of our 'treatment' model as a whole. It does not necessarily mean 'doing' new things, but is likely to affect the way that we listen. We may 'hear' about the lateness both with our own resistance in mind and in the context of what our modality informs us in terms of the psychoanalytical concepts of countertransference and transference, or with the person-centred core conditions in mind. This is a stage when an overall context, with a new sense of significance of the parts in relation to the whole, is emerging.

- **Transforming on an extended abstract level.** This is when connections are made not only within the given subject area, but also beyond it. We begin to generalise about a problem, put into context other situations, and transfer principles and ideas underlying the specific instance into other contexts. We may, for instance, put our own modality in the context of others, and consider aspects such as 'therapeutic relationships' and 'therapeutic outcomes' on a more general, generic level, for example in the context of reflective practice, evidence-based thinking and/or critical psychology. This can involve comparing psychotherapy with other mental health approaches such as psychology and psychiatry, or requires us to consider the role of the therapist with socio-economic, cultural and/or gender-related interests in mind. The original problem has now triggered a chain of new insights, which will affect the way we approach our role as a therapist. We can now look at the original problem of 'all clients stay over their allotted time' in a new light, with our own reservations around our sense of self and our role as a therapist, and put this into the context of what both our own and other modalities inform us about enactment, therapeutic relationships, etc.

SMART

Personal development builds, as suggested, on reflective practice theory. Reflective practice focuses on the underlying values and beliefs of the practitioner. However, personal development adds some of the demystifying intentions of evidence-based approaches. Evidence-based approaches address pitfalls of reflective practice theory in terms of being *both too nebulous and too difficult to quantify and evaluate* (Youngson, 2009, p14). This book is written with this tension in mind. The SMART aspect of the ACCTT SMART model is an encouragement to incorporate the valuable element of 'measuring' one's progress and to make one's development accessible for others, such as supervisors, managers, employers and colleagues, to evaluate.

The SMART model is inspired by Roffey-Barentsen and Malthouse (2009) and their adaptation of the model originating from Drucker (1954, in Webber 2008, p50). It refers to an action plan for 'measurable' goals and stands for:

- Specific;
- Measurable;
- Achievable;
- Relevant;
- Time-bound.

ACTIVITY 2.5

In Chapter 9 you will be asked to write a case study based on your own ACCTT SMART process. In that chapter, there is a case study and a questionnaire based on the ACCTT stages. Before you complete this, it is important that you familiarise yourself with the model, with your own problems and processes in mind.

- Take some time to consider if there is a unique problem or some recurring issues that you would like to explore in more depth. Write down what springs to mind and be prepared to revisit this later.

CHAPTER SUMMARY

- Personal development addresses a wide range of questions, from our emotional responses to situations to our basic beliefs with regard to knowledge, trustworthiness and truth. What drives us and why? What are our weaknesses and where lie our strengths? And how do different training and career options respond to our assets and vulnerabilities? What impact do we have on others? How do certain others affect us? These are some of the key questions – questions that concern our own past and future.
- Personal development also concerns basic beliefs and ways in which we generate knowledge and understand truth. What do we expect to achieve as therapists? On what do we base our understanding about therapy?
- Personal development is explored with reference to reflective practice and reflexive awareness, which are concepts that invite practitioners to position themselves in a linguistic, cultural, theoretical and personal context with underlying values, assumptions and potential blind spots in mind. Reflexive awareness is an underpinning concept for transformative learning. We looked at two types of reflexivity, namely:

- *reflexive self-awareness*, which involves reflecting on one's thoughts and reactions so that personal blind spots and potential new and different angles are brought to the forefront when problem solving;
- *critical reflexivity*, which is about looking at our work with cultural and theoretical values and biases in mind.
- The ACCTT SMART model starts with a problem and refers to the way in which we may conceptualise and discuss the process of 'recycling' experiences into useful, transformative learning.

CHAPTER 3

Trust and support for personal and professional growth

CORE KNOWLEDGE

- This chapter focuses on the support we need in order to enjoy our work and grow as therapists. The potential of supervision will be explored, together with personal therapy and other means of receiving nourishment, inspiration and knowledge.
- We will explore what Orlinsky and Ronnestad (2005) found in their research in terms of quickly escalating 'cycles of depletion', as a result of not addressing difficulties in time.
- Therapists are sometimes good at hiding their weaknesses, and receiving the support that supervision can offer is sometimes easier said than done. We will explore obstacles in terms of shame and difficulties involved in trusting others for help.

NIBBLED TO DEATH BY DUCKS . . .

Many helpers are ambivalent about asking for help and support for themselves. This is particularly so for helpers at the trainee stage, but probably in many cases on an ongoing basis throughout their careers. Helping is indeed a privilege, but it also has its problems. As suggested in the previous chapter, the founder of person-centred therapy, Carl Rogers (1961, 1995), often captures the wonders and the sparkling moments, of which there certainly are many in therapy. Rogers' accounts of therapy are punctuated by such lyrical remarks as:

> When I can really hear someone, it puts me in touch with him; it enriches my life . . . It is like music of the spheres.
>
> (1995, p8)

Later, however, Rogers (1995) reveals a darker side to our work. He uses the phrase 'nibbled to death by ducks' to describe how he felt at one point when 'harried' by outside demands. *I have always*, writes Rogers, *been better at caring and looking after others than I have been at looking after myself*. He continues:

Three years ago a workshop group helped me to realise how harried and driven I felt by outside demands – 'nibbled to death by ducks' was the way one person put it, and the expression captured my feeling exactly. So I did what I have never done before, I spent ten days absolutely alone in a beach cottage . . . I asked for help – and got it – from a therapist friend. I explored and tried to meet my own needs.

(1995, p80)

Self-reflection and reflexivity are usually of extreme importance during counselling and psychotherapy training (Ronnestad and Skovholt, cited in Trotter-Mathison et al., 2010). Counselling and psychotherapy training rests on exploring experiences through group activities, personal therapy, regular reflective practice exercises and ongoing supervision. These are the key components of training, which lasts between three and five years. There is, however, still a risk that therapists are assumed to be 'sorted out' and forever 'repaired' (Sussman, 1992; Kottler, 2011; Skovholt and Trotter-Mathison, 2011) after their challenging training. Sussman (1992, p246) contends that *unlike traditional shamen, modern day healers are expected to be psychologically strong, robust and stoical.* Sussman continues:

As incongruous at it may seem, the profession that aims to assist people in accepting and coming to terms with their feelings and needs often fails to tolerate or to even acknowledge such human concerns in its practitioners.

In Chapter 7, Marie Adams describes her research into the field of therapists' personal crises. A significant finding was the amount of depression experienced by therapists while working, and the shame that prevented many from addressing their own level of suffering. Of the 40 therapists whom Marie interviewed, more than half (24) admitted they had suffered depression. Sixteen described their experience as episodic, and referred to themselves as suffering 'chronic' depression. Some therapists described their depression as debilitating, but Marie found that those who experienced 'chronic' depression tended to function regardless, often through the support of therapy and sometimes in conjunction with medication.

ACTIVITY 3.1

- Look at the ethical guidelines below. Notice the last one – self-respect. To what extent to do you apply the guidelines to yourself?
- Write for ten minutes about an imaginary therapist who breaches at least three ethical guidelines with regard to herself. If you need a trigger to get you started, begin your story with the following sentence: *Bethany had decided not to take on any more evening clients. The telephone rang. There was an elderly lady at the end of the line: 'I am looking for some help, my husband has just died . . . I can only do evenings . . .'.*

ETHICAL GUIDELINES

As a member organisation for therapists, the British Association for Counselling and Psychotherapy (BACP, 2010) expects its accredited members to adhere to a number of ethical guidelines. One of them is self-respect, which involves the therapist applying the guidelines to him- or herself. Below are the guidelines, with some questions that may arise as a result.

- Fidelity and keeping one's word: *Can I do what I said I would do? Am I able to keep my word?*
- Autonomy and allowing clients to make informed choices: *When and how do I admit to my own limits and restrictions? On what basis do I, for instance, reach common consent in assessment and ongoing with my clients?.*
- Beneficence and duty to care: *Am I qualified, appropriately trained and equipped for this particular client-work?*
- Non-maleficence and 'never doing any harm' to anyone: *How do I reach professional opinions and decisions? What harm can I cause indirectly to clients?*
- Justice and treating clients fairly: *Can I give all clients equal treatment, time and energy? How do I relate to cultural diversity, gender issues, disability, etc.?*
- Self-respect: *Self-respect involves checking that you have applied all the ethical guidelines to yourself!*

Self-respect involves the need to address the following questions.

- Fidelity: *Am I being true to myself? Do I really want to see this client? Is it right for me, my family and friends, to take on this client at this stage? Do I need more time for myself?*
- Autonomy: *Am I considering all factors in my own life when I take on this case? Am I making an informed decision with regard to my own needs and interests right now? Do I 'know' what I am doing, right now, with my own needs in mind?*
- Beneficence: *Where are my own interests in all this? Is this choice serving my own best interests? Am I considering both short- and long-term effects, for myself and my family, both psychically and emotionally?*
- Non-maleficence: *Am I possibly doing myself harm with my decision to take on a new client, to work evenings or to continue working in general, etc.?*
- Justice: *What price might I be paying to help others? Am I doing myself justice; am I fair to myself? If not, then why? What do I need in order to find a comfortable balance?*

WHAT CAN WE EXPECT FROM SUPERVISION?

Supervision is an obligatory requirement for all registered therapists, usually for at least 1.5 hours per month. Our own input is invaluable. The more we prepare for the supervision with our own needs in mind, the greater are the chances that we will find the supervision useful. It is easy to feel lost at the beginning of the process; it is not therapy, but we are not 'reporting back' to a boss or a manager either. It is something in between. Proctor (1986) refers to ethical, educational and personal needs in terms of 'normative', 'formative' and 'restorative' needs:

- your normative needs concern issues such as professional and ethical guidelines, norms and laws;
- your formative needs involve skills, theoretical knowledge and personal attributes as a practitioner;
- your restorative needs revolve around being supported and sometimes constructively challenged with regard to your personal issues, doubts and insecurities.

Scaife et al. (2001, p80) assert that strong feelings will inevitably be evoked during our kind of work and that *the task of the therapist is not to deny them, but rather to make meaning of them in order to most usefully employ them in the service of the client*. We will refer to personal therapy, further training and the support of colleagues and peers at different stages in this book. Supervision is, however, the most consistent and often the first port of call for any therapist who wants to discuss their reactions, doubts and perceived progress. Supervision is an invaluable place for therapists to learn, but also to be nurtured, and perhaps regain a sense of direction. As therapists, we tend to travel between understandings as part of our daily work; we tune into 'different frequencies', abandon ourselves for jointly lived moments with the aim of sharing our clients' 'phenomenology' or lived experience; and it is easy to lose, if not oneself, then one's sense of direction.

Gilbert and Evans (2000) suggest that the challenge for supervision is to help the therapist to move between their client's and their own experience and reality. They assert that at *the heart of effective dialogue* lies what Buber referred to as 'inclusion':

> *[I]nclusion is the back and forth movement of being able to cover the other side and yet remain centred in my own experience . . . The challenge in supervision is to facilitate in the supervisee a flow between these polarities whilst at the same time encouraging a view from above of the interaction between.*

> (cited in Gilbert and Evans, 2000, p10)

Gilbert and Evans (2000) emphasise the importance for the practitioner of being able to 'let go' in a safe and contained way. The supervisory triad offers the therapist the opportunity to let the supervisor 'hold the client's perspective'. Gilbert and Evans write:

> *The supervisee is offered the safe space in which to feel his feelings unedited and for that period not to hold the client's perspective.*
>
> (2000, p11)

The supervisory relationship can help us to step back and reflect at a 'safe' distance. It offers the option to momentarily withdraw from an intricate web of emotional and cognitive processes that normally involve both the therapist and their clients.

The ability to empathise can be a complicated 'talent'; it is something that therapists are assumed to bring with them as a natural asset. However, a common problem for novices is often to 'care too much', as Skovholt and Trotter-Mathison put it:

> *[T]he problem for many in the helping fields is caring too much – excessively feeling the distress emotions of the other . . . Repeatedly forming optimal, positive attachment is often especially difficult for practitioners or those in training who have serious attachment distress in their personal lives.*
>
> (2011, p26)

The different stages of the caring cycle are likely to throw up different issues for different therapists, as Skovholt and Trotter-Mathison (2011) highlight; and depending on our own background some will find certain areas easier to deal with than others. The training can help us to conceptualise and address what Sedgwick (2005, p112) refers to as a self-awareness that involves *a fluid awareness of new and old shadow as well as a concern not to rationalise it or project this upon the client.* Sedgwick (2005, p112) proposes that *the therapist need not eliminate their pathology, but know it and utilise it [rather than] enacting it.* The psychoanalyst Herbert Strean (1993) also warned against the risks of enacting our own issues in the sessions. On an everyday basis we are confronted with strong emotions and can easily become overwhelmed or, as suggested by Eleftheriadou, *make the client's experience too similar to ours:*

> *If we follow this path (i.e. over-identify with the client) because it triggers so much of our own experience, it will, in turn, be reflected in our interpretations that we do no longer see any differences with our clients.*
>
> (2010, p177)

These are aspects that we take with us into supervision. Many helpers also run a general risk of living through their clients. This is a common problem for therapists that we will explore from different angles in this book. To examine the issue in supervision can be essential. Yet, it is also something that therapists sometimes refuse to admit. The actual circumstances of our work in terms of isolation and confidentiality highlight the need for sharing experiences in supervision. We simply cannot speak freely about our work and need to feel able to 'vent', chat and complain. But, for some of us, the reluctance to find a voice of our own stems from having grown used to the helper role and finding it difficult to relate to people in ways other than through listening. Strean warns against the temptation to put pressure on others to achieve the success we may have wanted for ourselves:

> *Like parents who experienced unhappiness in their own childhood and want their sons and daughters to have happier lives than they experienced, clinicians can feel the same way . . . If therapists want to relive their own lives vicariously through their clients every time a residue of one of their own conflicts emerges, they prolong the treatment by trying very hard to achieve the success they wanted for themselves by pressuring their clients to achieve it for them.*
>
> (1993, p228)

However, Strean supports Sedgwick's idea that the therapist's weaknesses can often be transformed into strengths and specialities. He admits, for instance, to having developed separation into a personal speciality:

> *For me, it has never been easy when a patient threatens to quit treatment . . . I feel that my own anxiety at the threat of separation is stronger than most of my colleagues.*
>
> (1998, p126)

Strean suggests that we always ask ourselves: 'Who does this client remind me of?' In the case above he writes that *it has to do with my father.* He explores how this particular woundedness has become a subject for much learning, personally and professionally:

> *Through my experience of warding off feelings of helplessness, weakness, desperation and anger when a patient threatens to leave, I have become an expert in dealing with such patients and I have helped other analysts salvage untreatable cases.*
>
> (1998, p126)

Hawkins and Shohet (2005, p9) also highlight the importance of not investing our clients with our own needs. They regard a willingness to examine our motives, 'good' or 'bad', as a *prerequisite for being an effective helper.* During our training, conclude Hawkins and Shohet:

> *we are taught to pay attention to client needs, and it is often difficult to focus on our own needs . . . even considered selfish, or self-indulgent . . .*

[It is however] not the needs themselves, but the denial that . . . can become so costly.

(2005, p9)

They continue:

Aware of what Jungians call our 'shadow' side, we will have less need to make others into the parts of ourselves that we cannot accept. The crazy psychiatric patient will not have to carry our own craziness, while we pretend to be completely sane; in the cancer patients who cannot face their impending death, we will see our own fear of dying. Focusing on our shadow, we will be less prone to omnipotent fantasies of changing others or the world, when we cannot change ourselves.

(2005, p9)

A defining feature for personal development is thus, as Scaife (2010, p48) puts it, *when I make a purposeful effort towards personal growth specifically in relation to my work.* For therapists, however, this invariably requires a *willingness to become more aware of oneself and one's fears . . . often by examining 'ghosts' from the past* (Scaife, 2010, p50).

ACTIVITY 3.2

- Using the following sentence as a starting point, write for five minutes without stopping: 'I remember it was a school day, maybe a Tuesday or a Wednesday. I was sitting on my bed, looking for a sock, thinking that . . .'.

REFLECTION POINT

Think about Activity 3.2 and answer the following.

- How did it make you feel?
- What issues arose for you?
- How old was the person you wrote about? What was the person experiencing at that time?
- In what way, if at all, are there any links between the themes that emerged in your writing with how you are today? What is different, what has changed? Discuss in pairs if possible.

COMMENT

Some people express surprise over the amount of detail that comes up in uninterrupted writing, such as smells, sounds and other vivid memories linked to time and place. Others sometimes reflect upon how little came up. In one writing group, for example, a member described feeling almost paralysed – unable to write a single word. He was later able to reflect on how this actually coincided with his feelings both at home and in school at this particular time. Many describe how strong feelings return in their writing, such as sadness, helplessness and loneliness, or, in some cases, excitement. One person remembered the day his mother was hospitalised and memories flooded back of trying to make sense of all this when he was at school. This triggered a discussion about how many in the group were 'wounded healers' who could recall a sense of leading a double life as children, coming from a messy household and with an urge to fit in and be a 'normal' child at school. Often, the writers are surprised afterwards to recognise that the age wasn't specified and that the feeling that they had about being asked to write about themselves with a special age in mind is linked to their own way of prioritising events. In one writing group, a member said afterwards that she found it easy to write. 'It was the grey sock that did it for me,' she said; she recognised only afterwards that this was in response to what had come up for her, rather than being specifically addressed in the question.

TEACH OR TREAT?

To explore our own reactions to our clients is not only a cognitive process, stress Frawley-O'Dea and Sarnat (2001) in the relational model. As therapists, we need places where we can acknowledge and connect with experiences that so far have only been around for us on an 'acting out' level. The supervisory relationship should, assert Frawley-O'Dea and Sarnat (2001), contain the supervisee's regressions and dissociations if and when they occur. As illustrated in Case study 3.1, supervision should allow for the unconscious means of mirroring either the client's process at the time or *something that she [the therapist] felt vulnerable to within herself* (Frawley-O'Dea and Sarnat (2001, p134)).

Case study 3.1

Aida is an experienced integrative counsellor whom Marcus, her supervisor, usually finds considerate and insightful. There is something different about Aida today, though. She speaks rapidly about the beautiful weather and has commented twice on Marcus's 'lovely curtains'. Marcus is reminded of the feeling he has when

---

watching his three-year-old girl racing around in a slightly overtired state. Aida's 'joy' makes him nervous. He wonders if she is enacting something that has not yet been formulated into words.

'I'd like to talk about a new client today,' chirps Aida. 'He's called Dan.' She starts on a detailed bibliographic account of Dan. Marcus notices that he is beginning to feel tired; he is struggling to keep his eyes open. He reflects on how this can happen to him when there are too many conflicting messages in the room.

Aida continues: 'He's got a very important job at the hospital. I think he's above the status of a consultant, you know when they stop being called a doctor and take on the mister again.'

Aida goes on to discuss Dan's family situation, and explains how his wife 'never understood him'. Marcus wants to interrupt her flow, but finds no entrance. 'We settled on quite specific targets. Dan thinks that we should . . .,' she continues.

Marcus finds himself to raising his voice to make himself heard. 'How do you feel in the room with the client?' Aida looks taken aback. She grows quiet. 'Good . . .,' she begins in a lower voice. 'It's good when he's pleased.' She looks pensive, and continues: 'But . . . to be honest, I think I am a bit worried about upsetting him.'

Marcus's intervention turns the focus on to Aida's feelings. She turns to a third-person perspective on the dynamic between the client and herself. She explains feeling taken aback from the start; the client's age and his way of walking and talking made her feel 'very young'. Dan's presented problem was panic attacks, but Aida explores how his behaviour contradicted his words. 'I think it was a mixture of him projecting an image of himself as self-sufficient at all costs, and me being caught up in my fears of not being good enough,' concludes Aida.

REFLECTION POINT

- The case study with Aida highlights the difference between talking about and enacting events and emotions. Gilbert and Evans (2000, p11) encourage the supervisee to regard supervision as a place where he or she *is offered the safe space in which to feel his feeling unedited.* Does this reflect your own experience of supervision so far?

Sigmund Freud regarded supervision as a space for dealing with professional, rather than personal, issues. After some personal analysis, the analyst was usually expected to be able to separate his or her emotions from work. If the therapist experienced strong emotions in the sessions, it was originally regarded as something that belonged to the client. Indeed, there is still, as Frawley-O'Dea and Sarnat assert (2001, pp136–7), an *ongoing dispute* within the therapeutic community with regard to what the therapist should do with his or her personal emotions. Outside personal therapy, there is a 'teach/treat' boundary that can be difficult to define. Frawley-O'Dea and Sarnat write about how the 'teach/treat' concept is often a source of anxiety in supervision:

> [T]he teach/treat question probably elicits more doubts and anxiety in supervisors and supervisees than any other aspect of the supervisory relationship.
>
> (2001, p136)

Frawley-O'Dea and Sarnat (2001) emphasise that this process is a matter of co-creating patterns during the supervision session, rather than assuming that the supervisor 'knows' the 'truth'. The supervisor can indeed help with reframing problems with, for instance, the supervisee's own internalised object relations in mind, but it is a matter of co-constructing links rather than 'teaching facts' to the supervisee. Hawkins and Shohet (2005) suggest a model where different roles and focus points in supervision can be addressed openly between the supervisor and supervisee. Their 'seven-eyed' model involves a shift between different focuses. Depending on the presented issues, supervision can allow focus on the client, on the client–therapist relationship, on the therapist's ongoing situation, on life in general, or on organisational matters. Sometimes it is the supervisee–supervisor dyad that needs to be brought into focus. Is, for instance, the supervisee bringing experiences from the client sessions that have not yet been contained or understood? The material and experiences for the sessions can be brought into supervision in an enacted way, which reverberates in the supervisor–supervisee dyad. Case study 3.1 showed how emotions have sometimes unknowingly been stirred in the therapist.

PARALLEL PROCESSES

The term 'parallel process' is often used in psychoanalytically inspired therapy to address how material outside our direct awareness at the time, that is 'unconscious' material, imposes on the therapeutic relationship. The most common form of parallel process happens when therapists tell their client's 'story' through enactments rather than with words. It is often something that the therapist is unaware of, but it offers a clue for the supervisor through changes in behaviour. Page and Wosket write:

> Most supervisors welcome such parallel phenomena as the resulting dynamic provides a more direct way of experiencing the counselling process than second-hand reporting by the counsellor . . . An example of this would be a counsellor who, when working with a particularly passive client, starts to act in an atypical passive manner towards his supervisor. Thus the

passivity within the client–counsellor relationship is paralleled in the counsellor–supervisor relationship.

(2001, p113)

The parallel process can, however, also go the other way; experiences from the therapist–supervisor relationship can become enacted in the client–therapist relationship. If, for instance, the supervisor is uninterested or overly critical in ways that the therapist feels unable to address or acknowledge, there is a risk that the therapist may bring this material into the client relationship. Page and Wosket continue:

[I]t is equally possible for supervisory dynamics to be reflected in the counselling relationship. An example of this is when the supervisor acts in a rather punitive and critical manner towards his supervisee, who in turn acts in a similar manner towards the client.

(2001, p113)

With the risks for parallel processes in mind, Frawley-O'Dea and Sarnat stress the importance of addressing a need to 'know it all' if it appears to be there. Like therapists, supervisors can be under a cultural pressure to 'know':

Supervisors also have to overcome the powerful cultural pressure to feel like competent, objective experts in order to acknowledge their . . . responses.

(2001, p122)

Hawkins and Shohet compare the supervisory relationship with a 'nursing triad':

Winnicott points out that it is very hard for any mother to be 'good enough' unless she herself is also held and supported, either by the child's father, or another supportive adult. This provides a 'nursing triad' . . . Supervision . . . provides a container that holds the helping relationship within the 'therapeutic triad'.

(2005, p3)

Being good enough involves listening inwardly for signs of stress and burnout before they occur. The term 'burnout' originates from the helping professions and refers to *someone in a state of fatigue or frustration brought about by devotion to a cause, way of life, or relationship that failed to produce the expected reward* (Freudenberger, 1980, p13). Burnout happens to those who, as Freudenberger 1980, p14) puts it, *hide their weaknesses well.*

When used constructively, supervision can help in letting go of old, restrictive frameworks of understanding. In my own experience, and indeed from what I have learnt from becoming a supervisor myself, therapists really are very good at hiding their weaknesses. It can, therefore, take some time to make use of the help and support that supervision offers. I suspect that, had it not been for the trust that I was able to build up in personal therapy, I would have struggled to move forward to consider my personal needs in supervision. Part of this would be down to shame.

SHAME

Shame (Gilbert and Evans, 2000; Carroll and Gilbert, 2005) is a common obstacle in supervision. As mentioned earlier, Kottler (2011) and Sussman (1992) found, in their research, tendencies within therapy that collude with the idea of the 'forever-sorted' therapist. Many therapists have, as Carroll and Gilbert (2005, p13) highlight, a fear of being *shamed and humiliated for 'not knowing'* and will, as a result, avoid seeking help. This is a pity, continue Carroll and Gilbert, since it prevents us from learning:

> *Where a supervisee comes from a shame-based system . . . such a person may, in response to any feedback that they construe as critical (whether from outside or from their own internal response to their work), descend into a place of shame and the annihilation of the self makes any further learning impossible until they can regain a more balanced third-person perspective.*
>
> (2005, p13)

Hawkins and Shohet (2005) raise the same issue as an obstacle for exploring cases freely. Shame prevents us from exploring the dynamics in the therapeutic relationship. Hawkins and Shohet write:

> *We have often seen very competent workers reduced to severe doubts about themselves, and their abilities to function through absorbing difficulties from clients.*
>
> (2005, pxx)

A distinct feature of supervision is, however, as Mehr et al. (2010, p111) highlight, that it evaluates the therapist with the client's interest in mind. In contrast to supervision, personal therapy does not involve evaluation. Supervision may complement but not replace personal therapy, as Philips suggests. He continues:

> *[S]uccessful integration of personal and professional development may best be accomplished through personal psychotherapy without fear that personal exposure may lead to lower evaluations.*
>
> (cited in Klein et al., 2011, p277)

An overly evaluative supervision, however, runs the risk of missing valuable information about the therapeutic relationship. Rather than raising standards, this kind of supervision encourages non-disclosure instead. Mehr et al. (2010, p103) conclude that *nondisclosure by trainees appears to be a frequent and normative aspect of supervision*. Their study of trainee non-disclosure indicates that *within a single supervision session, 84.3 per cent of trainees withheld information from their supervisors*. Issues that trainees chose to keep to themselves were often related to the trainee's:

- negative perception of supervision;
- personal life concerns;
- feelings of professional inadequacy.

Mehr et al. (2010, p111) conclude importantly that *it appears that trainees would be more willing to disclose information if the supervision environment was less anxiety-provoking*. As suggested earlier, in the context of parallel processes, a negative supervisor–therapist dyad can seep into the therapist–client relationship and it is always important to address this.

HEALING OR STRESSFUL INVOLVEMENT CYCLES

In their research of nearly 5,000 therapists, Orlinsky and Ronnestad (2005, p169) identified among therapists an experience of a rapidly accelerating cycle as a result of feeling unsupported. The experience of *effective, constructive and affirming relationships* with their clients was usually a rejuvenating experience in itself. These positive experiences would trigger a *renewal of interest and optimism*, which would then feed back into the therapeutic relationship again and contribute to a *felt importance of further development*.

Stressful moments would always need support. If not, the therapists experienced something that Orlinsky and Ronnestad called *stressful involvement with a premature closure*:

> *Premature closure means interrupting the reflection process before the assimilation/accommodation work is completed. It is an unconscious, predominantly defensively motivated, distorting process that sets in when the challenge is too great.*
>
> (2005, p172)

As Orlinsky and Ronnestad (2005, p185) point out, trainees in particular are *likely to feel anxious and overwhelmed* at the best of times:

> *Educators need to recognise this and structure the learning situation so that anxiety-related emotion can be kept to a level where [it] can be mastered.*
>
> (2005, p184)

Once started, Orlinsky and Ronnestad found that the stressful cycle (see Figure 3.1) quickly escalates and can be difficult to get out of. Typical for stressful involvement is the sense of *awkwardness, insecurity and defensive rigidity*, which prevents the therapist from seeking new solutions in supervision, personal therapy and further training. The lack of input feeds into a sense of stagnation, boredom and general lack of motivation, which impacts upon the therapeutic relationship further in a negative sense. This balance between growth and depletion naturally fluctuates and shifts organically over time depending on the work and life in general. But when feelings of anxiety or boredom become overwhelming, they usually engender the earlier-mentioned 'premature closure'.

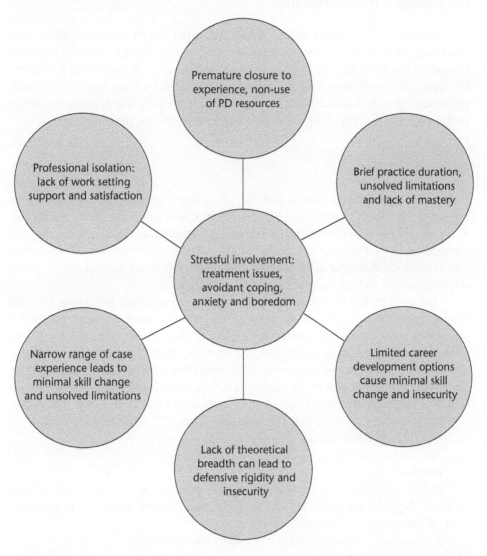

Figure 3.1: Components of the stressful cycle, as identified in Orlinsky and Ronnestad's (2005) research of 5,000 therapists and their experience of work

Orlinsky and Ronnestad continue:

> *Stressful Involvement in therapeutic work is the main source of currently experienced depletion and acts in two ways. The primary source of difficulties with patients that are not constructively managed; such difficulties arouse in the therapist's feeling of anxiety, boredom, or both. As these threaten to become overwhelming, they engender a reaction that Ronnestad and Skovholt (1995) defined as premature closure.*

(2005, p172)

If dealt with at the time, problems can become a source for new awareness and transformative learning. If avoided or ignored, the impact on the relationship can be detrimental.

In Case study 3.2, Helen brings a case to supervision where some of her reactions are outside her own awareness at the time. She has reacted strongly to one of her clients. Read the case study with some of your own reactions to clients in mind. If not discovered and explored in time, the therapeutic relationship may take unwanted directions. Can you think of an example when supervision has helped you to explore such reactions?

Case study 3.2

Helen is a 45-year-old counsellor with ten years' experience of both individual and couple work. When Helen was 16 years old, she was told that she was adopted as a baby by her grandmother. Her biological mother was Laura, whom she had considered to be her sister up to this point. Helen's supervisor was reminded of this experience during a session when Helen referred to an assessment of a self-referred couple seeking help at her private practice.

'I felt sorry for the husband. The wife was the ruthless kind, you know, the real bitchy type who just don't care,' concluded Helen in what came across to the supervisor as a careless way. Helen spoke louder than usual, and used slang and gestures that reminded the supervisor of a teenager. Helen had normally struck the supervisor as a reflective person who considered her own reactions carefully. Her detachment from her new client stood out as unusual and the supervisor wondered if Helen communicated something from the session in both words and behaviour.

'What makes you think that the wife doesn't care?,' asks the supervisor.

Helen shrugs her shoulders.

'Don't know,' she says.

'You don't know . . .'

'Well, I suppose it's the whole package. You know, the type with heavy makeup. Giggly, loud, probably just thinking about herself and when to have fun next. Almost tarty . . . well, insincere.'

'She seemed to have stirred some strong feelings in you . . .'

'I can't stand that type of woman.'

> 'Can you describe what feelings you experience in her company?'
> Helen shifts restlessly in her chair, gesticulates, pulls a funny face and laughs a little.
> 'I just feel very sorry for him, her husband . . .'
> The supervisor remains silent.
> 'He must feel so . . .'
> Helen shrugs her shoulders again.
> 'Well, so boring. So unwanted.'
> 'Unwanted?'
> 'Well, that's how you feel with that kind of woman . . .'
> They both remain silent. Helen's body language changes, she grows still, sighs and adds:
> 'She reminds me of my mother, the "sister" who went out dancing all the time . . .'
> Helen and her supervisor use the rest of the session to unpick the assessment session in a new light after this. Helen recognises that she has assessed the couple through inappropriately tainted lenses, and she appreciates the safe space to explore 'what is what'.

COMMENT

In the case study with Helen, the therapist's 'lenses' were temporarily blurred by prior personal experiences. Helen did not connect with the female client; she assumed that the client had an agenda, which later on in supervision she could explore in a new light. She could see that something in the client had reminded Helen about her own mother's lack of commitment and consideration of others. Helen had brought this experience to supervision in an 'undigested' way; her supervisor picked it up from her behaviour. Supervisors must be prepared for 'listening' to spoken, unspoken and enacted messages in order to learn about the clinical practice of their supervisees. Helen's own training had, in turn, prepared her for being open to these kinds of events, and the supervisory relationship was safe enough for Helen to quickly pick up on the supervisor's hints and make use of the opportunity to bring blurred aspects into awareness.

Withers suggests that therapists inevitably become part of the assessment. She writes:

> *Through the intellectual, emotional and countertransferential considerations of the material gleaned during the initial interview, the therapist becomes part of the client's story and a structure for the subsequent work emerges.*

> (2007, p27)

ACTIVITY 3.3

Think of a case where your own personal experiences may have seeped into the assessment.

• Can you identify an example from a client situation that has reminded you of a conflicted part of your life? If so, to what extent do you feel able to explore such issues in supervision?
• How does your modality inform you to deal with the impact of your own emotions on work? How does that theoretical understanding fit in with you? Are there any objections, or anything that you would like to add or feel a need to learn more about?

Shame and lack of trust are, as suggested, common obstacles for keeping problems to oneself. To what extent we face and deal with these obstacles will impact upon our involvement with our clients. Orlinsky and Ronnestad (2005) found that therapists rated personal therapy highly. Regardless of modality, therapists expressed an appreciation of their own therapy, both in moments of distress and for a more general sense of growth:

> *At every career level, personal therapy was ranked as one of the most important sources of positive influence on therapists' current development. Moreover, personal and professional growth was cited by our therapists as the leading reason for seeking therapy . . . Therapists in general are clearly well aware of the benefits that personal therapy offers; four-fifths of those in our study had at least one course of therapy.*
> (2005, p199)

GAINING INSIGHTS INTO VULNERABILITY

An ability to trust is something that Klein et al. (2011) emphasise is an essential part of the therapist's learning experience. The therapist needs to trust others to fully engage with their clients and risk personal exposure and vulnerability. Klein et al. write:

> *[P]eople who have been damaged and have not successfully worked through these experiences often lack this ability [to trust]. A successful therapeutic relationship is one in which patient and therapist learn to trust one another.*
> (2011, p273)

The therapist's own personal therapy is often regarded as one of the most important training experiences within both psychoanalytic and humanistic approaches. It brings the opportunity to rebuild our trust. Many helpers 'set themselves up' for a cycle of depletion by avoiding help and support, and maintain the image of 'I always need to be there for others.' Personal therapy can be difficult for trainee therapists. My own experience of therapy was described earlier, with reference to working with Janet and Andy; I not only struggled with receiving the support that my supervisor wanted to offer, but initially found personal therapy very difficult too. I somehow expected to 'look after' my therapists and found it very difficult to turn up when I felt sad or downtrodden. It took us a long time to work through my irrational fear of 'destroying' my therapist if I turned to her with too many troubles. This kind of resistance felt impossible to deal with through rational means; we needed time. Some therapists need shorter therapy; others – like myself – need time to work through deep-seated, stubborn patterns and at the same time gain real-life experiences around trust.

REFLECTION POINT

- What is your experience of personal therapy? If possible, discuss in pairs.

Personal therapy also brings an invaluable awareness of how vulnerable one can feel as a client, how confusing it can seem at first with time-limited slots and just how difficult it actually is to change old patterns. Personal therapy has traditionally been considered as less important within cognitive behavioural training. However, as addressed earlier with regard to the growing interest in the impact of the therapeutic relationship, the view on personal therapy for therapists is changing. Phillips also notices a shift with regard to personal therapy as part of therapist training. She writes:

> In the past 20 years, while not viewed as a standard training element . . . personal therapy has been increasingly acknowledged by cognitive behaviourists as helpful in enhancing important training goals . . . One cognitive behavioural therapist shared that it was not until he was a client he could recognise how difficult it was to change patterns and how much he valued his therapist's patience.
>
> (2011, p152)

Case study 3.3

Millie is in her third year of training.

'I have some issues,' said Millie when she first began her personal therapy, as part of the training. She told her therapist, Margot, about having been sexually abused by her father between the ages of five and eleven. She said she felt that she had dealt with the issue in therapy before, and hoped to be able to 'focus on other things now and move on'.

Millie is cheerful, engaging and exceptionally neat when she does turn up. She has, however, a tendency to cancel sessions at short notice. When eventually addressing her irregular attendance, Millie responds with anger. She says that she feels abused by 'unreasonable' requirements on the trainees. She is fed up with having to work voluntarily and pay for her own therapy, which she doesn't see any need for anyway. She cancels her next session, but agrees to come for a final session to say goodbye.

Millie comes to the session and recounts a dream from the night before. In the dream, she moved slowly in circles around her father, who sat on a bed with a 'blanket over his thing'. In the dream, his presence felt like a magnet, which Millie did all to resist, until she eventually caught sight of a door.

'I felt so happy, so very relieved,' begins Millie and then grows quiet. Margot notices that she is crying.

'But when I got out on to the street, I realised that I couldn't speak to anyone. I walked up and down the streets, they were crowded with people, but I got this sick, kind of sinking feeling in my stomach.'

Millie reflects over how she 'knew' in her dream that she would never be able to connect with anyone about her experiences; it was only her father who would really understand. In her dream she had returned to the room where she'd known her father had been waiting for her.

Millie and Margot remain silent for quite some time. Eventually Millie says: 'I think what I hadn't really realised until now, is just how impossible it has seemed to get help from outside.'

They agree to continue the therapy, with a renewed focus on trust and the difficulties in letting go of the shame and the sense of exclusivity that was fostered in her abusive relationships.

ACTIVITY 3.4

Alice Miller (1997, p19) asserts that the therapist's curiosity, empathy and *powerful antennae* indicate *that as a child he probably used to fulfil other people's needs and repress his own*. Miller links curiosity with hypervigilance and lack of trust, and addresses the need to 'work through' issues of this kind before we make helping others into our profession.

- What is trust for you? Where does this negative or positive idea of trust stem from?

CHAPTER SUMMARY

- In this chapter, we have explored the potential in supervision to assess our own work, while at the same time receiving support and inspiration. We also looked at hindrances to making the most of this kind of support.
- Therapists are sometimes good at hiding their weaknesses, and receiving support can sometimes be an issue for therapists. We looked at shame and other obstacles for admitting to mistakes and addressing difficulties as they occur in our practice. It was suggested that personal therapy is used as a way to regain trust. It is necessary for a therapist to receive support and to engage with clients in an authentic relationship based on trust.
- We looked at what Orlinsky and Ronnestad (2005) suggest in terms of a quickly accelerating cycle of depletion as a result of not addressing difficulties as they occur. Personal therapy, supervision and peer support are key factors for preventing depletion.

CHAPTER 4

The anatomy of healing

CORE KNOWLEDGE

- In this chapter we will look at 'therapeutic mastery' in terms of recognising and constructively managing subtle effects, while being able to put our understanding of a client's experience into context, *and* conveying this understanding to the client.
- Therapeutic understanding is linked to 'phenomenological' understanding, characterised by our willingness and ability to see reality as it appears to the other. The importance of phenomenological understanding is relatively undisputed. It is when we come to how best to organise, evaluate and convey the information gathered that disputes often arise. On what basis do we arrive at knowledge and 'truths' within therapy?
- As therapists, we are requested to choose between different theoretical orientations. How do we do that? We will look at the meaning of an underpinning philosophy, and consider some differences and overlapping features within psychoanalytic, person-centred and cognitive behavioural therapy.

WHAT IS THERAPEUTIC MASTERY?

Klein et al. (2011, p19) assert that *it is possible to identify certain characteristics to be a good therapist, regardless of the theoretical approach employed.* 'Therapeutic mastery' involves learning to recognise and constructively manage subtle effects of the therapeutic process, while being able to put one's understanding of a client's experience into context, and conveying this understanding to the client.

A 'good' therapist needs, first, an ability to understand another person. This skill involves, as Klein et al. (2011, p19) put it, the ability *to accurately [understand] the phenomenological experience of those who present themselves for treatment.* This involves both seeing and feeling what the client is going through. Klein et al. continue:

[patients] who experience their therapists as being able to feel, and vicariously experience, what they are going through in their lives have a much better chance of finding the treatment beneficial than those who do not.

(2011, p19)

We looked at the complex issue of empathy in Chapter 1. Over-identification is a close relative of empathy. The kind of understanding referred to here is linked to 'phenomenological' understanding, where the therapist is willing to see reality as it appears to the other, at that time. Sometimes we need the therapist to help us 'digest' (Bion, 1962) overwhelming emotions. As Fonagy states:

The repeated experience of finding himself in the mind of his therapist, not only enhances self representation but also removes the patient's fear of looking.

(cited in Baradon, 2003, p141)

The therapist also needs to safeguard space for the client to experience and feel the changes. Therapy is not just cognitive but also an affective and bodily experience. This is made more tangible through recent neuro-scientific findings, which, as Klein et al. (2011, p10) put it, highlight *that interaction with the environment, especially with other people, has an impact on the structure and function of the brain.*

As suggested in Chapter 1, the importance of phenomenological under-standing is relatively undisputed. It is when we come to how to *organise, evaluate and convey the information that is gathered* (Klein et al., 2011, p275) that disputes arise. The intention of the following section is to explore some of the differences that might arise regarding the issue of what to do with our understanding of the client's experiences.

Case study 4.1

Claire is a middle-aged woman who is seeking therapy for panic attacks. When she was 14 years old she was raped by a neighbour for whom she used to babysit during summer holidays from her Catholic boarding school for girls. She never spoke about the event at the time; she felt it was 'her fault' for having dressed inappropriately. The trigger for seeking therapy was a car accident, 12 years ago. She was physically unharmed, but has not been able to leave her house since the accident. Talking about the event brings tears to her eyes.

   'I keep thinking about what happened and it feels like the driver just went for me, like he singled me out and thought I'll nail her, I'll show her!'

Claire sobs, and continues:

'That's why I won't go out any more, anyone can suddenly launch . . .'

The therapist nods.

'I'm right, aren't I, it's just not safe anywhere!' cries Claire.

'What's that like for you, not to feel safe anywhere?' asks the therapist.

Claire thinks for while, and continues:

'It's like you need to watch every step . . . how you walk, how you dress, how people are looking at you . . . . It's like that summer. All I did was be myself, I just wanted to dress like a teenage girl, you know. He was just waiting really, wasn't he? Just waiting to launch at me, like a predator . . .'.

COMMENT

Claire is able to explore the meaning of the car accident in her therapy. She feels safe to say what comes into her head. She senses a genuine interest from her therapist and this motivates her to explore events more thoroughly; they are 'partners in thought' (Stern, 2010). The therapist invites Claire to look at her general assumption that 'it is unsafe to go out' with a more specific reference. 'What does unsafe mean to you?' asks the therapist. As Claire explores the accident, she associates with other events and begins to see links to how she has experienced herself as helpless in the past. Therapy can offer her a place to explore her pre-understandings of herself in relation to others, with the potential for new understandings of the world in mind.

Ogunfowora and Drapeau emphasise the impact that our modality can have on our outlook on work:

> A psychotherapist's theoretical orientation serves as his/her foundation for understanding the nature of human change, the aetiology and prognosis of presenting issues, case conceptualisation, therapy goals and therapeutic techniques.
>
> (2008, p151)

In this section, we look at three core modalities:

- psychoanalytic;
- person-centred;
- cognitive behavioural therapy.

THE ANATOMY OF HEALING

TRANSFERENCE AND COUNTERTRANSFERENCE

The psychoanalytically inspired therapist might have approached Claire with an interest in the 'point of maximum pain'. It is a key concept in Hinshelwood's theory about assessing the client with a relationship tripod in mind:

> *Clinical material is best approached as pictures of relationships with objects. There are then three areas of object relationships which I try to bear in mind:*
> 1. *the current life situation;*
> 2. *the infantile object relations, as described in the patient's history, or by hypothesising from what is known;*
> 3. *the relationship with the assessor which, to all intents and purposes, is the beginning of a transference.*
>
> (1997, p157)

So, while the rape is important to consider, a psychodynamic therapist might also be interested in what rape means for Claire in particular. Why did she keep the incident to herself? What were Claire's early relationships like?

Psychoanalytically inspired therapy is often caricatured as cold and detached; the therapist sits behind his client who lies on a couch four or five times per week. The 'blank screen' approach is characterised by silence and 'abstinence' on the part of the therapist; but it is easy to get stuck within stereotypes. My own memories from psychoanalysis are full of warmth. It is easy to forget that one of the original intentions with the blank screen approach was to avoid giving in to the temptation of acting as parents, teachers or idealised role models. That would, argued Freud (1959), involve repeating the damage inflicted by overly dominating parents in the first place. Together with his colleague Josef Breuer, Freud discovered that clients' anticipations of their therapists often coincided with their experiences from other, earlier relationships. Freud writes:

> *[The patient] sees in his analyst the return – the reincarnation – of some important figure out of his childhood or past, and consequently transfers on to him feelings and reactions that undoubtedly applied to this model.*
>
> (1959, p38)

The idea of 'transference' soon became an underlying principle for psycho-analytic practice. Transference is 'ambivalent', writes Freud (1959, p38); *it comprises positive and affectionate as well as negative and hostile attitudes towards the analyst.*

Positive transference can be particularly difficult to work with. It is tempting, admits Freud, to perceive positive transference as genuine praise. *It serves us admirably*, writes Freud (1959, p39). It feeds into our desire to please. It is tempting, continues Freud, to play into the role of a saviour, teacher and infallible helper, but we must *shamefacedly admit* that it is often a question of the client's underlying *aim of pleasing the analyst, of winning his applause and love* as a means of repeating earlier patterns:

> However much the analyst may be tempted to act as teacher, model and ideal to other people and to make men into his own image, he should not forget that is not his task in the analytic relationship . . . He will only be repeating one of the mistakes of the parents, when they crushed their child's independence, and he will only be replacing one kind of dependency by another.
>
> (1959, p39)

Transference was offered as a means of living through experiences, rather than simply thinking and talking about them. Freud (1959, p41) considers the lived experience as a crucial aspect of the talking cure and asserts that *the patient never forgets again what he has experienced in the form of transference.*

THE THERAPEUTIC FRAMEWORK

The 50-minute session is regarded as an important component of psycho-analytic work. It is common for client novices to feel perplexed when the framework is violated, asserts Gans (2011). Sometimes *a cigar is just a cigar*, continues Gans (2011, p96), and people, for example, arrive late or forget to pay, for good reasons. But, more often than not, aberrations from the agreed contract will be regarded as options to explore deeper and more complex problems. Gans continues:

> The therapeutic framework is not meant to be a set of rules to which strict patient obedience is expected. Just the opposite is true: they have secured the patient's willingness to take responsibility for honouring items in the contract precisely because experience has shown that as therapy unfolds, patients – and sometimes therapists – will violate these very conditions.
>
> (2011, p96)

Psychotherapeutic practice has developed radically since its beginning. Today, few therapists would argue in favour of rigid ways of responding to 'framework violations' such as lateness, cancellations, lack of payment, etc. Gans reminds us about the importance of contracts in terms of getting to know our clients. The different ways in which clients relate to pre-agreed boundaries can tell us much about the clients' relationships and expecta-tions of self and others. Gans writes:

Clinical experience teaches that the best approach is the one that keeps therapeutic space open . . . Only through exploration of the issues involved can the therapist determine what that approach should be. Such an exploration will take into account existing transference and counter-transference, the state of the alliance, the phase of therapy, past handling of this situation, and the real relationship.

(2011, p96)

ACTIVITY 4.1

Time, money and agreements around, for instance, unplanned contact are part of the so-called 'therapeutic frame'. Some modalities emphasise different aspects of the frame more than others. But, in general, there are certain fundamental boundaries that are agreed upon across modality borders.

- What does time-keeping mean to you? What kind of boundaries might be particularly important to emphasise for you, in personal therapy?
- On what guidelines do you base the therapeutic frame for your work – and why?

If possible, discuss in pairs.

Let us return to Claire in Case study 4.1. Claire has just started to elaborate on the bodily experience and the cognitive construct with which she approaches her reality; ideally, Claire would continue exploring her patterns of relating to others on the basis of blueprints. She would begin to challenge the patterns and explore new ways of relating to her environment. Instead, she seems to return to new threats each session: she feels her neighbour is unfair by asking her to move her bin on to the drive; she feels the shop-keeper wants to take advantage etc.

Case study 4.2

Today Claire returns to the theme of not trusting people.
    Claire: 'It's like you need to watch every step . . . You've got to watch out all the time!'
    Silence.
    Claire seems to seek reassurance; and the therapist might be tempted to smile, nod or say something encouraging or comforting. She decides upon silence in order to allow Claire's lack of trust to surface. She is hoping to address some of the feelings that Claire may harbour in the room. The therapist makes a point of keeping a straight face.

Claire: What?

Silence.

Claire: Why are you looking at me like that?

Silence.

Claire begins to shift nervously in her chair.

Therapist: I am wondering if you feel like you have to watch out all the time here too?

Claire grows silent. Eventually she nods and begins to open up about why she cancelled the last session. She looks different, more relaxed and somehow more 'grown up' as she can begin to address the relationship in the room. She explains how she feels sure that the therapist will grow tired of her. The therapist reflects on the sense of helplessness and 'stuck-ness' that she has experienced with Claire, as if her needs are overwhelming. The therapist wonders if this might be how Claire's mother might have felt. All she knows so far is that the mother 'didn't like children much'. Are they now, muses the therapist, perhaps beginning to gain insight into what Claire's life and early relationships were like, before the rape?

COMMENT

The way we choose to 'explain' our reactions will vary, depending on how we perceive the purpose of our interpretation. The therapist may choose to comment on the situation to:

- show an interest in her client, with the view of validating Claire's experience rather than leaving her feeling resentful and isolated;
- begin to make sense of the situation, and offer an interpretation to reach a shared understanding;
- offer Claire the opportunity to make the link herself, by addressing what 'has happened' but leaving the conclusion open for Claire to formulate what the situation might have reminded her of, perhaps opening up for reflections around her experience of not being able talk about the rape at home;
- help to access cut-off feelings, such as 'it is easy to feel vulnerable when you feel that no one will cope . . .', 'trusting others can be scary . . .'.

Howard sums up this dual cognitive and affective focus in psycho-analytically inspired therapy, as she writes about *interpretation as an aid to integration*. By linking feelings, thoughts and behaviour, we:

enable [the client] to create a narrative around his life, which can help him have a sense of where he came from and his place in the world. An interpretation can also be used to deepen the affective relationship between you and your client. The neuropsychoanalysts describe this connectedness as the result of right brain activity, which is similar to what happens between mother and baby.

(2010, p83)

REVISITING THE UNCONSCIOUS

Howard addresses how psychoanalytic theory, today, tends to include neuroscientific findings. As Green (2003, p1) asserts, *no single methodology can do justice to the complexity of the human mind*, and neuropsychoanalysis is an example of how original oppositional frameworks, such as biology and psychoanalysis, find common ground. The unconscious has, for many, a strange ring to it; it smacks of 'blank screen' thinking. Developments within neuroscience have brought new perspectives to 'consciousness', which can be adopted in a wider context than Freud originally proposed.

Most of what we do consciously depends upon implicit unconscious memory systems, assert many modern neuroscientists. Scientists such as Damasio (1999), Solms and Turnbull (2002, 2003), Schore (2003) and Kandel (2006) suggest that most of our moment-to-moment life is guided by connections within our memory systems, and that these are implicit and beyond our conscious awareness. Solms and Turnbull write:

[M]uch of human memory is unconscious, and it never becomes conscious – though that does not mean that it does not influence consciousness. Most of what we do consciously, in our moment-to-moment lives, depends upon implicit unconscious memory systems which exert their effects on us without us even realising it.

(2002, p279)

To grasp this process, Damasio (1999) suggests that we think of our conscious in terms of a 'movie'. To be conscious involves generating a 'movie-in-the-brain', including objects such as sound and images, people and relationships. This movie has *as many sensory tracks as our nervous system has sensory portals*, asserts Damasio (1999, p8), and is based on a script where *different emotions [are] induced in the brain and played out in the theatre of the body*.

To be 'conscious', writes Damasio (1999, p8) means that *there is a presence of you in a particular relationship with some object*. Consciousness involves 'replaying' interactions with ourselves in relation to objects (good, bad and indifferent) in our minds.

Some of the vast material that lies beyond our immediate awareness can be retraced through *conscious auditory and kinesthetic sensation*, write Solms and

Turnbull (2002, p253). Unconscious thoughts can be made conscious by representing them both by images, such as in dreams, and in words:

> *Unconscious mental processes are removed from the perceptual periphery [and] cannot be rendered conscious until they are associated with something perceivable. Since the memory traces of words – what Freud called 'word representations' – are derived from conscious auditory and kinesthetic sensation, they possess the requisite perceptual properties. Unconscious thoughts can therefore be made conscious by representing them by words.*
>
> (2002, p253)

Remembering will, however, as Kandel (2006, p281) puts it, invariably be a 'creative process'. When we 'access' memories, core memories are *elaborated upon and reconstructed, with subtractions, additions, elaborations and distortions*:

> *For all of us, explicit memories make it possible to . . . conjure up events and emotional states that have vanished into the past yet somehow continue to live in our minds. But recalling a memory episodically – no matter how important the memory – is not like turning to a photograph in an album. Recall of memory is a creative process. What the brain stores is thought to be only a core memory. Upon recall, this core memory is elaborated upon and reconstructed, with subtractions, additions, elaborations and distortions.*
>
> (2006, p281)

The 'replay', as Damasio (1999) puts it, means thus that personal memories invariably 'arrive' with distortions and elaborations, formed in the context of our unique personal, previous experiences – both in the past and in the present context of the 'replay'. Damasio uses the term 'reflexive consciousness' for the kind of level of our thinking that allows us to reflect on, think about and remember our conscious experiences as opposed to living them moment-by-moment'.

RECONNECTING WITH EMOTIONS

Alan Schore is both a scientist and a psychoanalyst. He has focused on the impact of interpersonal circumstance for the movie-in-our-brain, as Damasio puts it. Schore specialises in the development of our capacity to self-regulate emotions and assess how others feel about things. He focuses on how our affective and emotional development is influenced early on in life, and how it can be redeveloped at later stages depending on circumstances. Schore (2003, p43) refers to the right brain as the *locus of the emotional, corporeal and the dynamic unconscious* and links its *ongoing maturational potential* to our *attachment-influenced early organisation*. He asserts that a child's early social environment influences the evolution of structures in the infant's brain. Schore suggests that the maturation of the orbitofrontal cortex is influenced by dyadic interactions of the attachment relationship. Being 'seen' or, as Stern suggested earlier, being heard in the ears of the other, affects our future capacity both to self-regulate emotions and to understand the way other people feel. A neglected or impaired affect regulation can, argues Schore, be recovered, for example, through psychotherapy. The relationship combines a *felt* experience with verbal conscious and intense reflective experiences, based on actual experiences of relating to others.

ARE WE RETURNING TO AN EXPERT STANCE?

The neuroscientific findings could tempt us into putting ourselves in an expert stance, which Freud implied in terms of assuming that the therapist had the key to all that was hidden. It is easy to forget that, if the neuroscientific findings are correct, then we too will be faced with the ongoing dilemma of making decisions based on implicit memory systems, in need of constant tracing and reflective assessment.

Countertransference was initially a concept designed to understand what the therapist felt in relation to the client's transference. It was regarded as an indicator of the client's problems, as something that always 'came', or was projected, from the client. Racker (1982) argued that psychotherapy always involved a fusion between the past and the present for *both* therapists and clients, and he suggested different types of countertransference, for example concordant and complementary. The different types of countertransference described how, sometimes, reactions in the therapist would stem from the client's transference and projection towards the therapist – such as in the case of Claire, who felt that her new client might have acted out something in the room that could inform them both, eventually, about earlier experiences and how these may affect the way she expects to interact with people today. But it is also important, argues Racker (1982), to acknowledge how some issues tap into the therapist's own history. Some of our reactions to our clients may say more about our own fantasies and issues than about our clients. Did the therapist, for instance, read too much into Claire's reaction? Did Claire's reactions feed into the therapist's experiences of frustration from 'always listening' to her own alcoholic mother; did this perhaps make her overly sensitive? Or, did it perhaps help her to pick up cues that another therapist might have missed?

Clarkson (1995, p89) suggests that the therapists listen to their reactions in terms of 'reactive' and 'proactive' countertransference.

- **Reactive countertransference** describes the psychotherapist's feelings that are elicited by or induced by the patient.

- **Proactive countertransference** refers to feelings, atmospheres, projections, etc. that can be said to have been introduced by the psychotherapist him- or herself.

Jung (cited in Sedgwick, 2005) contends that these reactions are often interlinked, and that there needs to be a 'hook' inside each therapist for a client projection to latch on to in the first place.

Freud compared therapy with archaeology. He aimed to reveal an underlying, pre-existing truth about the human mind. Much has changed within psychoanalytic theory. The unconscious is not an already formed entity or thing, waiting to be found by an outside expert. As Stern puts it:

> There can be no single reality underlying any transference, no unitary truth can be uncovered. Transference and countertransference can no longer be viewed as distortions . . . but are created in just the same ways as any other interpersonal perceptions.
>
> (2010, p7)

More often than not, asserts Stern, these 'right' moments are spontaneous moments – 'Kairos moments' – when the therapist and the client become present to each other in the full meaning of the word.

ACTIVITY 4.2

Consider the therapeutic relationship from the perspective of a client. Read Case study 4.3 with your own experiences in mind.

- How does this experience of therapy compare with yours?

Case study 4.3

Ellen recalls:

I have a very fond memory of my therapist. I called quite a few therapists at first, and what made me settle for my therapist was that she dropped a pen while she was on the phone. 'Oh dear, I dropped my pen,' was all she said; but there was a warmth in the way that she said it. I've been thinking afterwards that it somehow made me feel that she was OK with making mistakes, and that felt really important to me. It was as if she could accept me not being perfect but also admit to making her own mistakes. My parents were never like that; I never felt any connection with either of them. They did terrible things to us children, but what hurt most was that they never knew when they were wrong. Parents who can't see when they are in the wrong are not safe to be around. I was quite scared in therapy too, during our first year together. It was probably the unknown territory that frightened me most. And I was expecting that she would 'turn' and become nasty. I tried to be polite, entertaining. One day, she quietly reflected on that. I think she said something about me working hard to please her. I began to cry, I felt so relieved. She had bothered to notice. I felt so cared for, my feelings really mattered.

The format was quite funny; she often sat there all quiet and I thought at first, what's this all about? Then, gradually, I felt both freer and safer than I've ever done before. I felt that we grew to know each other, we seemed to fit. She spoke with her eyes, I felt. She would hold my gaze, and really listen.

The time-keeping was very precise but in the sessions it was as if anything goes. Not in a bad way, but in a warm, safe, loving kind of way. Sometimes I'd walk out of sessions with roaring laughter ringing in my ears and we would have laughed together. With hindsight, I think that she might just have smiled or maybe just chuckled. I think that I often read in reactions. But when it mattered she would show her emotions; she would get angry with my father when he had cut me out of his will. She once raged over my mother, when she had smacked our youngest daughter like she used to do with us. That was a huge thing; she was on my side, on our side. I would carry her anger with me out of the session like a shield. My therapist got really angry, I would think, and that would help me in feeling those feelings myself. Most of the time she'd actually just give me space to say certain things myself! She would perhaps nod, maybe sometimes agree. But she probably just said a fraction of what I felt she did. She did feel very present, though, very real. She still does; I often think 'what would Erica say?' when I find myself in tricky situations. Our relationship lives on, inside of me.

THE PERSON-CENTRED THERAPIST

Humanistic psychology developed during the 1950s in direct opposition to the idea of therapy as a form of 'excavation'. Yalom writes:

> To Freud, exploration always meant excavation . . . Deepest conflict meant earliest conflict . . . There is no compelling reason to assume that 'fundamental' (that is, important, basic) and 'first' (that is, chronologically first) are identical. To explore deeply from an existential perspective does not mean that one explores the past; rather it means that one brushes away everyday concerns and thinks deeply about one's existential situation.
>
> (1980, p10)

As we have seen, Carl Rogers emphasises the importance of a phenomenological understanding. The person-centred therapist will, as suggested, bring the here and now to the forefront. Rogers (1951/1999, p151) emphasises the importance of relating to clients in such a way that our responses, attitudes and phrases *indicate that it is the client's evaluation of the situation which is accepted*. The example below is borrowed from Mearns and Thorne (1999, p10) and illustrates this way of talking, guided by an aim to restore the client's *own organismic valuing process* and tap into his or her own innate ability to grow, develop and evaluate events.

Case study 4.4

Client: I feel very sad: it's an overwhelming feeling.
Counsellor: As if you have no option but to give yourself to the sadness.
Client: That sounds very frightening – as if I shall lose control. But I never lose control [suddenly bursts into tears].
Counsellor: Your tears speak for you.
Client: But big boys don't cry.
Counsellor: Are you saying that you are ashamed of your tears?
Client: [Long pause]. No . . . for the first time in years I feel in touch with myself . . . it feels OK to be crying.

As part of being 'real', showing emotions becomes a more natural aspect of therapy within humanistic therapy. The way that warmth, for example, can be shown in person-centred therapy obviously differed from the way Freud had suggested with reference to his 'blank screen' approach. Mearns and Thorne (1999) include some of the following ways in which the therapist can communicate warmth:

- using a warm tone of voice;
- smiling;
- keeping eye contact;
- shaking hands;
- genuinely laughing when the client recounts something;
- taking the opportunity to let a client know that you have remembered what she told you some sessions ago; for instance, the name of her dog, a treasured childhood memory etc.

Rogers' philosophy was influenced by the therapist Godfrey Barrett-Lennard (1959, in Rogers, 1961, p263), who had researched the impact of empathic understanding. A sense of being cared for by a genuine, honest person who aimed to see things through the client's eyes with a 'no strings attached' – unconditional interest – was, according to Barrett-Lennard, the bedrock of what the clients in his research would experience as empathic under-standing. This became the foundation for Rogers' core conditions. In the security of the therapeutic relationship, writes Rogers:

[that is], in the absence of any actual or implied threat to self, the client can let himself examine various aspects of his experience as they actually feel to him, as they are apprehended to [him], without distorting them to fit the existing concept of self.

(1961, p76)

Being warm is sometimes an important aspect of this non-threatening environment.

The therapeutic relationship taps into something that is already there, 'implicit, but unverbalised' in most clients. One of the overriding goals with therapy, suggests Rogers (1951/1999, p150), is *the dawning realisation that [we] can base a value judgement [on our] own senses [and our] own experiences.* Rogers noted, not dissimilarly to Freud earlier, that many of his clients struggled with evaluating experiences. They found it difficult, as Rogers puts it, to 'experience the experience' and would doubt their senses on the basis of what they had learned in earlier relationships. Again, not that differently from Freud, Rogers warned against the temptation to leap in and 'take over'. Rogers writes:

In therapy, in the initial phases, there appears to be a tendency for the locus of evaluation to lie outside the client. It is seen as a function of parents, of the culture, of friends and of the counsellor . . . In client-centred therapy, however, one description of the counsellor's behaviour is that he consistently keeps the locus of evaluation with the client.

(1951/1999, p151)

Rogers emphasised the importance of 'therapist congruence' within the therapeutic relationship. Mearns and Thorne (1999, p99) assert that 'congruence' is a skill that often takes longest to develop in a therapist. To be incongruent involves deliberately concealing aspects, in the way in which the psychoanalytically 'blank screen' therapist could be argued to do. It also, with parallels to earlier discussions about countertransference, involves having an underlying feeling towards our client that we are unaware of ourselves. In other words, congruence requires the therapist to listen deeply both inwardly and outwardly, and to carefully consider how his or her own experiences may or may *not* facilitate the relationship. Rogers compares congruence with being 'real':

In place of the term 'realness' I have sometimes used the word 'congruence'. By this I mean when my experiencing of this moment is present in my awareness and when my awareness is present in my communication.

(1995, p14)

Rogers (1951/1999, 1961, 1995) addressed, as mentioned, certain core conditions for therapeutic change. In addition to therapist congruence, Rogers emphasises the importance of the following conditions.

- **Therapist–client contact**. There must be a relationship between client and therapist in which each person's perception of the other is important.
- **Client's motivation**. The client's fragility is often manifested in a lack of faith in their own judgement; there is usually an 'incongruence' between their experience and awareness. A client can, for instance, think that she *is* 'useless' and doomed to fail with everything she sets out to do. To make the most of therapy, she ought to show willingness in exploring where this self-image of 'useless' comes from. The client must be able to reflect on whether or not this causes her enough of a problem to consider a potential change. Does the client's symptoms cause him or her sufficient problems to justify therapy? Is there a strong-enough motivation to remain in a therapeutic relationship?
- **Therapist's unconditional positive regard**. The therapist is prepared to consider whether or not he or she is able to step into the client's shoes and accept the client unconditionally, without judgement, in order to give the client space to explore his own 'locus of evaluation'. Unconditional positive regard is, asserts Rogers, about 'non-possessive caring':

The therapist is willing for the client to be whatever immediate feeling is going on – confusion, resentment, fear, anger, courage, love or pride. Such caring on the part of the therapist is nonpossessive. The therapist prizes the client in a total rather than a conditional way.

(1995, p116)

- **Therapist empathic understanding**. Empathy is linked to being able to enter the client's internal frame of reference. Accurate empathy on the part of the therapist helps the client believe in the therapist's unconditional love for them. Rogers links this to what we earlier referred to as a 'sparkling moment' of 'deep hearing':

When functioning best, the therapist is . . . inside the private world of the other . . . This means that the therapist senses accurately the feelings and the personal meanings that the client is experiencing and communicates this understanding to the client.

(1995, p116)

- **Client perception**. The client is able to relate to and perceives the therapist's intention and empathic understanding.

COGNITIVE BEHAVIOURAL THERAPY

Both person-centred and cognitive behavioural therapy (CBT) emphasise the importance of transparency. CBT is, however, based on collaborative effort to the extent that the therapeutic alliance is often compared with 'negotiation' (Gilbert and Leahy, 2007, p92). As Aaron Beck and colleagues (Beck et al., 1987) assert, cognitive approaches often seem deceptively easy. Beck et al. emphasise both Rogers' core conditions and Freud's idea of transference in his approach to the 'therapeutic alliance'. Warmth, say Beck et al. (1987, p46), is essential in establishing a therapeutic relationship, although *it is crucial to bear in mind that the patient's response is his perception of warmth rather than the actual degree of warmth expressed by the therapist.* Beck et al. (1987, p48) also emphasise genuineness and empathy; the therapist must be able *to experience life the way the patient does* at the same time as being *careful not to project his own attitude or expectations onto the patient.* This empathic understanding will, continue Beck et al. (1987, p48), be balanced with *objective checking of the patient's introspection against other sources of information,* such as *testing the logic involved in the patient's inferences and conclusions.* Beck et al. (1987, pp50, 54) assert that *therapeutic interactions are based on trust, rapport and collaboration* and they view them as a *vehicle to facilitate a common effort in carrying out specific goals.*

CBT includes a variety of approaches and therapeutic systems; some of the most well known include cognitive therapy, rational emotive behaviour therapy and multimodal therapy. Beck, the 'father' of cognitive therapy, has developed most in the field of the therapeutic relationship. CBT emphasises overall, however, the collaborative problem-solving approach that Beck et al. referred to above. Questions that a CBT therapist might ask Claire from the earlier Case studies 4.1 and 4.2 might focus on what logical errors could be involved in the way she perceives herself, her future and the world around her. Claire's therapist might use cognitive techniques such as examining the evidence and thought records to identify and change maladaptive cognitions. The therapist may also use behavioural methods through systematic exposure techniques to reverse ways of avoiding certain things. The term 'consciousness' is used in CBT as a state in which rational decisions can be said to be made with full awareness. The term 'automatic thoughts' is often used to describe the opposite way of making decisions. These types of thoughts are what Beck called 'private cognitions'. Much of Claire's cognitions could be described as automatic thoughts. They are shaped by her earlier life experiences and have become core beliefs, or schemas, which create templates for the way she processes information in the present. CBT refers to the Socratic method, which encourages clients to contribute in asking questions of themselves: 'How do I really know that all people are dangerous; what is the logic in that; could they seem threatening because they are in a bad mood, or because I have approached them in a reserved, maybe defensive way?' etc. CBT emphasises rational thinking; 'What are,' Claire might ask herself, 'the facts for her belief that all people are threatening?' Homework is likely to become a part of Claire's therapeutic process if she is in CBT. She and her therapist would agree on tasks that Claire could undertake in between sessions to explore her automatic thoughts in terms of facts.

THE 'CURING FACTOR'

Efforts to draw on commonalities between modalities have been made. Wosket (2001, p15) refers to an emerging *common factor paradigm* and an increase in explaining effective outcomes in counselling and psychotherapy by common therapeutic factors across all schools, rather than with reference to approaches, specific strategies and procedures. Hofmann and Weinberger (2007, p107) assert that *the therapeutic relationship is, by far, the most written about common factor*, but they propose five common factors that *empirical data seem to support*.

- **The therapeutic relationship**. This appears to be most central to psychodynamic and humanistic/experiential approaches but is, however, *genuinely related to therapeutic success* across the modalities.
- **Expectations of treatment effectiveness**. Expectancy, assert Hofmann and Weinberger (2007, p106ff), has also been noted as particularly influential within all modalities. People who are able to put faith into the treatment, and who expect progress, can also expect to feel better. The cognitive therapies incorporate this factor into the actual treatment more than other modalities, and make sure that expectations are addressed. What, in medical treatment, is called the placebo effect is, as Hofmann and Weinberger (2007, p106ff) put it, *no less powerful in psychotherapeutic settings*. This therapeutic factor will be determined from the outcome, before the actual therapy starts.
- **Confronting or facing problems (exposure)**. There is usually a different emphasis on how to confront problems within the different modalities. Cognitive therapies value the use of 'exposure' in the treatment. This involves pinpointing specific issues and agreeing on ways to challenge them overtly. Self-defeating verbalisations or 'pathogenic', counterproductive cognitions and beliefs are some of the problems that the therapist and client may try to identify and alter during the course of therapy. Psychoanalytic theory suggests a less explicit and more indirect route to problems, while humanistic/experiential theories often take a more direct, collaborative and transparent approach to confronting or facing problems in the sessions.
- **Mastery or control experiences**. Similar to the therapeutic value of confronting and facing certain problems, attempts to explicitly foster 'mastery experiences' through structured tasks and well-defined goals are, again, central to the cognitive and behavioural approaches. This 'therapeutic factor' is *relatively neglected by psychodynamic and humanistic/experiential thinkers*, assert Hofmann and Weinberger (2007, p106ff). Rather than using tasks and activities, psychodynamic therapists usually rely on the fact that insights will indirectly lead to mastering experiences. Humanistic therapists also adopt the view that mastery will unfold naturally and 'organically'.

- **Attribution of therapeutic outcome.** While the earlier-mentioned 'expectancy of treatment' is formed before the therapy, the category 'attribution' will develop during therapy. Attributing the outcomes of therapy to a wonderful therapist can, assert Hofmann and Weinberger (2007), cause the client to believe that positive change lies outside rather than within him or her. Treatment success is markedly higher in those cases where the client experiences that positive change lies within themselves than, for instance, in terms of changed coping skills and/or altered personality styles.

Orlinsky and Ronnestad (2005) refer to theoretical breadth as an important factor for the earlier-mentioned 'healing involvement cycle' with clients (see pages 50–3). Orlinsky (1994, p105) suggests an approach in training based on *a generic model for psychotherapy*. This highlights *six functionally interdependent aspects of the therapeutic process*.

1. **The formal aspect.** The therapeutic contract including schedules, fees and negotiating a working consensus with regard to goals and reciprocal roles during different stages of the therapy.
2. **The technical aspect.** Therapeutic operations that include:
   a. eliciting the client's subjective complaint and patterns of thought, feeling and behaviour, and, as suggested above,
   b. putting this understanding in the context of a 'treatment model', with a
   c. strategy (appropriate interventions) in mind, in which
   d. the client can participate and recognise his or her own efforts.
3. **The interpersonal aspect.** The therapeutic bond based on interpersonal involvement and emergent dyadic processes.
4. **The intrapersonal aspect.** Self-relatedness, where each participant's self-awareness, self-control, self-esteem and so forth are being elicited and incorporated into the clinical progress.
5. **The clinical aspects.** In-session impacts where positive and negative effects on the therapeutic interactions are being elicited within each session in terms of, e.g., insight, self-understanding, catharsis, skill enhancement and emotional intimacy.
6. **The temporal aspect.** The sequential process, where developments are put into the context of the overall therapeutic course and explored with reference to events unfolding over time – for instance, at work or at home with family and friends.

When researching transcripts from different types of therapy session, McLeod and Balamoutsou (2001) found the therapists' statements to be, overall, relatively brief. Viewed separately it is, as McLeod and Balamoutsou (2001, p140) put it, *hard to see that they carry much narrative content other than merely reflecting what the client has said.* It can seem as if we are merely nodding, agreeing and feeding back what the client is thinking about and exploring at the time. McLeod and Balamoutsou found, however, that:

> *[Studies] have shown the importance of the therapeutic relationship in storytelling: the story the person tells in therapy is closely bound up with his or her moment-by-moment experiencing of self-in-relationship with the therapist . . .*
>
> (2001, p128)

Some ways of summing up or commenting were common; there were shared themes between therapists, while others would reflect the therapist's own unique style. McLeod and Balamoutsou refer to the themes as 'therapeutic metanarratives', and write:

> *This 'metanarrative' offers the client a generalised framework within which his or her specific story of trouble can be accommodated and, in time, re-told and transformed.*
>
> (2001, p142)

Many therapists would, continue McLeod and Balamoutsou, *consistently use language permeated by*:

- *the central significance of feeling, for instance, 'so when you're starting a fight you are actually feeling really scared . . .';*
- *the existence of an inner world, as in, 'so, are you saying that on the outside you're always happy, but inside you're actually feeling . . .';*
- *a self compromised of 'parts', like 'it's like a part of you still is very angry . . .';*
- *the value of experiencing what is felt here and now, for example, 'You looked tearful, right then . . . when you're talking about the dinner with your family. Can we perhaps try to stay with that feeling that came up, could you try to tell me what you're feeling right now. . .'.*

(2001, p142)

THE MESSINESS OF BEING HUMAN

Research has thus helped us to elicit common themes that have been noted in successful outcomes. Guidelines are essential but, as suggested before, psychological realities are likely to remain 'messy', ambivalent and chang-ing. Some would argue that the therapeutic space is one of the few places where this perhaps profound characteristic of human life is still allowed to be acknowledged and accepted; and that this is a healing factor in itself. The particular truth that we may hope to reach in therapy, *do[es] not have the property of extension or tangibility*, asserts Symington; *it cannot be measured but it does exist*:

Most psychological realities do not have the property of extension or tangibility; a dream, a hallucination, a belief, a thought. Truth is a reality of this nature. It cannot be measured but it does exist; the fact that it is difficult to define does not detract from this.

(1986, p17)

The remarkable philosopher and concentration camp survivor Victor Frankl asserted that:

It is never the task of the therapist to 'give' meaning to the life of the patient. It is up to the patient himself to 'find' the concrete meaning of his existence. The therapist merely assists him in his endeavour.

(cited in Friedman, 1999, p485)

This idea resonates with my own view of therapy. It implies an overriding aim to provide people with an opportunity to explore their own meaning-making processes.

NARRATIVE AND HISTORICAL TRUTH(S)

Our role as therapists is perhaps, first, as Polkinghorne (1988) suggests, to assist clients when exploring their 'narrative' truths rather than necessarily striving to discover 'historical' truths. One's past cannot be changed, but the interpretation and significance of these events can change, asserts Polkinghorne (1988, p179), emphasising at the same time that therapy should *not lead the analysand to create literal descriptions of or recover past events. Instead, the past is to be reconstructed in the light of the client's present awareness.* Polkinghorne continues:

Psychotherapy and narrative have in common the construction of a meaningful existence. When they come to the therapeutic situation, clients already have life narratives, of which they are both the protagonist and author. The life narrative is open-ended: future actions and occurrences will have to be incorporated into the present plot. One's past cannot be changed . . . However, the interpretation and significance of these events can change.

(1988, p179)

As suggested in Chapter 1, this book shares the psychoanalyst Donnel Stern's idea of therapy as a form of 'witnessing'. One of the most damaging effects of trauma can be the absence of a witness. This does not have to be witnessing in a literal sense, but is rather about the willingness to share the client's lived experience.

NO FIXED MEANINGS

The philosopher Maurice Merleau-Ponty specialised in the 'phenomenology of perception' and asserted, like all existentialists, that there is no one 'fixed' meaning with life to be 'found':

> *Phenomenology . . . does not believe that man and the world can be understood on the basis on their state of fact . . . We must not wonder if we really perceive the world. Rather we must say that the world is that which I perceive.*
>
> (cited in Friedman, 1999, p86)

The world *is not an object* but *a natural milieu and the field of all my thoughts and of all my explicit perception*, asserts Merleau-Ponty (in Friedman, 1999, p84), where we become *responsible for our own history*. But, as suggested earlier, our sense of reality does not take shape in isolation. Merleau-Ponty (in Friedman, 1999, p84) writes that the phenomenological world *appears at the intersection of my experiences with those of others by the enmeshing of one with the other*. Therapy can offer a *partnership in thoughts* to explore both old and new ways of making sense of our experiences. The therapist does not possess ready-made solutions; therapy involves a joint attempt to explore new, potential meanings where rigid and unhelpful understandings have got in the way.

A FUSION OF HORIZONS

Stern (2010) refers to therapy as an act of joint interpretation. He also compares therapy to 'hermeneutics'. Hermeneutics is the study and practice of interpretation. Hermeneutics revolved originally around interpretation of the Bible, with historical and cultural changes in mind. Hermeneutics encourages us to explore our pre-understandings, our 'prejudices', as part of this process. Today, it is a form of study that includes most aspects in the interpretative process – verbal as well as non-verbal forms of communication. Stern refers to Hans-Georg Gadamer's *fusion of horizons* (cited in Stern, 2010, p2), which is a key phrase in hermeneutics. Our horizon stretches as far as we can see, but, as in the case of reflexivity, hermeneutics invites us to try on new perspectives and expand our horizons. Stern continues:

> *From the hermeneutic perspective, reality cannot be directly apprehended; it can be perceived only through lenses of tradition, history, and culture . . . When offering an understanding . . . we do not reconstruct the literal history of the meaning that we find in the other's mental history. Each conversational partner interprets the meaning of the other, absorbs the answering reaction, and then interprets again, until a fusion of horizons comes about.*
>
> (2010, p2)

CLOSENESS AND DISTANCIATION

There is, asserts the philosopher Paul Ricoeur, a difference between knowing and understanding. Ricoeur suggests that therapy involves a 'dialectical relationship' between a 'narrative commitment' and an 'explanatory commitment' (see Figure 4.1), with one sparking off and influencing the other. Ricoeur (1970, p386) uses the concept of 'critical hermeneutic appropriation' to explain what he sees as the *dialectic of presence and absence*. The therapist attempts to immerse themselves in the other's 'world', but will occasionally retract into their own, separate understanding of the situation, in order to make sense of it.

Ricoeur's theory of critical hermeneutics includes the philosopher Wilhelm Dilthey's idea that our understandings involve moving back and forth between *Verstehen* (where we understand *with*) and *Erklärung* (explaining or knowing *about*). This distanciation in the *Erklärung* phase resembles an 'expert'-related stance. For a therapist, this can mean adopting any type of 'expertise' or framing, be it psychoanalytic, humanistic or CBT-inspired thinking. Critical hermeneutics can, as Steele (1989, p116) puts it, be *nourished by almost any form of inquiry*. The main thing is to be aware of when and how we retract into our own 'world', and how our own pre-understandings may 'prejudice' our interpretations.

My experience cannot become your experience, writes Ricoeur (1981, p15), *yet something passes from me to you*. Ricoeur describes this as the *'miracle of discourse'*, and he asserts that the *dialogical structure of discourse appears as a way of trespassing or overcoming the fundamental solitude of each human being*. This narrative commitment is linked to the earlier-mentioned

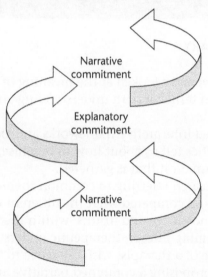

Narrative
commitment

Explanatory
commitment

Narrative
commitment

Figure 4.1: Ricoeur's dialectic process of understanding

phenomenological understanding, where the aim is to understand *with* the other. As Stern (2010, p31) puts it: *to understand is to overcome the division of two . . . and hence also to love, prove[s] to be basically one and the same.*

But we need, at some point, as Ricoeur proposes, to stand back and comple-ment our 'narrative', or immersing commitment, with a more 'explanatory' commitment. In other words, in addition to our attempts to merge with our clients' understanding, we need to view what has happened with some sort of informed opinion, a type of 'expertise' – whatever this may be. Merleau-Ponty also captures this when musing on the meaning of a dialogue:

> *It is only retrospectively, when I have withdrawn from the dialogue and I am recalling it, that I am able to reintegrate it into my life and make of it an episode in my private history, and the other recedes into his absence.*
>
> (1999, p132)

As suggested earlier regarding the concept of reflexivity, 'standing in the shoes of others' usually changes our old ways of looking at, and our feelings about, things. When we retract in the sense that Ricouer and Merleau-Ponty write about, we return with new perspectives in mind; our horizons are usually broadened. Our 'expertise' is thus never set in stone; it develops, ideally ongoing, in light of new experiences, but offers us (and our clients) a sense of being anchored in our work.

ACTIVITY 4.3

- Consider the potential need for understanding both with and about a client.
- In what ways can you explore these shifts in your supervision?

CHAPTER SUMMARY

- In this chapter we have looked at the meaning of 'phenomenological' understanding in terms of both understanding and feeling *with* the client.
- We also examined interpretive frameworks and explored what the different modalities tell us about how to organise, evaluate and convey the information that is gathered.
- We looked at research referring to common themes for 'mastery' and 'good' therapy, and compared what the different core modalities say with regard to knowledge and 'truths' within therapy.
- We considered ambiguities in therapeutic understanding, and explored the role of a therapist with reference to 'critical hermeneutics', proposing a combined narrative and explanatory commitment to our clients.

CHAPTER 5

Theory and the therapist as a person

CORE KNOWLEDGE

- In this chapter we consider the issue of 'rivalry' among explanatory frameworks in therapy, with reference to personal as well as cultural experiences and differences.
- We will look at attempts to *examine* our own underlying motifs, for example through reflective writing (which involves free association), creative writing and returning to the text with certain questions in mind.

In the previous chapters, we have explored overlapping features within modalities with regard to empathy and phenomenological understanding of the client. When it comes to the issue of our 'explanatory' commitment, different approaches will emphasise different strategies.

CHOOSING AMONG MAPS

In Chapter 3 we explored how supervision should involve room for growth. This is the case not only with regard to personal issues but also when it comes to our theoretical awareness. As therapists, we are required to choose between different theoretical orientations. How do we do that? On what basis do we arrive at knowledge and 'truths' within therapy? Some trainees experience a pressure to formulate a theory. Fitzpatrick et al. quote one of their studied trainees as saying:

> I felt bombarded by all the different theoretical approaches that I was exposed to . . . Each one seemed to say, 'Follow me! I am the best!'.
>
> (2010, p99)

Others felt pressure from outside to make up their minds:

> I feel an increased urgency to determine what my theoretical orientation is so that I can verbalise this to potential supervisors in my interviews.

We have already looked at some suggestions with regard to the therapist's choice of 'map'. One perhaps obvious factor behind the choice is the clinical setting. Orlinsky and Ronnestad (2005, p199) stress the importance of *working milieus*. Some settings offer *less backing* with more *frustration and disillusionment*, as Orlinsky and Ronnestad (2005, p199) put it. Inpatient institutions scored *significantly less [on] support and satisfaction* than outpatient settings. There can, as suggested in Case study 5.1, be a conflict between one's narrative understanding and agencies' expectations of the explanatory commitment that we carry to our clients. The appreciation and understanding of psychotherapy can, for instance, be less in medical settings where there is an emphasis on pharmacological treatment. There can be an 'epistemological' clash between how to generate knowledge about and deal with a problem.

REFLECTION POINT

- How do you experience your work setting? Do you work (or plan to work) in a private practice, hospital or some form of charity setting?
- How does this impact on, and overlap with, your personal approach to your clients?

When confronted with diagnosing and classifying clients' symptoms, the dialectics and movement between understanding *with* and knowing *about* is being pushed to the forefront. Below is an extract from an account of a child and adolescent psychodynamically informed psychotherapist, Jeanine Connor (2011, p12). Jeanine's account highlights the change that many therapists undergo as part of their everyday work, as they travel between knowing and understanding.

Case study 5.1

Child and Adolescent Mental Health Services (CAMHS) are receiving a growing number of referrals of violent and aggressive boys who are unable to concentrate, are failing academically and have no impulse control. In many cases, the referrer is seeking a diagnosis of, and treatment for, attention deficit hyperactivity disorder (ADHD). Darnell is a nine-year-old boy referred to CAMHS for a mental health assessment. The referral letter states that Darnell meets every one of the criteria for ADHD and is so extreme in his presentation that a diagnosis is inevitable . . . Darnell's mother confided that 'he has always been like this' and that even as a baby he was difficult . . . We learned that Darnell was an unplanned baby. His father once punched Darnell's mother in the stomach when she was pregnant and she gave birth with a black eye. The relationship ended and she began a relationship with Jason. But he raped her and she became pregnant with Jess and is now in a relationship with Jamie. Jamie is described as being 'like a third child' and they have heated arguments and sometimes use 'each other as punch bags' to 'let off steam'. When I spoke to Darnell alone, he told me that he hates Jamie because he is mean to his mum and that he is lazy and doesn't play football. Darnell has learnt that if he is naughty at school he gets to go home and that way can make sure that his mum is OK. Yesterday, the police came because Jamie had hit his mum . . . I asked Darnell what he likes to do when he isn't at school and was given the inevitable response of 'Xbox'. Fearing the answer, I asked Darnell which game he likes to play. I noticed he became excited and animated for the first time during the assessment. He said he liked the Grand Theft Auto and Call of Duty games and had just got Black Ops for his birthday which, said Darnell, features 'sex and killing' . . . Darnell is illustrative of countless young boys whose lives consist of real and virtual violence and who often present as ADHD-like . . . For many children, early 'care' is provided by screens portraying sex and violence . . . a mirror to their external lives . . . These boys crave things that are raw, loud and angry because they need [them] to match and master their own anxiety and anger.

Theory, assert Schön and Rein (1994), can give a false sense of belonging. Some would argue that practitioners are actually unable to move between frameworks without losing a sense of purpose and direction in work. People can become very protective about their theories. Schön and Rein (1994, pxiii) refer to the sociologist Joseph Gusfield's suggestion that clinicians and practitioners *cannot afford to stand outside the framework within which action occurs.* To examine their belief systems as only one among a number of possible frameworks would, in Gusfield's mind, require the clinicians to *give up that wholehearted commitment to a single set of beliefs that is indispensable to their effective action* (Schön and Rein, 1994, pxiii). Gusfield argued, in other words, that once we begin to question our theory as only one of many possibilities, we begin to doubt what we are doing and possibly lose our motivations altogether. Donald Schön based his thinking around reflective practice on the belief that clinicians were quite capable of working with maps while keeping an open mind that the maps required ongoing reassessment in light of upcoming problems and new challenges. Case study 5.1 illustrates the value of adopting different frameworks. Darnell's 'problem' might well be a reaction to someone else's problem.

THE POWER OF LANGUAGE

When we break down the grand ideas of psychotherapy and its role, we invariably find that therapists' everyday explanatory commitment consists of a multitude of mini decisions – implicit and explicit – regarding matters such as how a response to a client should be phrased. With regard to the way in which we communicate our understanding of the client's feelings,

Neuhaus (2011, p232) asserts that *there's much talk about therapy, but little about what the therapist actually says.* It is important to bear in mind how perceptions and one's sense of self can be challenged easily by applying certain subtle techniques in the dialogue – silences included. Below is another example of how a client, Lisa, and her therapist reframe Lisa's rigid personal construct about herself as being incurably 'greedy'.

Case study 5.2

Lisa is seeking therapy for problems with her eating patterns. She is above average weight and has a gastric band that has made no change.

'I'm beginning to think that this is me, I'm simply a greedy person. I just want food that tastes really nice, cream and sweets . . .'

Silence.

'Hmm . . . I have been a greedy pig all my life. I *am* greedy! I was fussy from the moment I was born, I wouldn't eat then . . . I'd be picky.'

'You feel that you have been greedy since you were born?'

'Well, yes . . .'

Lisa grows quiet. She looks pensive:

'I suppose you can't really be picky when you're newly born. I haven't thought of that. I just got used to thinking that I was awkward from day one, it was what my mum used to say. She felt I was . . . difficult and well, too much . . .'.

LET'S TALK ABOUT FEELINGS . . .

'Meanings', as Crossley (2000, p59) puts it, do not simply emerge from within an individual, they *develop in the context of specific interactive episodes and contexts*. Feminist theory, social constructionism and postmodern thinking lend critical perspectives to narratives as they develop between the therapist and the client. Narratives are explored with reference to their cultural meaning and impact. The idea of talking therapies as 'unpolluted' space for people to reconstruct events is, perhaps, a myth. Social constructionism is an example of a theory within the social sciences that is influenced by so-called postmodern thinking. Social constructionism takes the view that everything that we call 'reality' stems from experiences and culturally co-constructed meanings, and that the therapist's and client's dialogue moves as in a figure eight; they 'meet' and influence each other, veer off and then overlap again. Kenneth Gergen, the 'father' of social constructionism, writes:

> [P]sychotherapy may be thought of as a process . . . the forging of meaning
> in the context of collaborative discourse. It is a process during which the
> meaning of experience is transformed via a fusion of the horizons of the

participants, alternative ways of punctuating experience are developed, and a new stance toward experience evolves.

(1990, cited in Bager-Charleson, 2010a, p19)

Language is a particular concern for postmodern thinkers. Rather than seeing language as being used to illuminate something, postmodern theories suggest that *language should itself be illuminated and deconstructed* (Alvesson and Skoldeberg, 2000, p48).

Feminist theory is an example of thinking under the postmodern umbrella, which challenges the role of psychotherapy in a socio-cultural and political context. Freud's (1959, p39) emphasis on the importance of *not acting on the temptation of being a teacher, model or image to other people to make men into his own image* has been challenged heavily by feminist writers. One of his more infamous cases is one in which a female client was concerned about being approached by her father's friend. Freud wrote:

Instead of genital sensation which would certainly have been felt by a healthy girl under such circumstances, Dora was overcome by disgust.

(1905, cited in Gay, 1995, p184)

What Freud, presumably to his mind objectively, framed as Dora's 'repressed desire' towards a 'perfectly desirable, albeit a little older man' has later on been reconstrued as an example of an oppressing discourse and *phallocentric account of psychosexuality* (Gyler, 2010, p1).

The extraordinary analysis of 'madness and civilisation' by the philosopher and historian Michel Foucault highlights the power psychotherapists, psychologists and psychiatrists hold in society. Foucault examined the codes and concepts by which societies operate, with a particular interest in the 'principles of exclusion'. Each generation holds, highlights Foucault (1984), an 'us' and 'them' distinction, by which a society defines itself. He was particularly interested in distinctions between the sane and the insane, and the criminal and the law abiding, and he surveyed social attitudes about asylums, hospitals and prisons from the fifteenth century onwards. He argued, for instance, that since the disappearance of leprosy, madness came to occupy the position of 'the excluded' – the ones we can 'lock away'. Our thinking and our experiences are 'shaped' by a *repertoire of dominant narratives* (Foucault, in Dallos and Miell, 1996, p112).

To recognise just how embedded our thinking may be in cultural values and commonly held beliefs implies thinking outside the box of time and culture. This is difficult; some argue that it is impossible, as suggested by the Chinese proverb about the fish being the last one to know the water. Culturally guided ways of organising meanings, that is narratives, which serve as 'building blocks' (Dallos and Miell, 1996) when we seek to make sense of and communicate experiences, can be very restrictive to our way of thinking. Foucault refers to these collected sets of narratives in terms of dominating discourses. He offers the concept of 'l'episteme' to describe a kind of 'epistemological unconsciousness' of an era within which a discourse takes shape and begins to dominate our thinking. Epistemology is a branch of philosophy that deals with *how knowledge is arrived at* (Pistrang and Barker, 2010, p68). The concept of epistemology derives from the Ancient Greek words *episteme* ('knowledge') and *logos* ('rational'). Taylor writes:

> *Epistemology concerns itself with knowledge generation, validation and meaning that it tries to ascertain. [Epistemology is about] how to make new knowledge and how to judge whether it is trustworthy and 'true'.*
>
> (2006, p88)

Epistemology is largely concerned with breaking down a potentially infinite ladder of beliefs, and identifies patterns and structures in different inferences. Epistemology asks questions about the bedrock and the ultimate foundations for beliefs. What we hold as 'evidence' is in fact based on 'inference' from one set of beliefs to another. Inference is the *move that we make when we reason from one or more claims to a conclusion* (Cardinal et al., 2005, p11). The way we generate knowledge, asserts Foucault, is based on a set of fundamental and socially familiar assumptions that could be said to be 'invisible' to people operating within it.

It is easy to criticise therapists with sufficient distance and hindsight; how could Freud not see how he imposed stereotyped symptoms on female clients when he labelled them as 'hysterical' etc.? We have reserved a chapter to explore some of the basic beliefs in today's therapy. Chapter 8 approaches the talking therapies with questions around identity formation and role language from a multi-ethnic perspective. Beverley Costa, the founder of the bilingual therapy service Mothertongue, refers to the gap in training and services provided for clients who seek to explore their identity against the backdrop of cultural living. There is, suggests Costa indirectly, still a dominant white, middle-class way of thinking in how we perceive and conduct therapy. How can therapy respond to the current social and political climate with its global escalation of cultural conflicts?

Fook brings the concept of reflexivity to the forefront in reflective practice. Reflexivity encourages us to 'try on' other perspectives and regularly reconsider the impact of our own theoretical, political, personal and cultural underlying values and beliefs:

> *What we see and understand in a situation is influenced by our 'subjectivity' including our embodiment (e.g. race, gender, social position,*

sexual orientation, ability, age), biography, values, ethics, emotions, cognitive and theoretical constructions.

(cited in Stuart and Whitmore, 2008, p157)

REFLECTION POINT

Hysteria is often referred to as a socially constructed problem. ADHD is another diagnosis that is sometimes explored in terms of a reaction to circumstances rather than an 'illness'.

- Do you ever come across problems in your practice where you feel that the term 'socially constructed' problem would be appropriate?

MULTIPLE TRUTHS

Postmodernism is, by its very nature, a slippery concept. Rosen and Kuehlwein wisely conclude that:

Anyone who thinks he or she knows exactly what postmodernism is and offers a clear, precise and coherent definition to demonstrate this knowledge is probably mistaken . . . I mean this not as criticism but as a characteristic. Postmodern theories are self-consciously and self-reflexively aware of this.

(1996, p38)

Rosen and Kuehlwein continue, however, with a unifying theme within postmodern thinking:

Perhaps the one unifying theme . . . is that there does not exist an immutable truth in the 'real' world to serve as a bedrock or grounding upon which knowledge can be built.

(1996, p38)

Some regard postmodernism as implying that 'anything goes' in the sense that there is no point in seeking rights, wrongs or so-called 'truths'. Others, like myself, argue that postmodernism is an invitation to welcome different truths, developed with varying contexts and different motifs and interests in mind. The underpinning principle in the latter understanding is that dogmas and universal truths are unlikely ever to reflect the different needs of human beings. The postmodern debate has introduced a welcome emphasis on multiple truths in light of cultural, social and personal requirements and interests.

REFLECTING ON OUR MAPS

Fitzpatrick et al. (2010) refer to links between a trainee's personal philosophies and their theoretical frameworks. Someone who, for instance, describes themselves as a person who 'believes the glass is usually half full' also emphasises a positive way of thinking in how they construe professional beliefs. The glass-half-full person also speaks in terms of possibilities and emphasises a belief in 'the client's potential'.

The theory should first and foremost be a vehicle for the client, and help us understand him or her better, rather than trying to fit the client into a seemingly neat framework. At the same time, the theory must make sense to the therapist as a person. And this can be a question of 'making sense' on both a cognitive and an affective level. Educational research suggests that we learn differently. Gardner (1999) criticised the educational system for teaching as if everyone learns in the same way. In fact, people have their own kind of natural maps with which they learn more easily. It is, as (Gardner, 1999) puts it, unexpectedly difficult to teach things that go against people's early or 'naive' theories or strategies. Gardner identified several different learning strategies among students, for instance 'bodily-kinesthetic intelligence', with a natural propensity to link mental and physical activities and using one's body to solve problems; 'logical-mathematical intelligence', with a tendency to arrange information into patterns and reason deductively; and 'linguistic intelligence', with a tendency to organise new information and express oneself rhetorically or poetically, etc.

Ogunfowora and Drapeau (2008) suggest that there is a link between theoretical orientation preferences and therapists' natural propensity for openness, analytical thought or 'straightforwardness'. The humanistic therapist is described as particularly 'open', while cognitive behavioural therapists are found to be more frank or 'straightforward', and so on.

Rowan and Jacobs (2002) argue that, beyond separate modalities, there are common themes that unite different 'types' of therapist. They suggest that, regardless of whether the therapist 'belongs' to a psychodynamic, humanistic or cognitive behavioural theoretical camp, there are certain traits that transcend this. Rather than assessing therapy with regard to different modalities, Rowan and Jacobs suggest that we look at the *difference between their stances in terms of working as an instrumental therapist, an authentic therapist and a transpersonal therapist* (2002, p132). Rowan and Jacobs continue:

> *[This] creates a greater difference perhaps than between orientations. They have different aims, different beliefs and different notions of self.*
>
> (2002, p132)

In the instrumental position the client is usually regarded as someone who has the problem that needs to be put right.

In the authentic position, personal involvement is much more acceptable, with the therapist much more closely identified with the client and more openly concerned to explore the therapeutic relationship.

In the transpersonal position, therapist and client may occupy the same space at the same time, at the level of what is sometimes termed 'soul', sometimes 'heart' and sometimes 'essence'.

ACTIVITY 5.1

To become an 'accredited' psychotherapist in the UK requires full membership with a professional body such as the BACP (British Association for Counselling & Psychotherapy) or the UKCP (United Kingdom Council for Psychotherapy). To gain membership we are normally required to provide evidence of our theoretical orientation and 'speciality'.

- How do you see yourself as regards working with your clients? Could you, for instance, position yourself according to Rowan and Jacobs' three different 'types' of therapists?
- Is your view of your role as a therapist reflected in your training, now or in the past?
- What type of theoretical orientation have you chosen? How did you decide?

Schön (1983, p129) addresses *a rivalry between theoretical frameworks* among therapists. There is a controversy, suggests Schön, *not only about the best way of solving specific problems, but also what problems are worth solving and what role the practitioner should play in their solution*. In the previous chapter, it was suggested that therapists often adopt a similar 'narrative' commitment to clients, in terms of agreeing on the importance of a phenomenological understanding. Or, in other words, we usually agree on the importance of being able to see and feel (experience) the world as it appears to the client. But it is with regard to our explanatory commitment to our clients that what Schön calls 'intractable controversies' seem to appear between therapists. How does this level of controversy and 'rivalry' come about? What 'makes' a therapist choose an explanatory model characterised by what Rowan and Jacobs (2002) would describe as either an 'instrumental' or 'authentic' approach?

DOUBLE LOOPING

The earlier-mentioned double-loop learning invites practitioners to consider their judgements in light of underlying assumptions, with a shared aim to reach *beyond* familiar goals and strategies with their own underlying cultural, personal and/or theoretical beliefs and assumptions in mind. The issue of socio-cultural implications was considered in the previous chapter, and it is an area to which we will return in Chapter 8 with reference to Beverley Costa's account of wanting to provide a service offering multilingual therapy. But for now, we look at the experiences of a personal development group, with therapists of different theoretical orientations who have a shared interest in understanding more about themselves and their practice with double-loop learning in mind.

Personal development is, as suggested earlier, an extension of reflective practice and encourages us to explore the 'engine' that drives us. This includes exploring to what extent we may be more driven to invest our time and energy into certain areas than others might be. Sometimes this involves an attempt to 'get to know' our shadow, as Guggenbuhl-Craig (1991) puts it. We can, however, perhaps aim to adopt a third-person perspective when looking at ourselves, but in reality can probably only claim to revisit, or 're-search' some of our understandings of events. Reflection, as Moon (2004) puts it, is an attempt to restructure our knowledge with new themes in mind. In the next section, 'critical incidents at work' are a chosen theme, with which the members in our personal development group, myself included, aimed to re-search our practice.

To reflect like this moves the practitioner, researcher or, and as is the case here, the author from a comfortable 'know-it-all' place, to a sometimes embarrassing and always vulnerable position. Frame reflection involves a shift of power; it admits that the 'knower' has blind spots and puts actions and strategies into a perspective where others can access and assess one's meaning and subsequent decision-making processes. By admitting to our 'framings' we are also saying 'I may be biased or have a restricted view due to personal, cultural and/or theoretical circumstances and assumptions.' We are admitting to the fact that we may need to have our 'lenses' or 'glasses' (Knott and Scraggs, 2008) checked. We open up to critique, admit to prejudices and expect to confront our own underlying personal, cultural and theoretical assumptions.

COPING WITH AMBIGUITY

A certain theoretical 'agility' is necessary to reflect on the inherent ambiguity in our profession. The degree of 'impossibility' is inevitable, as Freud (1900/

1976) once suggested when he called psychotherapy 'the impossible profession'. Clinging on to single solutions is likely to provoke, or feed into, the sense of depletion that Orlinsky and Ronnestad (2005) identified as common among therapists when problems become debilitating rather than stimulating further learning. There are no clear-cut rights or wrongs in therapy, and an insight into the options is likely to help both the client and us as therapists to incorporate ambivalence into our practice with greater flexibility rather than confusion or frustration as a result. Supervision is, of course, again invaluable as a means of 'holding' and coping with the 'impossibility' of our profession. It is essential for a therapist to come to terms with ambiguity, assert Klein et al.; a trainee looking for certainties is unlikely to thrive in this profession:

> *Unless the therapist can tolerate the ambiguities inherent in clinical practice, they will often feel frustrated and even despairing about the work they are doing . . . There is no single, universally agreed upon way to treat patients . . . Unlike the work of the physical scientist or the mathematician the work of the psychotherapist is often unclear and inexact.*
>
> (2011, p274)

Indeed, *much of the time we don't know what we're doing*, as Kottler (2011, p209) puts it. He also rates this as one of the most taboo areas among therapists. Kottler refers to research by Theriault and Gazzola (cited in Kottler 2011, p210) and suggests that a quarter of therapists report often feeling 'clueless' in their work:

> *I don't mean to imply that therapists are not competent, skilled and highly trained experts who have a clear treatment plan and defensible rationale for what we do and why we do it, grounded in empirical research and evidence-based clinical experience. What I do mean is that a lot of the time we are operating in the dark . . . often clueless about what is going on with a client at any given time . . . Feeling clueless and incompetent isn't all that rare for most therapists, who admit to having questions about their effectiveness about 25 per cent of the time, often throughout their careers.*

ACTIVITY 5.2

Reflective practice encourages us to embrace ambiguity, and feelings of 'cluelessness' can involve being open rather than rigid, in a positive sense. This is a 'good' kind of not knowing. There are also cases that involve an unsettling lack of direction, with potential negative outcomes.

- Try to identify an example of each kind of 'not knowing'.

REFLECTIVE WRITING GROUPS

As a trainer, academic and clinical supervisor and member of different peer-support groups, I have enjoyed the company of colleagues who want to make sense of the helping profession. Double looping is an ongoing process; it invites us to reconsider our strong emotions and interpretive frameworks as part of our regular practice. Schön (1983, p130) offers reflective practice as an integrative model that can be used across classic borders, with a focus on *a fundamental structure of professional inquiry which underlies the many varieties of . . . therapy advocated by the contending schools of practice*. The reflective writing groups that have become a part of my regular work resonate with this thinking; reflexivity and double looping are key concerns for how these groups work. In this section, I have chosen to refer to one reflective writing group in particular. It was one of my first personal development groups in which writing played an important role, and the members of the group became very close.

Apart from the obvious interest in writing, this group was created with a relatively open agenda in mind. Therapy was for each of us a second, or in some cases third, career. We enjoyed our work, but also needed a personal development group within which we could discuss post-training-related disappointments and unexpected hardships. We shared the experience that the training sector had seemed something of a jungle. Compared to other vocational training, getting an overview of training routes within the therapy sector struck us as difficult. Did it or did it not, for example, lead to BACP or UKCP registration, which was ultimately required for advertising as an accredited counsellor or psychotherapy? This was not always easy to gauge; there seemed to be a lot of exceptions, options and alternatives that left trainees like us exposed to open-ended avenues and, at times, cul-de-sacs within the training world.

ACTIVITY 5.3

- Research (Skovholt and Ronnestadt, 2001, 2010; Orlinsky and Ronnestad, 2005) suggests that therapy students and trainees frequently experience stress and anxiety, which they struggle to talk about in their training. How does this resonate with you?
- Do you have access to personal development or general peer group support? If not, who could you consider instigating support with? And what types of issues would you like to feel free to explore in particular right now, with peers?

SELF-CARE ISSUES

Loneliness and isolation in our profession were other issues we shared concerns about. We all worked from home and wondered what impact this might have, particularly on our children. A particular trigger for beginning to write together was when one of our group members brought along an article about personal safety for discussion. The article was 'Risk assessment: the personal safety of the counsellor' (Despenser, 2007) and triggered concerns about and memories of our risk taking. In a study about therapists and safety, Despenser found excessive risk taking among most therapists:

> *In all the settings covered in my survey, the identified risks faced by counsellors are striking: physical isolation, dangerous premises, some clients being seen without pre-screening, neglect of safety by counsellors and managers. Why do counsellors accept this level of risk?*
>
> (2007, p17)

One of us, Susan, recalled meeting a male client with anger management in a badly lit, unsupervised and isolated spot. She had worked on a voluntary basis as part of her training and, when the usual secretary had failed to turn up, she had made the decision to see her client without anyone else in the building.

'I still wonder why I did that,' she said. 'I remember thinking, why do I do this to myself? Why do I put myself at risk like this?'

The memory triggered discussions about failing to look after oneself as part of looking after others. We agreed to gather in writing our cumulative experiences, ranging from training to eventual employment, mainly because we were all at a stage where we were interested in trying something new. Our experiences resulted in a minor research project entitled *Why therapists choose to become therapists* (Bager-Charleson, 2010b). It soon became clear to us that the question 'why work as a therapist?' was difficult to answer without talking about *how* we worked. Far from all reflective practice groups produce published works, but many groups do choose to collaborate on articles, papers for conferences, workshops and other forms of public sharing. Finding a 'voice' has always, in my experience to date, led to pleasant surprises in the reflective groups and a natural development has been to share the writing in some way outside the group. The writing in any reflective group involves many facets of writing. Some meetings will need to be reserved for creative writing. Others will revolve around a more focused reflective writing, for example around the theme of a problem session or a crisis. In this case, the reflective writing group agreed on exploring motivations for working both in general as a therapist, and the choices of modality in particular.

ABOUT CHOOSING MODALITIES

As mentioned, we all felt that we had childhood 'issues' of some sort and shared the experience that personal therapy had been invaluable in understanding what impact past experiences had on our adult lives. It was, however, interesting to note how the different modalities offered different kinds of framing to the dilemma. 'We lived at a time and in a place where no one talked about their emotions,' wrote Sheila (Lauchlan, in Bager-Charleson 2010b, p73) as she shared her experience of an early bereavement within her own family. Her writing invited reflections on how her childhood trauma could be linked to her systemic perspective and social constructionist thinking on the ways our lives take shape. The ways in which the bereavement had been dealt with felt typical for the time and place in which she grew up. The fact that the death of her mother had been hushed up had left Sheila to wonder about the impact of socially held values and beliefs on individuals and their sense of self. The extract below from Sheila's 'story' (Lauchlan, in Bager-Charleson, 2010b, p73ff) highlights how her choice of modality took shape.

Case study 5.3

My mother was never discussed at home again, and as it was beyond my friends' experience, it was difficult to have the conversation with them either . . . My therapist helped me to make connections with what was happening in the present with what had happened in the past. During the process of my own personal therapy, I became very intrigued with the practice, and this contributed to my desire to train as a therapist myself . . . I chose systemic/family therapy, as these ideas were very prevalent in the social services department where I worked, and I was influenced by how the communication within families could impact on an individual . . . Systemic/family therapy is a relatively new therapy which emerged in the 1950s. Rather than locating problems within individuals, family therapists became interested in the interactions that went on between family members, and how these communication patterns influenced individuals in the family. By consulting with whole families it was possible to experience the patterns of communication at first hand and to develop interventions. This created a shift from seeing symptoms as a reflection of the individual's internal conflict, to understanding symptoms as providing a function within the family's dynamics. By creating changes in the family's communication patterns, changes at the individual level became possible.

Sheila still works with families and couples in private practice and the ways in which families deal with issues have become a matter of ongoing interest to her. Her case study highlights a combination of factors for her choice of modality; systemic theory obviously resonated on a deep level with her, and enough aspects fell into place for her to want to pursue her training and clinical practice within this framework. But it was also, to a certain extent, a matter of timing and coincidence. Sheila took up her studies while working within the social services, and it was systemic training that was on offer at that time.

Ogunfowora and Drapeau (2008) suggest that we consider our choice of modality at an early stage of training, with certain personality traits in mind. According to Ogunfowora and Drapeau (2008, p152), research suggests a link between personality traits and theoretical orientation preferences.

Humanistic psychotherapists are described as particularly 'open'. The research suggests that they prefer novel experiences and are intellectually curious and highly imaginative, with broad interests.

The cognitive behavioural theoretical orientation positively correlates with the 'agreeableness' dimension, particularly the 'straightforward' (sincere and frank) and 'altruistic' (compassionate, altruistic and generous) facets. They are described as conscientious, and score significantly higher than psycho-analytic psychotherapists on 'conforming'.

Psychoanalytic psychotherapists score significantly higher on the 'intuiting' scale, which involves preference for the unstructured, symbolic and intangible rather than attention to observable and concrete phenomena. They show a tendency to rely on abstract means in processing information, and are often happy to step outside cognitive structures.

ACTIVITY 5.4

- Consider your own theoretical orientation at this time in your training or career. To what extent do any of these descriptors resonate with you?

COMMENT

In our writing group, we found it difficult to relate to the explanations proposed by Ogunfowora and Drapeau (2008) about a clear-cut link between modality and personality traits. Perhaps it is a matter of defining what personality traits are in the first place. Is openness, for instance, a fixed trait; or is it perhaps something that undergoes changes as we develop and learn more about ourselves? Skovholt and Trotter-Mathison (2011, p181) take another slant and refer to attachment research, which suggests that *therapists tend to re-create interpersonal patterns for relationship and treat clients accordingly*.

EXPLORING PERSONAL MOTIFS FOR THEORETICAL ORIENTATION

Theory can be a very personal matter. John Bowlby was the founder of attachment theory, which revolves around the impact of early attachment patterns for future relationships and the way we lead our lives. Bowlby (1983) has written about his heightened sensitivity to children's suffering with reference to his own experiences. He saw, for instance, his mother for only one hour a day. The nanny to whom he was attached died when he was four years old. He was sent to boarding school at the age of seven; he later said *I wouldn't send my dog to boarding school at age seven* (cited in Schwartz, 2003, p225). The link between one's own experiences and a passionate theoretical involvement with overlapping features is not unusual. In *Autobiography of a Theory*, Agazarian (2000) shares her experience of development with a group of therapists guided by system-centred practice. Below are some extracts from her introduction of herself, and the subsequent description of her choice of theoretical orientation.

Case study 5.4

Biography:
As a child of the early 1930s (I was born 1929) I was brought up to be seen but not heard . . . often played alone [. . .] There was a gate at the nursery door and I spent much time leaning over the gate listening to the house. I became very good at knowing what was going on by the noises and voices that drifted up the stairwell [. . .] My early life was a mixture of the nursery, the silence of watching and listening and waiting and playing by myself [. . .] At 7 years old I was sent to the Convent of the Sacred Heart where I remained as a boarder until I left school at 17. As much as I hated what seemed like every minute of the ten years I was at school in the convent, looking back I can see that the nuns were very good with me, they encouraged me to think through all the different heresies that I intuited (Agazarian, 2000, p13ff).

Theoretical orientation:
For me theory does not come from my comprehensive brain. Rather it comes from some subterranean force that has a rhythm of its own. [It] is like Aladdin's lamp to me, the more I massage it, the more the genie looks over my shoulder and there seems to be no end to the dimensions of new understanding that appear and transforms the world [. . .] System-centred thinking simplifies thinking about many levels of existence: self and others, small groups, large groups, departments, organisations, societies and cultures. Each is a system that survives . . . and moves in relationship to goals in the environment [. . .] Becoming a system-centred therapist depends upon learning how to see the group as a hierarchy of living systems . . . Each living human has geographical boundaries and time boundaries which are connected to goal and

---

purposes [. . .] System boundaries open to information and close to noise [. . .] generated whenever information is too discrepant to be integrated (Agazarian, 2000, pp222ff, 242).

COMMENT

Reflecting on one's practice in this way can help the therapist to understand particularly strong emotive responses, for example with regard to one's own modality in the context of others. A double-loop thinking about our theory can highlight, for instance, a personal investment in the theory and can help us to accept that others don't always feel as strongly about certain things as we do.

WE DO NOT STORE, WE STORY OUR EXPERIENCES

'Reflective writing' is a term used for writing for the purpose of *making sense of ourselves and the world* (Bolton, 2005, p4). Rather than storing experiences like computers, we story them, asserts Bolton. Bolton et al. contend that:

> *Writing is different from talking; it has a power all of its own . . . It can allow an exploration of cognitive, emotional and spiritual areas otherwise not accessible.*
>
> (2006, p2)

Reflective writing involves *examining our story, making processes critically, to create and recreate fresh accounts of our lives from different perspectives, different points of view and to elicit and listen to the responses of peers* (Bolton, 2005, p3). To question our 'story making' involves 'deconstructing' (Fook, 2002) and examining the narratives that we hold about ourselves and our world, in this case about ourselves as professional helpers.

ACTIVITY 5.5

This exercise is about your life story. You will be asked to write a brief piece, for no more than five minutes, about a significant life event, followed by a piece about your approach to work. Work in pairs if possible.

- A. Choose a significant event or an important personal memory and write down what you remember.
- B. Write something brief about your approach to work. Write something about your focus and special interest in work, as the thoughts come into your head.
- C. Compare the two stories. In what ways do they overlap or differ? There may be no links at all. If so, where do you see the inspiration for your interest in your modality coming from?

MORE WRITING

Group work offers good reminders of how nothing is black or white. What can be described as personal reasons have in fact, as already suggested, many dimensions. While Sheila explored her choice of modality with reference to her experience of bereavement, and how social and cultural aspects had had an impact on this experience, Francesca (Thorpe, in Bager-Charleson, 2010b, p87ff) explored how her sense of self had developed in the context of her growing up with a disability caused by Thalidomide. Her story revolves around an incident relating to counselling another person with Thalidomide-induced disabilities – something that she had waited many years to do. Francesca drew on a couple of first experiences and gathered these in a fictitious encounter with 'Janet'. Case study 5.5 is an extract after a critical incident with her client, where Francesca is reflecting on the link between her personal experience and the way she has decided to work.

Case study 5.5

I have been working as a counsellor in agencies, schools and in private practice for some ten years. My focus has been on relationships, I have worked with couples at Relate and with teenagers in school . . . I was born Thalidomide and have an upper arm disability. I never felt I had issues about having a disability but as I got older I began to realise I was feeling extremely angry. I decided to enter into personal therapy which I had for five years. I finally was able to let go of my anger [and] feelings of loss without feeling guilty. The guilt, I began to realise, was about my relationship with my parents. The guilt my parents felt about taking the tablet Thalidomide, and the guilt I felt for seeing their sad faces at times. My personal therapy was a life-changing experience and I feel it offered me another way of living my life. I began to realise that life involved choices despite the givens of being born different [. . .] I have recently become involved in setting up the first counselling service offered specifically to people born with Thalidomide. I am interested in working with the 'givens' of life, as the existentialists call it. There is an inevitable aspect to life for us all. There are things that we cannot easily change or make go away . . . Working existentially means different things for different people. To me it involves staying with what Heidegger called the Dasein. This is about both acceptance of who we are and taking responsibility for what we can be within the framework of givens. There is the sein-side to life which involves defining ourselves in relation to others. This involves taking charge of our being-in-the-world, with authenticity in mind. Van Deurzen (2002, p81) compares authentic living with 'being at home in oneself and with oneself'.

COMMENT

Writing can be a very powerful experience. In Case study 5.6, Francesca concludes that: *As I write this sentence I think about how frightening this meaning must have been for me as a little girl.* I have chosen another extract of Francesca's account, to illustrate some of the experiences involved in reflective writing. Francesca reflects on how her Catholic upbringing affected the way she perceived herself as someone who needed to repent and always to be good, which obviously affected her choice of career – nursing at first, and then counselling – which, later, Francesca (Thorpe, in Bager-Charleson, 2010b, p87ff) was able to consider in personal therapy.

Case study 5.6

. . . I was brought up as a Catholic and the meaning I made early on in my life as to why I was born Thalidomide was because I had done something wrong. God was punishing me. As I write this sentence I think about how frightening this meaning must have been for me as a little girl [. . .] Writing this chapter has been very challenging. I have put off writing it so many times, often due to negative thoughts. The main thought [is] 'I am not good enough to do this'. Being asked to write and to be part of a wonderful writing group did not match the meaning society put on me being Thalidomide. According to the medical world when I was born I wasn't meant to grow, they felt that my brain would be affected. The school I went to didn't think I would be able to cope with any academia. The meanings I had made which I spoke earlier about confirmed these statements [. . .] As I grew up I often thought what have I done wrong? I decided very early on I needed to be a good girl, and be this so called 'perfect' friend, wife and mother . . . Entering into personal therapy I began to see I could create another meaning for my life . . . I am able to accept that I am not 'perfect' and it's ok to make a mistake.

In our reflective writing group, Sherna also chose to write about how the individual develops a sense of self within a social context, but now with ethnicity and cultural issues in mind. Sherna (Ghyara Chatterjee, 2010, p97ff) chose to begin her story with a vignette in the third person, based on a supervision session in training.

Case study 5.7

The supervision group was tense. The three trainee psychotherapists sat in a circle slightly closer to each other with the supervisor making up the fourth. This was the time when they presented their case studies and one of their number was presenting her case. They looked like the usual group. One was clearly from another culture with her dark skin and black hair. She was presenting her case of providing therapy to a client from her own culture. The tension in the group increased as the case was presented and the supervisor spoke: '. . . the point is that you are not being congruent here. Your response is not real. During this session I sense that something is not in synch. You are not being real.' The trainee looked despairing, 'what can I say or do to make myself seem real to you?'

Sherna grew up in India and highlights an important aspect of personal development, in terms of cultural considerations in training. She expands on the theme of intercultural therapy and how she has integrated classic psychoanalytic thinking with an Indian understanding of self and reality. But this, wrote Sherna (Ghyara Chatterjee, 2010, p97ff), involved stages of feeling lost and misunderstood.

Case study 5.8

On completion of my counselling training I was aware that something was missing. Although my training had been stimulating and absorbing I felt that there was a void and that my own cultural and intellectual differences had played a peripheral role in preparing me to practise in this profession. Almost always, I was the only person from another culture on these courses and my response to the lack of any context other than Western was to constantly explain my own culture and its difference and to get exhausted in the process. Even basic concepts of congruence and the use of language needed further elaboration and were met with incomprehension and avoidance. The therapist in the first of my vignettes is myself. We were constantly urged to bring ourselves into the sessions, and were told that the type of relationship depended on the congruence of the therapist. But I felt very alone and felt compelled to present myself in language and form that made me acceptable within the Western concepts of my course . . . I finally found my professional home after many years of training

---

when I undertook the MSc in Psychoanalytic Psychotherapy in Intercultural Therapy at Nafsiyat/University College London. With its feet firmly in contemporary anthropology the study of psychoanalysis provided the broadest base from which to provide therapy across cultures. Intercultural therapy addresses all issues of difference. Nafsiyat Intercultural Therapy Centre was founded to provide the best therapy to those in society who could least afford it.

Susan McGrath shared her experiences of therapeutic practice with reference to sessions in which her own thinking about what brought her into the profession came to the surface. Like the others in the group, Susan drew on an amalgam of cases to formulate a fictitious-enough case not to breach the confidentially of one single client. The principle that Susan wanted to highlight was how she would react with reference to both prior personal experiences and her modality in the light of certain problems. Susan felt that a reference to a particular country captured the link she was after, and she wrote about a fictitious but not atypical client who originated from a country where Susan (McGrath, 2010) herself had lived and suffered from depression.

Like Francesca, Susan was brought up as a Catholic and her interest in spirituality has developed and had an impact on her choice of modality. Susan is trained in psychosynthesis and works as a student counsellor and in private practice. She refers to the term 'bi-focal vision' to describe her outlook on both life and therapeutic practice. Susan (McGrath, 2010, p113) writes:

> *The main thrust of transpersonal therapy is that it goes beyond the personal. It includes exploration of our divine nature as well as the personality and that the two are inextricably linked. Psychosynthesis hypothesises that we have an 'I' which is our divine essence beyond, but also including, our conditioning and wounding . . . I am struck with the idea that therapy is not just about reducing anxiety or psychological symptoms but about fulfilling potential and helping us fully engage with all life has to offer from an authentic place.*

WRITING TOGETHER

To engage with colleagues with or without writing is meaningful on many levels. Susan was particularly susceptible to group processes and helped us to observe how the dynamics in the group changed as we began to write. It was, for all of us, a peculiar experience to develop a voice in the sense that writing permits. For the listener, talking in this sense carries all sorts of connotations; it is unusual to say the least. It occurred to us also that many of the authors were men. This triggered discussions in the group about the experience of moving from a familiar role of being a listening receiver to someone who sets out to 'penetrate' the world with one's opinions, views and experiences. It often led to anxiety, and to a good few tears. But the overriding experience was one of joy, growth and stimulation.

Pam, another member of our group, chose to develop the research she had carried out for her Master's training. Pam (Critchley, 2010, p127ff) shared her interest in self-disclosure, which of course became another important issue to explore in our writing group.

Case study 5.9

From my study of this subject (MSc Surrey/Roehampton 2006) I came to understand the concept [self-disclosure] in a way expressed by Knox et al. (1997, p274), where self-disclosing and self-involving, the interpersonal and intrapersonal, are considered as:

'An interaction in which the therapist reveals personal information about him/herself, and/or reveals reactions and responses to the client as they arise in the session.'

'Interpersonal' here refers to the therapist revealing feelings evoked by the client in contrast to intrapersonal where the therapist discloses information about their present and past that is outside the therapy room. [. . .]

It seems the therapist can self disclose in different ways and on different levels. I am aware from my own private practice of very subtle disclosures of my lifestyle that are experienced by potential clients when they first make contact. My voice on the phone has been commented on by a number of clients.

My office phone is a fixed phone and sits alongside my home phone. I remember speaking with a nervous young man enquiring about therapy when the house phone started to ring, he nervously asked 'should you get that?'; 'No I replied, don't worry it will stop.' It did stop, only to be immediately replaced by my mobile going off (the ring tone, incidentally, had been set by my children to a very loud setting following their frustration with me for not hearing it!). At this point in the conversation I started to laugh, apologising to the enquiring client for the background interruptions. He subsequently came for therapy and stayed with me for a number of years and commented quite early on about what a relief it had been that day to hear me laugh and realise I was human.

I have a piano in my consulting room and this too is an interesting focus. Questions do arise as to whether I play and I am very conscious of putting away any music as this could indeed self disclose an awful lot about me and/or my mood!

So knowingly or unknowingly we disclose from the onset of the first contact.

- *Our website style or our voice as we answer the phone.*
- *Our geographical location.*
- *Those in private practice who work from home disclose their house; indications of wealth/status . . .cars in the drive.*
- *Choices of furnishings, decorations etc. and maybe the tell tale signs of other occupants in the house, or pets.*
- *Our dress, our style, our manner.*
- *Wedding rings, photographs.*
- *Our professional qualifications and training.*

COMMENT

Many therapists, suggests Kottler (2011, p2), are drawn to counselling and psychotherapy *to understand oneself more fully and feel understood by others*. Reflexivity encourages therapists to 'own' their underlying needs and carefully consider how one's personal development is being integrated into professional practice. Reflective writing groups are offered here as an example of activities in which this kind of reflection can take place. They are additions to, and not replacements for, personal therapy and super-vision. Reflective writing will inevitably involve some form of self-disclosure, and publishing some of these explorations needs careful consideration. As Pam highlights above, self-disclosure can find its way into the session indirectly. Published books, articles or research papers about a therapist's own behaviour, reactions, emotions and underlying values are examples of such indirect self-disclosure. Each therapist needs to consider how this fits in with their modality and the ethical guidelines of their accrediting membership organisation. My reflective writing groups usually adhere to two rules.

1. Never publish a first insight in writing. It is not the 'purging' and 'telling' that is going to be of interest to other readers, it is the learning experiences, the transformational learning, that matters in this context. While Francesca shares strong emotions that emerge during her writing, the experiences that surface fit in with a carefully selected theme about 'not being good enough' and about the existential emphasis on accepting the role of creating meaning for our own life.
2. Never use actual client material. Confidentiality should never be breached. Therapy should, as clearly stated in the ethical guidelines in Chapter 2, always be conducted with the client's best interests in mind and any potential indirect harm should at all costs be avoided. Sometimes research and therapy can overlap, but only if the research can be argued as directly beneficial for a particular client. With regard to writing, clients may sometimes agree to be written about, but can

easily feel differently afterwards once they read about themselves or simply have had some time to think. Be creative, seek inspiration from characters in books, magazines or other public places and allow yourself to be inspired. It is best to be fictitious and/or draw from several client experiences and write the generics; focus on the themes that you want to illuminate and sift out events that the readers can identify with, relate to and learn from.

A reflective writing group will be successful to the extent to which its members are able to commit to a genuine attempt to understand where the other is coming from. A reflective writing group relies on trust in order to work. Reading others' texts can be as important as writing one's own. Knowing that someone will read the texts we are writing can improve, stimulate and give the writer a purpose to write. But it can also cause the kind of premature closure that was earlier described with reference to Orlinsky and Ronnestad (2005), in the context of the stressful cycle. Reflective writing groups rest on what the philosopher Jürgen Habermas (1986) calls 'communicative rationality', where the aim is to understand each other rather than trying to prove a point, convince or in other ways manipulate the other to act according to our wishes. Like Rogers (1961), Habermas concludes that we often meet others with an assumption that, in order to be 'right', someone else needs to be wrong, and the way we communicate often reflects an underlying purpose of getting our own point across. The person whose text we are reading should be able to ask what he or she wants the readers to look out for.

Sometimes there are particular areas of feedback required, for example in terms of grammar, style or characteristics of the story. Offering praise is an essential part of the process – being too critical of one's own writing is a common problem, which prompts many to think that they simply cannot write at all. Combating this inner criticism is fundamental for the writing to flow, and for a writing group to be sustained. There will usually be general questions to attend to. The reader may give their feedback with regard to its overriding purpose: What is the text about, to the reader? Who is in it? What happens? What is its theme? How has the writer chosen to arrange and present these themes? There is no 'right' in the reading, on the basis of being technically right. It is a bit like holding up a mirror to the writer and his or her text, saying 'This is what I see – is this what you intended and wanted the reader to see?' As suggested, the clearer the writer is with regard to what he or she wants feedback on, the better.

RESEARCHING

To me, reflective writing groups are, by definition, a form of research, or perhaps better put, re-searching. Reflective writing encourages us to revisit experiences and search through events again with new perspectives in mind. The more transdisciplinary such research can be, the better. Therapy is not a clear-cut science. Restricting one's attention to distinct themes and features may be limiting, in the way Barkham et al. suggest with the parable of the six blind men and the elephant:

> *The man who felt its [the elephant's] side said the elephant was like a wall; the man who felt its tusk, like a spear; the man who felt its trunk, like a snake, and so forth. Each inference was different, but all were partly justified and described the same animal. Although the blind men in the parable failed to listen to each other, the point is that the elephant (like counselling and psychotherapy) has many aspects.*

(2010, p92)

Wheeler and Elliott conclude that:

> *a key feature of competent professional practice is a thirst for new knowledge and understanding'. Professional therapists today need to know:*
> *   *what their methods are, and be able to discuss their merits and limitations;*
> *   *how to find new information from the literature (including electronic sources) that might help them with a particular client;*
> *   *how to access evidence to support their practice.*

(2008, p134)

The word 'research' can sound intimidating. Many think of research as something that is done in laboratories by scientists in white coats. Chenail (1994, p8) distinguishes between 'private' and 'public' research:

*   **private research** is the *reflexive posture therapists take when they reflect upon their interaction during or after the session with a client;*
*   **public research** is *systematic inquiry, intended to be shared primarily in textual form with colleagues through dissertations, journal papers, and conference papers.*

McLeod (1999) asserts that all therapists are by nature practitioner researchers. Research is a broad concept. Some of the key characteristics of practitioner research in counselling are:

*   that the research question is triggered by personal experience and a 'need to know';
*   a goal to produce knowledge that makes a difference to practice, and that the research is designed to enhance the counselling process;
*   an aim to use reflexive awareness to access underlying meanings of the study.

The objectives above are often the basis for reflective writing groups. Discussing, comparing, writing and reading in the company of others bridge what Chenail above calls private and public research. An underpinning belief in reflexive writing groups is that, as Barkham et al. (2010, p92) suggested with the parable of the blind men and the elephant, the more angles we can cover and the better we can communicate with others about the findings, the greater are our chances of 'getting it right'.

CHAPTER SUMMARY

- In this chapter we have looked at choosing one's modality with several different interests in mind. We have discussed different modalities in terms of theory as well as personal experiences of how theoretical orientations evolve.
- This involved considering how personal experiences, socio-cultural backgrounds and coincidental circumstances, as well as links to personality 'types' and general cognitive learning, may impact on our choice of theory.
- Reflective writing was explored with reference to its 'relative permanence', which allows us to explore our meaning-making processes in different ways from how speech may allow us to do. Reflective writing involves three phases: pre-writing, writing and rewriting. Uninterrupted and creative writing were explored as examples of the first two phases.

CHAPTER 6

Accountability and transparency

CORE KNOWLEDGE

- In this chapter we return to the concept of lifelong learning, with different ways of improving knowledge, skills and personal qualities in mind.
- Research can sound intimidating. We will explore the link between everyday practice and research. We will look at the rationale for practice-based research, and explore some of the stages in terms of problem formulation, literature review, choice of method etc., with reference to a therapist's account of her research into sex offenders' development of victim empathy through role plays.

EVIDENCE-BASED PRACTICE

'Evidence-based practice' is currently a commonly used phrase. It aims for accountability and transparency in therapy, albeit from an epistemologically almost oppositional angle to the postmodern critique of therapy. Evidence-based research has contributed to a more open discussion about therapy, and has brought with it a refreshingly demystifying perspective on psychotherapy. Orlinsky (1994, p101) saw this development coming. He referred to the *crisis in the development of psychotherapies*. At the heart of this crisis *is the widespread questioning amongst therapists about the scientific basis of their practice.* Orlinsky continues:

> *This is not an age that honours prophecy or venerates tradition. Healing practices associated with older forms of cultural authority, such as Asclepian incubation (Meier 1967) and the 'king's touch' (Geertz 1983), have been forgotten, disregarded, or relegated to the possession of a lunatic fringe. Rational authority, derived from sustained critical reflection on verified observations, is the standard of modern culture.*
>
> (1994, p101)

There is, as Barkham et al. (2010, p3) put it, *pressures on the delivery of psychological therapy, which have challenged the autonomy of clinical judgement.* Barkham et al. continue:

> *These pressures have led to a desire to modify the basis of decisions in health care, away from autonomous judgements made by a professional, and towards the objective and transparent forms of knowledge. This has often been identified with a movement called 'evidence-based medicine' . . . succinctly summarised by one of its originators, who defined it as 'the conscientious, explicit, and judicious use of current best evidence in making decisions about the care of individual patients' (Sackett et al. 1996).*
>
> (2010, p4)

The evidence-based approach thus involves an aim to be as explicit as possible, and to be well informed of alternative options. To be judicious means remaining neutral in the light of outside, irrelevant pressures.

The emphasis on this type of research is on accountability, and one of its 'gold standard' methods is the randomised controlled trial (RCT), which has developed from the classic experiment within natural sciences with its focus on cause and effect. RCTs involve comparing a randomly chosen 'case group', exposed to a certain intervention, with a 'control group' subjected to a benign or placebo intervention, with the view of assessing the effect through the comparison.

Is evidence the same as 'facts'?

It is easy to confuse evidence with facts. Evidence is defined in the dictionary (cited in Webber, 2008, p4) as *one or more reasons for believing that something is or is not true.* The term 'evidence' refers in this sense ultimately to *the basis for a belief* (Barkham et al., 2010, p5; Cardinal et al., 2005), from which different sets of further conclusions can be inferred. Barkham et al. write:

> *What is evidence? Simply put, it is the basis for a belief, such as the belief that a treatment will work for a patient. Beliefs may arise from a number of sources. Two major sources of relevance to health services are personal experiences and scientific research . . . EBP [evidence-based practice] imposes a hierarchy of trustworthiness, with forms of evidence lower in the hierarchy only to be used when higher forms of evidence are unavailable.*
>
> (2010, p5)

The evidence-based approaches are thus not based on fixed truths but suggest that there is a hierarchy of *trustworthiness* among different types of beliefs, from which healthcare decisions can be made.

A dilemma with research that explores outcomes on the basis of what large populations hold in common is that the unique is lost or kept outside the focus. Clinical trials miss out on all the complexity and messiness that usually is what human life comes down to. This, argues the cognitive behavioural therapist Edmund Neuhaus (2011, pp218–19), is one of the reasons why personal development has become such a relevant issue to consider in the first place. As suggested in Chapter 1, there is a growing interest in the therapeutic relationship within modalities that have previously regarded techniques as more interesting for outcome research than the impact of the therapist's emotions and reactions:

> *Evidence-based treatment has become a lightning-rod issue . . . a major problem exists 'on the ground', or as some describe it in the 'real world' . . . of clinical practice that is quite unlike the highly controlled world of clinical trials.*
>
> (Neuhaus, 2011, pp218–19)

PRACTICE-BASED RESEARCH

In response to the problem of approaching real-life situations through research, another approach called 'practice-based research' has been developed. Practice-based evidence emerges from experiences developed through active engagements with clients in a wide range of real-life settings. It encourages therapists to engage in ongoing evaluation of their own practice, and often suggests that we arrive at knowledge with an openness for nuances and greater variety than evidence-based methods allow. Practice-based research does not exclude evidence-based research. It can, however, include research of a more idiographic and inductive nature, to learn more about unique, individual experiences and allow for unanticipated themes to emerge. Perhaps the most significant feature of practice- and work-based research is, as Costley et al. (2011, p1) put it, its 'situatedness', which arises from an interplay between the researcher as a person, the particular set of circumstances that the researcher is positioned in, and the overall context – the where, when and general background. This means, as Costley et al. (2011, p1) put it, that practice-based research assumes that *organisational, professional and personal context will affect the way a piece of research and development is undertaken.* Rather than striving for research that excludes as many factors as possible, practice-based research often aims to capture them with an increased understanding about the complexity of real life in mind – be it on an organisational or personal, unique level. This does not, for instance, exclude a medical, objective standpoint in the research. It does, however, require the researcher to address this standpoint and compare it critically with other perspectives; for instance, with the idea of a socially constructed world view, or with reference to a phenomenological per-spective with a focus on the unique, individual experience. *Reflective practice is an invaluable approach, to think about theory building and conceptual frame-works* (Costley et al., 2011, p120) in work- and practice-based research. The double-loop thinking referred to earlier, that is the importance of paying attention to how practitioners' personal, cultural and theoretical framing may impact on the outcome, is thus applicable to practice-based research. This critical view of our own involvement means that we more often than not will learn something new about ourselves as part of the research process. We will look at this further on in this chapter and in Chapter 7, when Marie Adams shares her experience from practice-based research into therapists' personal lives. An example fresh in my mind is from a good friend who, together with some colleagues, recently undertook some research into changes in the way their clients spoke during the process of therapy. My friend shared her dismay on recognising how influential her own voice was in the outcome of her clients' narratives:

> *We're at a stage of our research when we feel appalled by our own practice. My colleague who recorded my sessions allowed me to read the transcripts, and I was appalled to learn about how much I actually speak in my sessions. I've almost pictured myself as a bit of a nodding listener, with occasional well-chosen intervention. Seeing the transcripts gave me totally new insight into how the clients' narratives take shape; I had naively thought they somehow developed in isolation from me. My research has prompted me to think long and hard on how I interact with my clients.*

It is possible that psychotherapy will never become an exact science; but both the evidence-based and the postmodern critique have invited us to demystify and explore more freely what is going on in the room. It could be argued that therapists today work within a tension between the postmodern critique of truth and the evidence-based supporters yearning for it. It could, however, also be suggested that the two 'extremes' can nourish each other.

RESEARCH AS CONTINUING PROFESSIONAL DEVELOPMENT

Continuing professional development (CPD) safeguards this need for being able to explore and learn more about therapeutic practice. CPD is defined as:

> *any process or activity that provides added value to the capability of the professional through the increase in knowledge, skills and personal qualities necessary for the appropriate execution of professional and technical duties, often termed competence.*
>
> (Professional Associations Research Network,
> cited in BACP, 2012)

Once registered with one of the member organisations, such as the BACP, UKCP or the British Psychological Society (BPS), therapists are required to undertake CPD to maintain their status as registered members. The precise requirements differ between the different organisations. The BACP, for example, expects its members to undertake 30 hours of CPD annually.

The CPD requirement implies a commitment to lifelong learning. Lifelong learning involves, as suggested in Chapter 1, *looking inwardly as well as outwardly* (Klein et al., 2011, p281). Apart from daring to explore new aspects of self, lifelong learning is learning about new approaches, cultural aspects and meta-theoretical concerns. In the next two chapters, we will look at different ways in which therapists may increase their knowledge, skills and personal qualities with an improved 'competence' in mind. Our focus will remain on the ACCTT model's emphasis on using recurring problems and particular challenges as invitations for transformative learning (see Figure 6.1).

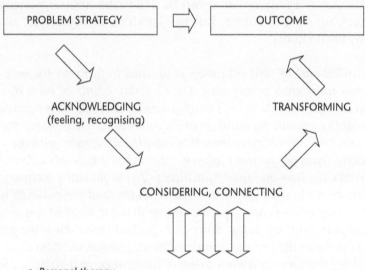

Figure 6.1: The ACCTT process, for transforming critical incidents and avoiding depletion in work

EVERY THERAPIST IS A RESEARCHER

Making use of research is, as McLeod (1999, p23) puts it, *a valuable way to stand back from practice and to engage in constructive and critical reflection.*

Therapists are under-represented in public research, compared to other health-related professions. One of the reasons for this, suggests McLeod, may be the sense of betrayal that therapists feel when talking about their clients. We normally work with our individual clients in mind, and tend not to think about 'doing research'. McLeod writes:

> *Counsellors engaged in clinical activity necessarily focus mainly on the issue presented by individual clients, and find it difficult to apply findings or conclusions derived from research on groups or populations.*

> (1999, p6)

Yet, our everyday practice is full of research. We form hypotheses that we 'try out' with our clients, usually with a focus on exploring the clients' lived experiences as if we were trekking and mapping out unknown landscapes together. But we often stand back and adopt a more evidence-based approach, with conclusions derived from observation and 'experiments' in which we have tested certain hypotheses. Yalom's example below illustrates how subtle our everyday research can be. He writes about 'growing rabbit ears' to pick up on the subtle, but informative, idiosyncratic responses brought by each client:

> *An essential part of your education is to learn to focus on the here and now. You must grow rabbit ears. The everyday events of each therapy session are rich with data . . . I develop baseline expectations because all my patients encounter the same person (assuming I am reasonably stable), receive the same directions to my office, enter the same room with the same furnishing. Thus the patient's idiosyncratic response is deeply informative [to identify the here-and-now equivalents of your patient's interpersonal problems] – a via regia permitting you to understand the patient's inner world . . . My office is in a separate cottage about a hundred feet down a winding path from my house. Since every patient walks down the garden path, I have over the years accumulated much comparison data . . . I give all patients the same directions to my office for their first visits . . . Some patients comment on the directions, some do not . . . [Other times, like when] the latch on my screen door was broken, preventing the door from closing snugly, my patients responded in a number of ways. One patient invariably spent much time fiddling with it and each week apologised for it as though she had broken it. Many ignored it, while others never failed to point out the defect and suggest I should get it fixed.*

> (2002, p52)

As in Yalom's example, we move between trying to merge with our clients for a 'real understanding' to exploring idiosyncratic responses with a particular 'hunch' or a hypothesis in mind, which we try out as part of our explanatory commitments. Every day, in this sense, we 'do' research.

CASE STUDY WRITING

One way of analysing and researching our session is through case study writing. Case study writing represents, as McLeod (1999, p205) puts it, *the most successful body of research in the history of psychology*. Within psychotherapy, it represents a tradition of practitioner research that has been in existence for almost 100 years.

'Case study' is a concept also used within research for in-depth investigation of one or more phenomena.

Looking back at your last couple of sessions:

- Can you think of any of the 'idiosyncratic responses' that Yalom refers to above? Is there anything in your session that remains the same for all clients, for instance time keeping, money etc., and to which one client may have reacted differently compared to others?
- If possible, divide into pairs and discuss your experiences regarding 'researching' your sessions.

REAL-LIFE RESEARCH

Practice-based research takes place in our everyday practice and is carried out by the practitioners themselves. Barkham et al. (2010) refer to practice-based research as a form of 'bottom-up' research as, in contrast to most evidence-based research, it approaches research from the grass-roots level rather than with experts and clinical trials in mind. Du Plock writes:

We get into difficulties, it seems to me, when we . . . begin to see research as something different and separate from what we are already intimately involved in . . . We need to take more seriously the idea of research as a personal journey of discovery . . . a continual transformation process rather than a discrete event.

(2010, p122)

Therapists who want to explore and seek understandings about their practice do have, of course, multiple choices at hand.

Different focuses and interests

- **Efficacy research** is interested in specific, measurable aspects of treatment. It focuses on the effects of particular interventions with an interest in questions of *safety, feasibility, side effects and appropriate dose level* (Barkham et al., 2010, p23).
- **Effectiveness research** often explores efficacy research in a wider context, and explores if the isolated treatment effects can have a *measurable, beneficial effect when implemented across broad populations and in other service settings* (Barkham et al., 2010, p23).
- **Practice research** focuses on variations in care and human processes rather than seeking to isolate or generalise 'facts'. It often takes an interest in the unique and seeks an understanding of therapy with a focus on meaning-making processes with subtleties and inter- and intrapsychological dynamics in mind.

- **Service system research** focuses on *large-scale organisational, financial and policy questions* (Barkham et al., 2010, p23), with delivery and optimal accessibility in mind.

DIFFERENT METHODS

Depending on whether we are interested in learning more about the individual or the unique, or hope to understand about what might apply on a more general level, two research strategies are at hand, namely qualitative and quantitative research, which offer different approaches to gathering and analysing data.

- **Quantitative researchers** usually focus on larger sample groups and explore data that tell us something about shared reactions to specific interventions. As an example is the questionnaire in Chapter 2 targeting 238 therapists with six alternative options as to why they chose to become therapists. Quantitative researchers use surveys and questionnaires to gather information, and adopt accessible ways of communicating the results, such as pie charts, tables and diagrams.
- **Qualitative researchers** often see their aim as *achieving in-depth understanding of a phenomenon, usually by studying a small number of participants* (Pistrang and Barker, 2010, p69). This is often presented in the form of case studies or themes from interviews, where the reader can follow, for instance, the clients' or the therapists' ways of thinking and reasoning around experiences. The researchers' understanding is guided by the choice of method and with reflexivity in mind.

HOW TO RESEARCH

To *have any impact on professional practice [the research] must be disseminated, and evaluated by our peers, colleagues and clients,* concludes du Plock (2010, p126). But this does not, as suggested, mean that research needs to be seen as something separate from daily life. Practice-based evidence emerges from experiences in real-life settings and invites us to revisit, or research, in the sense of looping back on to our own practice with new questions and different perspectives in mind.

In an earlier chapter, Francesca Thorpe's contributions to our reflective writing group were referred to. Shortly after the writing process for our book about therapists' motivations for practice, Francesca embarked on further research into the field of disability and therapy in general, and with a focus on Thalidomide. Francesca's progress in an example of how therapists' own special interests can trigger further and more systematic inquiries. In an article (Thorpe, 2011, p11ff), Francesca refers to some of the findings.

Case study 6.1

Last year, I was approached by the Thalidomide Trust to run a pilot counselling service specifically aimed at people affected by the Thalidomide drug. The pilot project included twelve counselling sessions paid for by the trust, for a group of eight Thalidomiders, with evaluation at the end of the project, to establish a way forward regarding Thalidomiders' up until now neglected emotional support [. . .] I began to research the role of disability in counselling, but found surprising silence there . . . As I began to unpick stories [I found different themes]. Themes were anger . . . there were accounts of bullying . . . isolation and of being 'tired of fighting' . . . Being stared at was a struggle for all participants . . . The time when they felt different was when people's attitudes were negative towards them, or when people were avoiding contact with them [. . .] The project confirmed the value of therapy, particularly with regard to the clients' recognition of their choices. Almost all clients began to explore their behaviour from new angles, often with constructive changes in their relationships with others.

COMMENT

The case study above highlights how a practitioner may take their interests further from a general concern to a more systematic inquiry. Franscesca's first step was to read up on the matter; but as she began to look for other forms of research about the role of disability in counselling, she found 'surprising silence' in that field and focused on gathering information through her research with Thalidomiders within the pilot study of the funded 12-week counselling project.

Case study 6.2 illustrates some further stages that practitioners might go through as part of their practice-based research. Daniels (2011) decides to conduct research about a victim empathy programme that she has worked with for over 20 years.

Case study 6.2

Daniels is a psychotherapist who has worked with role plays for sex offenders since 1994. In the light of a discussion about 'reorganisation', she recognises opportunities to develop the programme further both within the prison service and possibly in other settings such as the probation service. She has trained group leaders who conduct role-play groups in different prisons. She feels certain that the programme has increased victim empathy, but realises that she does not have much else than her own, her colleagues' and the sex offenders' word for it. She finds that there is little written by anyone else in the field, and recognises a need to make some form of evaluation. Daniels decides to enrol on research training, and she chooses the DPsych programme, a 'professional doctorate' with a practice-based approach. She brings a 'hypothesis' with her on to the programme, in terms of the belief that the role play does contribute to sex offenders' victim empathy. If empathy can be taught in this way to offenders, it could be an inhibitor to reoffending in the future.

COMMENT

Daniels' first step is to explore what 'evaluation' actually involves. She realises that there is no one way of evaluating; there are many different ways of describing and assessing a service and its outcome. Literature review and research into the field of evaluation becomes an inevitable step. The research involves a balance between being systematic and particular, on the one hand, and being transparent about herself and where she comes from, on the other.

The terms 'objectivity', 'validity' and 'reliability' are often used in research. The evidence-based meaning of objectivity assumes a neutral stance, which researchers within natural sciences usually take; this fits more with the traditional image of the researcher in a white coat – the 'sterile surgeon'. Validity implies here that different ways of studying something should lead to the same conclusion. Validity in this sense is meant to guarantee that the actual research has not influenced the outcome. The term 'reliability' traditionally involves the requirement *that the study remains stable over time rather than being liable to change* (Parker, 2004, p137). Social sciences, psychology in particular, can never be objective in this natural scientific sense, asserts Parker (1994, 2004). To gather data that reflects the complexity of human life, we need to reconstruct the concept of objectivity. Rather than trying to eliminate the impact of the researcher, we need to understand it and use it as part of the findings in the research. Parker writes:

> We arrive at the closest we can get to an objective account of the phenomenon in question through an exploration of the ways in which the subjectivity of the researcher has structured the way it is defined in the first place.

(1994, p13)

If we are to 'replace' or reconstruct the meaning of objectivity, validity and reliability, we need to think about the following requirements, as identified by Parker.

- **Objectivity**. Have you described what theoretical resources you use and rely on, to turn your subjectivity into a useful device? How can others understand and evaluate how your input has impacted on the research and its outcomes?
- **Validity**. Have you made clear the ways in which you give the study its distinctive difference from other perspectives?
- **Reliability**. Have you traced a process of change in your own and others' understanding of the problem? Have you explored how views of the problem or topic may continue to change?

Parker suggests that we think of the criteria for 'good' research with the following key concepts in mind. Research should be:

- grounded;
- coherent;
- accessible.

Parker continues:

> *Qualitative research does not pretend that we can fill the gap between objects and representations one and for all. Rather, because it is an essentially interpretive enterprise, it works with the problem – the gap – rather than against it.*
>
> (1994, p4)

This puts reflexivity at the forefront. As mentioned, reflexivity represents *an effort to reflect upon how the researcher is located in a particular social, political, cultural and linguistic context* (Alvesson, 2000, p179). The way we collect, select, ask certain questions and interpret the answers will, as Parker puts it, invariably affect the outcome of the study:

> *The way in which we theorise a problem will affect the way we examine it, and the way we explore a problem will affect the explanation we give.*
>
> (1994, p13)

In Case study 6.3, Daniels (2011, pp3, 6, 27) chooses to trace her interest in role play to school, and explains how she has developed this interest from a hobby into work with sex offenders in prison, describing what her work revolves around today.

Case study 6.3

Describing who you are and what you do

- *My interest in role plays started when I was a child at junior school where I loved being involved in plays . . . I studied drama in Birmingham and then embarked on a successful career as an actress . . . I had always been interested in psychology . . . and this led me to study an Open University BSc degree [in psychology]. . .*
- *. . . Over the course of the last ten years, I have been delivering role-play training for facilitators working with the Adapted Sex Offender Treatment Programme, for men with learning difficulties . . . I also deliver role plays for relapse prevention in the Core Sex Offender Treatment Programme (Daniels 2008, Fentham 2010) for medium- to high-risk sex offenders. The role plays are integrated in the cognitive behavioural model, and yet there is a list of psychodrama techniques . . .*
- *As a result of being involved in offending-behaviour programmes in Wandsworth prison, I was asked . . . to deliver role play for the victim empathy programme . . . Core SOTP is principally a cognitive behavioural-therapy programme and is very much focused on 'skills' training but also includes the exploration of thoughts, feelings and behaviour during the victim empathy modules and the relapse prevention block (Beck 1967). For the victim empathy exercise I have developed two types of role plays . . ..*

LITERATURE REVIEW

An essential part of research is, as mentioned, to undertake a literature review where the researcher reports back on current literature in the field. To 'do' a literature review involves reading, analysing, evaluating and summarising other forms of research relating to the specific topic, for instance role play and victim empathy among sex offenders. It is important to be exact with regard to the referencing, so that readers can trace the references and read more or simply check if they agree with the way the researchers have interpreted the literature. Below is an extract to give a flavour of Daniels' otherwise extensive literature review (2011, pp9–10), where she aims to position her own research in the context of others.

Case study 6.4

While researching the literature on role play, I found a wealth of information and studies that have been conducted over the last seventy years. These use inter-changeable terms such as 'role play', 'role enactment', 'skill training', 'psychodrama'

> *and 'drama therapy' . . . Role play was born out of three psychotherapeutic approaches that included sociometry and psychodrama (Moreno 1934), behaviourism (Wolpe 1958, Wolpe 1969 and Lazarus 1966), personal construct theory and fixed-role play (Kelly 1955) . . . The evolution of the term 'role theory' during the 1930s is based on three significant theorists . . ..*

COMMENT

By comparing with other ways of dealing with the topic, we get a clearer picture for ourselves about what it is we want to focus on and what feels less relevant. This is usually an exciting phase, when our original idea grows and changes shape in the light of what we learn from other people's research processes and outcomes.

A sometimes quite daunting project is choosing the most appropriate method to gather and analyse the information; for example, in this case the information that tells us something about victim-empathy role plays. This becomes another area for literature review; what are the appropriate methods at hand? Of course, this question depends on what it is that we want to know more about. Daniels wants to avoid tick-box questions, which could be affected by the research subjects trying to give the 'right' answers. Her real interest is how the experience of the role play impacts on the sex offenders' way of thinking. How does the programme impact on their ways of making sense of their meaning-making processes, with regard to their offences? How do they perceive their own role in the offences, and how do they make sense of their victims' reactions? Is there any difference before or after the programme? If so, are there any stages that the sex offenders could go through, which could be helpful in identifying further programmes?

Below is an extract from Daniels' attempt to put her choice of method into a context of her research interests. She explains (2011, p82) that she is interested in 'idiographic' thinking, which involves a focus on the unique and the individual, and reflects on the different options at hand in her field of interest.

Case study 6.5

I deliberately chose a phenomenological method to elicit the 'experience' of prisoners when undertaking victim-empathy role plays . . . What is clear from the literature is that a number of phenomenological research methods emerged over time (Moustakas

1994); ethnography (Mead 1928); grounded-research theory (Glasser and Strauss 1967); and phenomenological psychological research (Giorgri 1985, Roy et al. 1999, Smith and Osborn 2008, Smith, Flowers, Larkin 2009). Smith (2004) developed a method of combining phenomenology and psychology in order to give a structure in which to examine the phenomenological data and named it interpretive phenomenological analysis (IPA). This methodology also acknowledges the relationship between researcher and participant, in that there is always an interpretation on the part of researcher. Smith (2004) describes features that are characteristic to IPA, such as the idiographic – the individual experience – the inductive, allowing unanticipated themes to emerge, and the interrogative, in that it is a shared psychological perspective . . . IPA is multi-layered in terms of its epistemological assumptions and it agrees with Heidegger's and Gadamer's philosophy of the hermeneutic circle, whereby the researcher is both the 'whole' and 'part' while analysing the data (Smith, Flowers, Larkin 2009). During the analysis, the researcher may shift positions in their thinking, and then change again when further through the analysis . . . The process is idiographic in nature in that it is concerned with the particular; in other words, the detail of one individual's experience, as opposed to a group of people (nomothetic) in a given context.

Daniels also explains how her chosen method, IPA, is used in her analysis of the data, that is the lengthy interviews:

> *IPA uses semi-structured interviews, with questions being open ended and non-directive, and the data is analysed by the researcher engaging in an interpretative relationship with the transcript. The process is repetitive and researchers repeat the process reading and analysing the data until the themes are clustered and then finally drawn together under the superordinate headings, or major themes. The writing up of these themes is still part of the interpretive stage, which is identified by Eatough and Smith (2008) as having two levels: (a) a more descriptive, empathic level to allow the researcher to enter the participant's world; and (b) another level of interpretation that takes it beyond the participant's own words. However, there can be ethical issues around this, given the complexity of meanings (Willig 2008) . . . so I endeavoured to find out more about the method.*

> (2011, p83)

COMMENT

Methodology is, as Robson (2002, p549) puts it, *the theoretical, political and philosophical backgrounds to social research.* Daniels explains how her choice of methodology has been guided by her interest in *capturing the quality and texture of individuals' experiences* (2011, p83). In Case study 6.5, she explains how she explored different alternatives within the family of phenomenological methods, for instance grounded theory, thematic analysis and narrative analysis. Daniels concludes that, among the different methods at hand, IPA suited her dual purposes best in terms of being able to both *keep the idiographic quality and not lose the individual voice, yet still cross reference themes*:

> But when I read articles . . . I decided the themes and outcomes were more generalised, rather than idiographic, in the sense of getting a rich, deeper understanding of meaning and seeing the world through the offender's eyes . . . I wanted to keep the idiographic quality and not lose the individual voice, yet still cross reference themes.
>
> (2011, p86)

By using both themes and stories as told by the research subjects themselves, the research is easy to present – the themes can be bullet pointed and presented with ease in documents for funding, at conferences etc. But the narratives, the full stories, give the reader with time on their hands a real insight into what happens in the offenders' minds as they undergo the programme.

Selecting sample groups can be a problem. There are always ethical concerns with therapy-related research. Researching on one's own clients is usually so riddled with issues that many avoid it altogether. The overriding interest is always on the client's well-being. The fact that research may be introduced does not alter this fact. Anyone who considers involving their own clients in research needs to be able to argue that this added dimension to the therapy, that is research, is likely to improve the treatment not just indirectly (benefiting clients in general) but directly.

ACTIVITY 6.3

The ethical guidelines explored in Chapter 3 (see page 40) can be valuable to return to in order to help us explore the potential impact research may or may not have. One particularly obvious dilemma is confidentiality; how will the research be presented? Another fundamental difficulty is to what extent the client is free or not to express what they really think about the therapy to his or her own therapist. It is likely that the therapist who seeks to evaluate his or her own practice will end up hearing what the clients think they ought to say.

- Imagine that your personal therapist explained that she wanted to evaluate her own practice in order to improve her overall service. What might be your immediate concern?

The ethical progress in Daniels' case was rigorous and had to be approved by an ethical committee both within the prison service, and within her training institute. Her sample solution in this case was resolved by interviewing prisoners who had undergone role play in other programmes. Daniels was able to distribute invitations to interviews via treatment managers in three different prisons. Daniels explains:

> *Three prisons were selected to source participants for the research . . . Each treatment manager from the three prisons [was asked] to identify and select three prisoners with different offences – a child offender, rapist and female or adult offender – in order to have a broader scope of offence types.*
>
> (2011, p48)

As suggested, this kind of research does not perceive the researcher as isolated or cut off. Instead, the researcher's involvement is expected to be as transparent as possible. In these final extracts from Daniels' research, reflexivity is put to the forefront. Daniels describes how natural supervision is in her clinical practice. She had, however, expected to react differently as a researcher:

> *As a conscientious clinician, I know how to be non-judgmental, empathic and supportive to offenders in helping them to disclose information and work through the difficult aspects of their lives. However, I am also human, experiencing conflicting emotions that I will take to supervision in order to make sense of it by exploring the countertransference (Freidrich and Leiper 2006). Strangely, I did not do this after the interviews because I was in a new role of researcher and did not equate this with being a clinician and needing to seek personal support.*
>
> (2011, p66)

After interviewing the sex offenders, Daniels transcribed the interviews. However, during the reading she noticed how she became increasingly affected by the readings. She began to put off reading certain transcripts, as described in Case study 6.6 (2011, pp67–8).

Case study 6.6

Although I have many years' clinical experience working with this client group, I was not prepared in my role as researcher for the disturbing and vulnerable feelings that were evoked in me when I analysed the data . . . My first interview involved a man who had abused his daughter from the age of twelve years, continuing through her leaving home and going to university . . . I struggled at the part where he said it was like 'having a love affair' . . . reading his account line by line, immersing myself in his

> *experience, left me on an emotional roller coaster . . . I avoided the analysis . . . and would make excuses and do something else . . . I would look at my own children, especially my sixteen year old daughter, and think about how this could happen. . . I knew I had to find specific supervision . . . I also wanted someone who was a trained therapist, as I realised this material was no doubt triggering my own issues, and in order to be clear about what belonged to me and what belonged to the offender, I wanted a professional who could help me explore my own personal material . . . It was this latter area that made me realise the importance of reflexivity. . .*

COMMENT

Daniels highlights the importance of considering our own emotions carefully during research. Our own reactions can seep into the actual research process, as Daniels writes above, when she seeks supervision to help her *to be clear about what belonged to me and what belonged to the offender*.

MORE ABOUT CONTINUING PROFESSIONAL DEVELOPMENT

Practice research can have a positive impact both on one's practice and on the therapist as a person. In the next two chapters, two therapists will share their accounts of their personal development. Each explores transformative learning in the way that their prior learning from difficult situations is woven into their therapeutic future in creative and constructive ways. In Chapter 7, Dr Marie Adams explains her own learning experiences from researching. Her account offers a good example of practice-based research, with a focus on the therapist as a person, and the potential impact a personal crisis may have on his or her professional practice. Adams' research also raises the issue of a complaint, which in her case was withdrawn at an early stage but nevertheless impacted on her enormously. In Chapter 8, Beverley Costa explains why and how she ended up establishing a therapy agency focusing on bilingual therapy.

CHAPTER SUMMARY

- Once registered with one of the member organisations, such as the BACP, UKCP or BPS, therapists are required to undertake continuing professional development (CPD) to maintain their status as registered members.

- CPD is defined as:

  any process or activity that provides added value to the capability of the professional through the increase in knowledge, skills and personal qualities necessary for the appropriate execution of professional and technical duties, often termed competence.

  (Professional Associations Research Network,
  cited in BACP, 2012)

- We looked at the meaning of evidence-based practice and practice-based research as forms of CPD. It was suggested that each session is a piece of research. In each session, we piece together information and understandings, followed by testing the validity of conclusions and actions based on shared knowing. Case study writing was suggested as a way of documenting these intricate processes.
- Finally, we looked at some examples of practice-based, 'real-life' research.

Placing ourselves in context: research as a personal narrative

Marie Adams

CORE KNOWLEDGE

- What happens when a therapist experiences a crisis in their own life? When should we work and when is it best not to work, when problems surface in our own lives? This chapter illustrates therapist Marie Adams' practice-based research about how therapists' own problems may impact upon their clinical work.
- Marie explains the background and rationale for her research. She reflects on the outcome of interviewing 40 therapists from three different countries about their ways of handling the boundary between their personal and professional selves. Marie's story highlights how research throws new light on both our practice and ourselves as *for the most part we all struggle to be the best we can be within the limitations of our human imperfections.*

MARIE'S STORY

This section concerns my practice research about how our personal lives may impact on our clinical work. My research involved interviewing 40 therapists across three countries and ten therapists in each of four major traditions: psychoanalytic, integrative, humanistic and cognitive behavioural. As discussed in the following section, I wanted to know how they believed their personal lives affected their work with clients/patients and how other therapists had experienced themselves as professionals working through hard times. This section revolves around where this interest came from, and what happened when I pursued it.

We all need to place ourselves within the context of the greater world, to give us significance perhaps and certainly a sense of place. We need to create a story for ourselves and make sense of who we are. When I was young I used to scribble in my notebook: *Marie Adams, Monstrose Street, Winnipeg, Manitoba, Canada, North America, the World, the Universe.*

I feel both a million miles, and yet not so far away, from that little girl writing out her address across the front of her exercise books, unconsciously working hard to place herself in context. Research, I believe, is often simply the grown-up version of that same preoccupation.

Researching 40 therapists across three countries – the UK, Canada and Australia – helped me to place myself within the greater therapeutic community and gave unexpected texture to my personal story – an evolving narrative that has profoundly affected how I see myself in the world, in the universe, and within my profession.

My research began after struggling through a particularly difficult period of five months, following a professional complaint. We all need meaning in our lives (Frankl, 1959; Yalom, 1980), but it is difficult to find purpose in an experience that appears devoid of anything positive, for example the loss of a loved one, a random attack, or a professional complaint as I had faced. The only intention here, it had seemed to me, was destruction and annihilation. Despite Frankl's assertion that there must always be meaning in suffering, there appeared to me nothing redeemable about that five-month period when I had lived in a state of almost overwhelming anxiety and fear that the career I had worked so hard for might be yanked from underneath me; and linked with that, of course, would be profound shame when the news became public.

My response to this 'attack' was to fight it, and to fight hard, clearly a defence honed early on in my history. And in that robust defensive action, I believe, is evidence of how deeply I felt the wound. This wasn't just the 'here and now' being affected, but something primal and difficult and painful, even life-threatening in its way, rooted of course in my past (Adams, 2008).

I had not crossed any ethical boundaries but, of course, as with any client, I had made mistakes, many of them within transference and counter-transference, both of us enacting elements of our history, including abandonment and sadistic impulses of persecution and rejection. I had also been frozen by terror at her potential to make a complaint (she was a 'vexatious litigant' with a history of grievances taken against colleagues, neighbours and medical practitioners) and I was full of regret that I had accepted to work with her in the first place when my instinct had suggested it was not a good idea. Instead, the gunslinger in me had accepted the challenge, finally meeting her at dawn, to work it out over a complaint's procedure.

In my case I was fortunate enough that the complaint was dropped but, nonetheless, if trauma can be evoked from what we *imagine* might happen, rather than what actually takes place, I was certainly affected.

I did spend some time in a dark tunnel. When eventually I emerged, I felt both grateful and overwhelmed by the number of 'stories' I was told by other therapists who had faced traumatic events while working. The stories included life-threatening illnesses, bereavement and professional crises, among them redundancy and professional complaints.

From this apparently unfortunate beginning, the seed of my research was planted, helping me to give meaning to my experience and place myself within the context of a greater therapeutic community.

WHAT'S OUT THERE?

There is not so much written about the personal lives of therapists; most of the literature focuses on the client or on the impact of the client on the therapist. There are also exceptions, of course, such as Rice (2011), who describes how a therapist's personal process has unconsciously played out or been enacted within the therapy room, and Mann's evocative description of the impact of his blood phobia on one of his patients (Mann and Cunningham, 2008). Bager-Charleson (2010a) focuses on the historical reasons for therapists choosing to become therapists, while Guy's (1987) seminal work focuses directly on the personal lives and motivations of therapists, inviting the reader to take a more critical role in assessing his or her own competence. Ragen's moving account (2009) of her time working in New York after the 9/11 attacks focuses almost exclusively on her personal process, and Gold and Nemaiah's (1993) book highlights the struggle of therapists facing divorce, old age and pregnancy, among other life events, while still working with clients. In Gerson's *The Therapist as a Person*, Chasen (1996) writes of continuing to work just a few weeks after the death of her only beloved child in a freak car accident. Like many of the therapists I spoke to, she found refuge in her work, a few hours in her day when she was not persecuted by unbearable grief. Chasen writes:

> *Freud was right about the nature of productive work. At least for the time that I was in session, I could escape a little from the horror of what my life had become.*
>
> (1996, p7)

THE RESEARCH

I wanted to know how other therapists had experienced themselves as professionals working through hard times. If faced with the same circumstances again, would they conduct themselves differently? Would they continue working? In learning about them, I thought, I might learn something to my benefit and, by extension, so might others. Perhaps what I really wanted was reassurance, to know that I wasn't alone in my experience. Like any child in search of an empathic mother, I was unconsciously trying to find my 'mirror' (Kohut, 1977; Stern, 1985; Winnicott, 1990).

What I hadn't planned on was to what an extent I would learn, and to what degree it would affect me in my work as a therapist. Through considering how other psychotherapists had coped, I was forced to look at my own feelings of omnipotence, my vulnerability to shame, the impossibility of perfection and that reassuring certainty that I belong to a community – the world, the universe.

ACTIVITY 7.1

- What are you interested in and what would you like to know more about? Is there anything you would consider researching? If so, what would your research question be, and how might you answer it?

As mentioned above, the formal aspect of my research involved interviewing 40 therapists across three countries and ten therapists in each of four major traditions: psychoanalytic, integrative, humanistic and cognitive behavioural. All but a very few were complete strangers to me, while several were colleagues I had known through training or conferences in the past but with whom I had nothing to do in the 'here and now' of my professional life. I wanted to know how they believed their personal lives affected their work with clients/patients. Interviews lasted approximately one hour, which of course limited the depth to which some subjects could be pursued, but as any therapist will tell you, an hour is certainly long enough to hit the lodestone of tragedy and grief, and to penetrate long-established defences, at least for a moment. In many cases, these interviews were like the first session with a new client when you learn everything, if only you knew it, and months later you return again and again to that first session when the truth was named so coherently.

CAPTURING THE STORY

'This will start off about me, but it will end up about you,' said a patient to me once in his first session, after which I had to remind him over and over again as time passed that he continually forfeited his own experience to the demands of others. The history, or the life story, of this client was written in this first, simple sentence and, in retrospect, I began to understand its significance, as did my client. He had spent a lifetime caring for his vulnerable mother and warding off the demands of a powerful, autocratic father. Nothing in his young life had been about him, but rather the focus was on meeting the needs of others, a scenario he enacted in all his relationships and that played out in his transference with me. Over the years we weathered this enactment until he was able to *articulate* his story – give words to the experience rather than simply play it out in an endless loop with everyone he encountered.

THE PERSONAL NARRATIVE WITHIN RESEARCH

So, too, was the story of these 40 therapists written in what they spoke about in their hour-long meetings with me. Unlike with my client, whatever came up in the 'session' could not be resolved in future meetings. We were a 'one-off', but the experiences were no less powerful for that, at least for me. I can only speculate on the significance of what each therapist said. This was a phenomenological study (Smith et al., 2009), and so it is my *interpretation* of what they said that is often highlighted, and I cannot know if what I took to be so significant in the interview would be reflected back as their 'tell' in therapy – the sentence that so eloquently summed up their life experience and the manner in which they conduct their relationships, particularly those within the therapy room. However, as Ogden (1997) points out, whatever transpires in the room is a co-creation between the therapist and patient, creating an 'analytical third'. Whatever the therapist considers or dreams, or how he or she responds, is information concerning both the therapist and the client. Ogden (1997) more or less sums up the truth that I could not possibly investigate the lives of therapists without learning something about myself. In every question where I asked them which significant events in their lives led them to become therapists, I could not leave out consideration of significant events in my own life, for instance my mother's grief after the death of my sister, or my struggle with 'difference' within the family. In asking them to consider their histories, I had to consider my own, whether I wanted to or not. In other words, I could not leave myself or my own story out of the experience. We were a co-creation.

ACTIVITY 7.2

- What in your own life do you think could impact on your work with clients?
- What might you focus on, or avoid, as a result of your current difficulties or archaic distress?
- How does your history interact with your clients'?

DEPRESSION AND ANXIETY

One of the most significant results from my research was the amount of depression experienced by therapists during their period of working. Of the 40 therapists interviewed, more than half (24) admitted they had suffered depression in the course of their working lives. Of these, 16 psychotherapists said their experience was episodic, while the remaining eight described themselves as suffering 'chronic' depression. Breaking this down even further, 13 therapists in this group suffered a form of abandonment as children, including parental death, an alcoholic parent and neglect. Only three therapists who named abandonment of some kind in their childhood did not experience depression.

While some therapists described their depression as completely debilitating at times, those who described their experience as 'chronic' tended to live with it and function regardless, often through the support of therapy and sometimes in conjunction with medication. One therapist, though, admitted that therapy did not work for her – she knew all the 'tricks', and she relied on drugs to help her through the difficult periods.

In 1988, Norcross et al. canvassed over 700 psychologists, psychiatrists and clinical social workers concerning the process and outcome of their personal therapy. Twenty per cent reported that they had sought therapy due to marital conflict, while 13 per cent named depression and 12 per cent cited anxiety as their reason for seeking help. The survey was repeated 20 years later (Bike et al., 2009) and little had changed, with 13 per cent again reporting depression and 10 per cent anxiety. Once again, 20 per cent cited marital stress as their motivation for seeking therapy. In both these studies women were more likely to seek help than their male colleagues.

In a deeply sobering study, Pope and Tabachnick (1994) considered when, and if, therapists returned to therapy after completing their training, and for what reasons. A startling 29 per cent reported having contemplated suicide, while 4 per cent of the 500 therapists questioned said they had actually made an attempt. A full 61 per cent reported suffering clinical depression.

More recently, Geller et al. (2005) investigated therapists' distress across the modalities, including Jungian, Freudian and cognitive behavioural. As they point out, *it is often easier to be wise and mature for others than for ourselves;* they continue: *therapists who cling to a sense of strength and mastery are threatened by the dilemma of 'needing help'* (2005, p6).

PERSONAL RESPONSE

If these studies, and my own investigations, are a reflection of my 'therapeutic community', how then do I fit in? Once again, I could not ask the questions without reflecting on my history, my own tendency to 'cling to a sense of mastery', questions I would rather, of course, ignore, and certainly keep hidden in the background of my personal and professional life so I can hold on to that very sense of 'mastery', or omnipotence, as one therapist so eloquently described:

> *I became very stressed and actually was diagnosed with being clinically depressed, so I kept working for a couple of months, but eventually I had to stop, I had to take time off. Because it's the first time I've ever become depressed, there was a bit of me – probably an omnipotent part of me – that thought I can cope, I can cope and certainly that was a huge learning curve for me.*

Asking the research questions did not necessarily prompt self-reflection, but rather it was in the receiving of the deeply moving, and personally revealing, responses of my interviewees that I was forced to consider my own story.

As in the therapeutic process, shafts of light kept piercing through the membrane of my defences where I keep hidden my shadow side, certainly from the world and often myself.

According to the therapists I interviewed, having suffered depression notably contributed to a deeper understanding of their clients' experiences. However, as one therapist put it, continuing to see patients while in the midst of depression often meant she was 'listless' in the room and less likely to be 'proactive'. Another therapist, who later took time out to recover, admitted:

> *I wasn't paying enough attention to what was going on between me and the client and I was stuck in more heavy automatic responses than really paying attention to what was going on for me.*

THE EXPERIENCE OF 'DEPRESSION'

Depression can manifest itself in many forms, from the chaotic disturbance of bipolar to the 'empty bed blues' of Bessie Smith. Depression can span the spectrum from one lousy day, to the chronic, disabling illness so eloquently described in William Styron's *Darkness visible*, where he names the experience as *despair beyond despair* (1990, p37). Depression can also manifest as 'anxiety' rather than as the terrible despondency described by so many who have suffered the condition, including those in my study. This may, in fact, be a manic activity to ward off a slump.

The distinction between depression and anxiety within the therapy room is actually crucial, if the therapists in my study are to be understood. While working when suffering despair can increase our empathy towards our clients in the therapy room, anxiety invariably acts as a current of interference. Depression, if you like, opens us up to the deepest of wounds, enabling us at times to bear the suffering of others. 'S' felt strongly that her grief after the death of her partner actually enabled her to work more deeply with her patients:

> I've often felt I'm in a rather worse state than people in front of me at times, and it's very interesting about how you use that, or how you find yourself umm being used through it, using it yourself . . . I suppose the way I think about it is that actually I was able to feel the bereavement very intensely because I was very well held within my profession, and within my friendships. I knew other widows who would say you just feel you're never gonna feel any better but you will, and it takes a long time but something does happen because you just feel so terrible, and you can understand why people take anti-depressants . . . they feel that other people actually don't really understand the level of pain they're in or they feel they shouldn't be in that level of pain. That's very common, (they believe) that somehow there's something wrong with them, so you know a lot of the time in a way I would feel that I was probably feeling more pain in a way than they were in relation to my situation.

But if depression can open us up to the suffering of others, anxiety tends to cut in the other direction. Despite its purpose to avoid underlying distress, anxiety also brings with it a curiously self-absorbed quality, as if with so much manic activity we actually can never quite forget ourselves. Rather than tuning in, we may tune out, as 'M' so poignantly describes when facing redundancy at his mental health clinic:

> My sleep and appetite was disturbed and then the service didn't look after us at all, so I think that invariably impacted on my clinical work. I can't think it didn't. I was probably not as engaged with the clients. I think I was distracted, you know, I mean you're going into these clinical rooms that you've been using for years, and you're aware that you're going to be kicked out of here.

ACTIVITY 7.3

- Do you tend to experience depression or anxiety, or both?
- How do you manage either/both within the therapy room?
- How do you think this has impacted on your work with clients?

WORKING THROUGH THE CRISIS: BRACKETING

Psychotherapy may manifest itself as a 'vocation' for some therapists, but it is also a career choice and, like anyone else facing hard times, we sometimes feel the need to throw ourselves into our jobs to avoid distressing thoughts and feelings. For a few hours, with clients and patients, we can forget who we are, escape ourselves and immerse ourselves in the world of those who sometimes appear to be in more distress than we are.

We can delude ourselves, perhaps, that we can 'bracket' our anxieties and 'keep them out of the room' – a phrase I heard from many of the therapists I interviewed. However, not a single therapist could actually say what 'bracketing' actually comprised and I am left feeling, as a result of both interviewing them and taking a hard look at my own experience, that 'bracketing' is a phrase of convenience, allowing us to continue working at times when we should not. In the aftermath of my experience, a number of supervisees said, 'I thought something was wrong, I just didn't know what.' So much for bracketing. I had conveniently convinced myself that work was a healthy refuge during those months, and that I was working normally. The truth is I likely looked tired, as I certainly was not sleeping well and, like those therapists who admitted they were less effective when suffering depression, I may have been 'listless' and less 'proactive' and, like 'H', I was often functioning simply on automatic pilot. I may not have done harm during those months, but from speaking with other therapists I realise I probably evaded subjects that tapped into my own distress, or veered away from deeper issues involving primal impulses of unarticulated hatred, particularly within the transference (Klein, 1986; Winnicott, 1947).

In listening to those therapists I interviewed I also had to admit that my habitual defence against depression is anxiety. I am more likely to ratchet up the pace, rather than close down. Certainly I had continued to work during those very anxious months facing the complaint. I had very low moments, of course, but they often acted as a prompt to take some action and protect myself. I was not given to hiding away, and I had continued to work. Unlike 'S', in my anxious distress I may not have been so able to tune in to my clients during that period, but rather my anxiety may have meant I missed them at times, unconsciously absorbed as I was by the distractions of my private life.

ACTIVITY 7.4

Every therapist faces personal difficulties at one time or another.

- How have you managed through difficult times?
- What might you put in place to ensure you are well supported in case of a personal crisis?

WHEN TO WORK; WHEN NOT TO WORK

How can we tell when we are all right to work and when we are not emotionally equipped to carry out the tasks of therapy, at the very least to stay tuned and provide empathic concern for our clients?

The single most repeated note of regret repeated through my research of the 40 therapists was that they had not taken enough time out at times of stress, including illness, depression or family anxieties.

It is, of course, simple enough to say that every therapist should take the time out they need to recover and repair themselves, but the hard truth is that this is also our job, our livelihood and the way we pay our mortgages, support our children's education and keep the wheels going, particularly in these hard times. Most of us need to work, both emotionally and financially.

The other side of this truth is that our job is not like other jobs. We have an obligation to keep the client in mind at all times, and perhaps we also have to consider how we occupy ourselves at times of stress. What else, other than client work, might we throw ourselves into as a point of refuge? We all need, at some point, to take a break from our anxieties and heartbreak, and find a way to feel good and productive about ourselves. We all need to have meaning in our lives, and I believe that our profession is one that allows us that sense of productivity and purpose more substantially than many other professions. Only those therapists who worked within the hard-core environment of various mental health systems expressed feelings of disenchantment with their work, in every case specifying the need to 'produce results' and 'show evidence' as the single most difficult thing they had to cope with. For those of us working within the luxury of private practice, we have many advantages, but we do not have 'sick pay' to back us up during difficult times. How, then, do we cope and manage those crises that will invariably erupt in the course of our working lives?

CONCLUSION

I may have been looking for answers by conducting this research, but the result was simply more questions. I learned a great deal about the struggles of other therapists and, as a result, I was forced to consider my own responses and motivations as a practising psychotherapist. I learned that I am part of a community, throughout the world in fact, which has more in common than it has differences: for the most part we all struggle to be the best we can be within the limitations of our human imperfections. We are also loath to admit them and often suffer terrible shame at the notion that we are not coping. To do so is to offer up our sense of omnipotence and our need to be 'better than' our clients, when in fact we are all part of the same human pool.

At every stage of our lives, I believe, we may have to renegotiate old ground, revisit the traumas of our histories and place them within the context of our current lives and relationships. As Faulkner (1951) says, *The past is never dead. It's not even past.*

CHAPTER SUMMARY

- This chapter focused on practice-based research as part of a transformational learning experience in the aftermath of a complaint issued – and withdrawn – by a client.
- Of the 40 therapists interviewed, more than half (24) admitted they had suffered depression in the course of their working lives. Of these, 16 psychotherapists said their experience was episodic, while the remaining eight described themselves as suffering 'chronic' depression. Breaking this down even further, 13 therapists in this group suffered a form of abandonment as children, including parental death, an alcoholic parent and neglect. Only three therapists who named abandonment of some kind in their childhood did not experience depression.
- Exploring the amount of silent suffering among therapists, Marie suggests a rethink. It is always good to talk. To leave our own problems unaddressed would be to *offer up our sense of omnipotence and our need to be 'better than' our clients.*

CHAPTER 8

A therapeutic journey across cultural and linguistic borderlands

Beverley Costa

CORE KNOWLEDGE

- What happens if we cannot find our niche within existing services? This is a second case study about transformative learning, as told by the therapist herself.
- In this chapter Beverley Costa, the founder of the multilingual therapy agency Mothertongue, reflects on how cultural tensions have impacted on her life and her subsequent choice of orientation as a therapist.
- Beverley offers a personal account of some of the complexities involved in finding training that reflects one's ethnicity.
- Upon recognising a gap in her training, as well as a lack in services provided, she decided to establish an agency herself geared towards the needs of bilingual therapy. She shares some of the practical, theoretical and emotional learning as part of this process.

BEVERLEY'S STORY – CULTURAL TENSIONS AND LACK OF BELONGING

In order to explain how I came to be in the situation of founding a new voluntary sector therapy service in 2000, it may be useful to provide a reflective account of what led me to this point. I grew up in a dual-heritage family. I was surrounded by cultures that were very different from the mainstream external environment in which we lived, and a range of languages, some of which I did not understand. There were a number of complexities and tensions that faced my family, including acculturation stress, the impact of migration and the loss of a homeland for political reasons, and tensions between the cultures within the home and outside the home. There was also a core dynamic that ran through our family life and manifested itself in response to feeling misunderstood and 'mis-seen'. This inevitably impacted on me. One of the strategies I developed to cope with this (with some but not total success!) was to try to seek out creative ways, as opposed to destructive ways, of managing these tensions.

One factor that was an invaluable source of support to me was my experience of school from secondary school age. Not only did it furnish me with another intellectual identity, but it also gave me a sense of containment and structure with positive role models and extremely nurturing, supportive and optimistic relationships with my peers. In the organisation that I was to found nearly 30 years later, it was those qualities that I would seek to reproduce so that others might have a similar opportunity for a reparative group/organisational experience. A sense of belonging and the inclusion of people's multiple experiences have been very important factors in the life and development of the organisation. We have been able to provide a point of attachment and a sense of belonging and community for people for whom migration has brought experiences of loss, displacement and disconnection. In fact, the art project we have conducted over the past two years from 2009, with local schools for newly arrived students, is called 'A Place to Belong'. It has been important to be able to attend to this sense of belonging for staff, volunteers and clients.

EXPERIENCING A GAP IN THE TRAINING

To return to my background influences, at university my choice of subjects, drama and Spanish, was informed by an interest in social and psychological roles and identity, and the role of language in developing different identities/selves. This choice of subjects was to reverberate down the years with my developing interest in the impact of multilingualism and migration on the development of the psyche. My years in Spain, speaking Spanish and teaching English, contributed to that reverberation as I added more versions of myself and my identities that led me further away from my core self. This facility of reinvention and assimilation, by people from migrant communities, has been described as the creation of a 'proxy self' by Lennox Thomas (1995). This has been a factor that has had a profound influence on the development of our therapeutic model and service delivery.

In all of my training as a psychotherapist, I was left with a sense of dissatisfaction that the models of therapy presented failed to take into account people's different world views and migration experiences. The models of therapy on offer in mainstream services tended to be based on an individual-centred world view and ignored the experience of people from collective-centred cultures.

REFLECTION POINT

- What are your experiences of training so far? What has resonated particularly with you, and what – if anything – has felt less 'right'?

ABOUT UNMET NEEDS WITHIN THE THERAPY SECTOR

One of the training initiatives with which I was involved was the Workers' Educational Association (WEA) Multicultural Learning Centre in Reading. This was a voluntary sector training organisation established to offer women from black and minority ethnic (BME) communities the opportunity to learn a range of skills in a safe and accessible environment. Courses included: Crèche Worker Skills, First Aid, Community Interpreting, English and Interpersonal Skills. I taught a range of classes including one on Bilingual Counselling Skills. Although I did not have a therapeutic brief in the Multicultural Learning Centre, students would want to talk to me about very troubling experiences as soon as they felt some kind of trust with me.

Many of the students I worked with – in fact, this is the case for our clients to this day – were isolated and unable to call on their traditional forms of support and coping. These may consist of talking and offloading feelings with their family and friends around them. In terms of provision, there was no service that was available and relevant to my students at the WEA. Statistically, although BME communities are over-represented nationally in secondary services for mental healthcare, their routes of access are normally via the police or accident and emergency services as a result of a crisis. They are starkly under-represented in primary mental health services. This was also the case locally where I was working.

FOUNDING AND SETTING UP THE SERVICE

At this stage in my career I had no experience of setting up and running a service and, without the help, knowledge and support of key people around me, it would have been impossible. Fortunately, I had some excellent colleagues in the local voluntary sector and Primary Care Trust (PCT) who helped with guidance. A Steering Group with representatives from a range of voluntary and public sector services was set up with the aim of forming a registered charity and company, and of securing initial funding. With support, I was able to gain funding from the local PCT and Health Authority in order to fund a feasibility study and to run an initial pilot counselling service based in a local GP surgery.

Together with the Steering Group, we decided to conduct a feasibility study in order to check out if what we were observing informally as a need and a gap in services was backed up by evidence and information we were able to gather. Although I was confident that what I was observing was in fact sufficient evidence, at this very early stage it was unreasonable to expect those who would be investing money into a service to trust my observations blindly. The feasibility study revealed that a number of factors created barriers to access to mental health services for the BME communities, including experiences of racism and discrimination in services; fear of stigmatisation; lack of cultural sensitivity; and language needs. Mothertongue multi-ethnic counselling service was created in an attempt to address all of these concerns. Mothertongue is a culturally sensitive, professional counselling service where people are heard with respect in their chosen language. It provides a space for people's real and not 'proxy' (Thomas, 1995) selves to be seen safely and understood.

MOTHERTONGUE: THE FIRST STEPS AND MY EVOLVING ROLE

The feasibility study and charitable and company status were achieved. The six-month counselling pilot was a success and we were able to attract further funding. At this point a Management Committee and Chair had been established, and we were able to recruit a part-time project manager and further counsellors. My role encompassed managerial duties, clinical responsibility for the service, including clinical supervision of all workers, and promotion and fundraising. Over time this role has developed into a Chief Executive role. The organisation, as a charity, has continued to have the governance structure of a Management Committee. The style of governance has been that of a 'critical friend'. I am very fortunate in that I have been guided to this day by an excellent consultant – an outside mentor. From my previous experience I had observed the pressures that people in leadership positions in the voluntary sector were under. I felt it would be important to have somebody external to the organisation to guide me, especially at the beginning, as to the differences between the roles of therapist and manager.

ACTIVITIES

Mothertongue provides a bridge between individualism and collectivism by offering possibilities to meet with people from a wide range of cultures and languages. For those who have needed it, it has provided a safe community space to try out a range of activities and roles, to move between dependency, independence and the ability to offer support to others. There is therefore the possibility of combining different heritages and of creating new cultures so that people can find their 'place to belong' in the wider society.

Although Mothertongue is principally a counselling service, it has taken a holistic approach to therapeutic provision from its earliest days. This seems to us to be the best way to make the service relevant and usable for our clients. The organisation currently comprises the following:

- the core culturally and linguistically sensitive counselling service;
- the Mental Health Interpreting Service and training programme;

- the Volunteer Language Support service;
- the groups: English classes; Knitting Support Group; Cross Cultural Parent Groups;
- schools work: art workshops for newly arrived students; training programme for young interpreters;
- a training programme for professionals in therapy across languages and cultures;
- a research project in multilingualism and therapy.

We provide a culturally sensitive, linguistically appropriate and relevant counselling service to members of the BME population that aims to respond to their specific social and psychological needs in a manner that takes into account their expectations and values. For instance, we weave together the needs of the community and the needs of the individual according to a Community Engagement model. We aim to engage individuals and small groups so that they can feel fully part of, participate in and contribute not only to their own lives but also to the wider society.

THE UNDERPINNING PHILOSOPHY OF THE COUNSELLING SERVICE

I am often asked about the model of counselling we use. The answer is that there is no standard cross-cultural counselling model to which we subscribe. I am sure my answer often disappoints. If that is the case, it is not for want of thinking! I am hoping that this disappointing answer may be offset somewhat by some words about the underlying philosophy that has led us to this conclusion. At first glance, the philosophy that underpins, for example, the person-centred approach may seem universal. However, as Ian Parker (2007, p114) reminds us, *All models of the mind in psychology are culturally specific*, which presumes the white *middle-class individual as the ideal standard.*

If we look at some of the following values that underpin person-centred philosophy, we can clearly see that all communities do not share them:

- *expressing your emotions with a stranger can be a good thing;*
- *separating from parental/family influence is something to be aimed for;*
- *we have freedom of choice;*
- *hierarchical structures are oppressive.*

(Laungani, 1999; Costa, 2002)

Other writers (Eleftheriadou, 1994; Laungani, 1999) discuss cross-cultural counselling models that challenge us to rethink assumptions about the values and beliefs we may think we share with our clients. Interventions that may be culturally adapted and appropriate for people from one culture may not be applied universally across ages, genders or, in the following example, class. In this example, the writer has been discussing the knitting circle set up as a psychosocial intervention for traumatised women in the former Yugoslavia.

Case study 8.1

After many talks with the women who participated in the project, the international NGO staff had realised that sitting in a circle and knitting and drinking coffee was an old peasant tradition among women from the region. It was a 'self-healing' circle that had been practised for centuries during all the former wars and hardships people had gone through. By distributing wool and supplying coffee they were setting the scene for a communal practice to develop among these refugee women, who often did not know each other and who needed new social networks. However, this would not have been the optimal approach among middle-class women in large cities, where psychotherapy was a normal activity that had been financed by the health system during the socialist government.

The adjustments that people have to make when they are moving between cultures include finding a way to respond to the new values that underpin the culture they are moving to. This can cause a kind of stress referred to as acculturation stress (Eleftheriadou, 1994). All of our clients have to make these adjustments.

Furthermore, we have discovered that, by paying attention to one under-examined aspect of cross-cultural therapeutic work, we can learn a great deal about how to understand and intervene therapeutically more effectively with our multilingual clients. As described at the beginning, my own experiences of cultural tensions and feelings of misrepresentation have certainly contributed to my heightened interest in language and culture. It was fascinating to learn more about what impact first and second languages can have on one's therapeutic experience.

THE ROLE OF LANGUAGE IN THERAPY FOR BILINGUAL AND MULTILINGUAL CLIENTS

The role of language in therapy for bilingual and multilingual clients with multilingual therapists is surprisingly under-researched in the field of talking therapy. It has also attracted relatively little interest compared with that dedicated to culturally competent therapy. Language is at the centre of our ability to influence how we see the world (Whorf, 1956) and gives meaning to our experiences. The way in which language is used to communicate is a reflection of social and cultural norms, which help to regulate the individual and the community.

One's first or native language has a heightened emotionality because of the family context in which first languages are learned; because first-language learning co-evolves with emotional regulation systems; and because first language has greater connections with the subcortical brain structures that mediate arousal (Harris, 2009). In the early years, acquisition of the first language can be understood in attachment terms as the main way in which the infant begins to separate from the mother (Winnicott, 1963) as well as the means to relate to others (Stern, 1998). The relationship the child has to their acquisition of language and the experience of separation are therefore inextricably linked. This, in part, explains why some people find it so difficult to learn a new language when they migrate. It may excite all types of anxieties around separation and loss – not only from the mother but also from the motherland.

One of our preoccupations, therefore, in providing a multilingual therapeutic service is to attend to the clients' relationships with the languages they speak, whether or not they are competent speakers of English as an additional language.

For the multilingual person, however, it can also be therapeutic to speak in a latterly acquired language. It may be that emotions are only accessible in one of a person's languages depending on when and how they have been learned. A non-native language can permit or facilitate the expression of emotions, which may have been discouraged when we were growing up. From research and evidence, I have observed that there are three psychological functions that speaking an additional language can serve.

1. **Defence**. Language can help us to create a new 'proxy self', which provides the opportunity to hide difficult or unsafe feelings.
2. **Protection**. Gilbert (2005) suggests that the self-soothing neuropathway, which needs to be activated in healing processes, is developed in childhood and is often associated with the native language. However, the language in which a trauma is experienced will carry an emotional charge, and research shows that subsequent languages may be able to provide the soothing factor. Research also shows how bilingual differences and language switching in therapy can increase emotional mastery and how exploring past problems in a new light can be aided by a new language.
3. **Expression**. There are many situations where emotional expression is facilitated by speaking another language, and it can be argued that being able to access a range of languages gives one the possibility of the expression of different emotions.

Not to be able to speak your language and to speak another language only partially may bring with it a sense of loss and inadequacy at one's ability to converse with eloquence. This is often accompanied by a sense of infantilisation – of being able to operate in society only in a restricted and childlike way. The ways in which people's identities are formed and their sense of self is developed are linked to the languages they have learned and choose to speak.

In Mothertongue, we encourage people to think about using more than one language in a session. Moving between languages can reinforce the sense of accommodation of tensions caused by differences between their original culture and the country in which they live. It can also, as already described, provide a facility to express and to integrate emotions.

The following case study shows how a client is able to access very deep-felt emotions in her mother tongue – a language that is not shared by her therapist.

Case study 8.2

Teresa was a refugee from Ethiopia who was haunted by the death of her mother – by the fact that she hadn't been with her at the time and that she had not been able to attend her funeral. Eventually, after many meetings, she came to a session and repeated the words to a religious service for a funeral in Amharic, with her counsellor – a non-Amharic speaker. It was only then that she was able to express her grief and begin to make some sense of her experience. Expressing the grief in the language in which she had related to her mother allowed her to experience it more deeply, connect with it and integrate it into herself. The counsellor was able to tolerate not understanding the words. The meaning was clear and could be explored after the expression of grief had taken place.

ACTIVITY 8.1

- Have you ever worked with bilingual clients? Would any of the following questions be relevant to ask your clients?
  - What have your experiences of learning a new language been like?
  - What does proficiency in the language represent for you?
  - What do you think you might gain in achieving proficiency in the new language?
  - What do you think you might lose in the process?
  - In which language is it easier to get angry/express affection/be professional?

- We think about the way in which we use English. We also think about the structures and world views embedded in other languages. In some languages there is no pronoun for the word 'I'. What impact might that have on psychological formulations?
- We try to consider issues of power in communication. Does the therapist speak the language used in therapy better or worse than the client? Do they address differences in accents? Are the therapist and /or the client speaking in the language of an oppressive coloniser and, if so, what are the implications for the therapeutic alliance?

CONCLUSION, IMPLICATIONS AND POTENTIAL RELEVANCE FOR OTHER THERAPISTS

In an attempt to describe, illustrate and reflect on my journey with Mothertongue's multi-ethnic counselling service, I hope I have encouraged the reader to ask questions and to think of differences, improvements, things to learn and changes they would like to engage with in their own environments. Starting with our own therapy, we need to view ourselves as a whole person: engaging at the interpsychic level with our social and family groups and engaging at the intrapsychic level with our personal and internal preoccupations. All our work with others can then flow from this.

We can also benefit from exploring all aspects of our psychic selves and trying to find parts that are often ignored. For me, that has meant paying attention to my relationship with the languages I speak as well as the languages I come into contact with that I do not understand. This helps me to understand the experiences of my multilingual clients. These are all useful areas for inclusion in our training courses and the material of our clinical supervision.

REFLECTION POINT

- I hope that I may have encouraged you to think about initiating some new aspect in your work. It could be a piece of research. It could be an extension of the client group and the material attended to in clinical sessions. It could be an idea for a new service.

From my own experience it has been utterly rewarding to found and to establish Mothertongue. It has been hard work and it has often been a scary and lonely venture, but I suppose these are the inevitable companions to any creative endeavour.

To quote Anthony Giddens:

> *individuals are striking out afresh like pioneers. It is inevitable in such situations, whether they know it or not, that they start thinking more and more in terms of risk. They have to confront personal futures that are much more open than in the past, with all the opportunities and hazards this brings.*

> (1999, pp27–8)

Essentially, any pioneering and creative activity will be risky to a certain extent. This is a hazard but it is also an opportunity that I, for one, would not have missed, not only for myself but also for all those people who have benefited from the creation of Mothertongue.

ACTIVITY 8.2

- Is there anything you feel tempted to explore further as a therapist?
- Have you perhaps identified a niche or unmet needs that you would like to act upon?
- If so, what are they? And what could be your first step towards meeting them?

CHAPTER SUMMARY

- The chapter revolved around the challenges that therapists face today as part of living in a multicultural society. The chapter explored the many layers of what we refer to as lifelong and transformative learning.
- Lifelong learning is about looking both inwards and outwards, and Beverley's report is an example of what happens when questions of identity and language are considered in a multicultural context. Why is there so little research about the role of language in talking therapies for bi- and multilingual clients with multilingual therapists? If therapy is about exploring one's identity, why are cultural issues so often ignored? Beverley's account illustrates some of the critical issues therapy must address in order to respond to needs within our multicultural society.
- The therapy model developed for the work at Mothertongue draws from person-centred, linguistic and attachment theory; it aims to engage with clients on both an interpsychic and intrapsychic level and reflects a dual interest in social groups, and personal and internal preoccupations.

CHAPTER 9

Being a listener with a voice

CORE KNOWLEDGE

This chapter will focus on you. You will be invited to write your own case study, with ACCTT themes in mind. Some of the guiding questions will be as follows.

- Do you ever miss talking to someone casually about your work at the end of the day? How do you deal with this? Who can you speak to apart from your supervisor and therapist?
- Do you experience 'flow' at work? Do you have the right support and inspiration to experience the right balance for you?
- The chapter involves a 'smorgasbord' with activities and reflection points to pick and choose from as you wish, in order to find the right balance for you with regard to listening and being heard. Writing and drawing/painting are suggested as valuable additions both when on your own, and in personal development groups.

Therapy exists, as Kottler (2011, p117) puts it, *to provide a safe and private haven for people to resolve their underlying problems*. This level of exclusive encounter with our clients comes at a cost. We tend to live a kind of double life. We must pretend indifference if a client's name comes up in a social gathering. We will, says Kottler, *fade into the background* if we meet a client at a social gathering, and our daily work is spent *separated from the outside world, ensconced in a sound proof chamber* (2011, p117). How does what Kottler calls this *compartmentalised isolation* affect us as therapists?

Kottler continues:

> One of the most meaningful, interesting, and fulfilling parts of a therapist's life is the time spent with clients . . . Yet, we can tell no [outsider] about the people we work with or about the details of what we do . . . What are the effects of this compartmentalised isolation?

(2011, p117)

CAN WE BE A LISTENER WITH A VOICE?

Self-awareness may be the key component in the makings of a good therapist, yet we can easily become too reliant on our clients for feedback. Isolation is a common problem among therapists. Our impressions are expected to be compartmentalised and dealt with either with our supervisor or our own therapist during carefully slotted appointments. While others can walk around simply venting their frustrations, and saying 'Oh, what a rotten day I've had!', therapists are expected always to accompany their venting with a purpose: 'Why am I feeling this? What can I do about it?' Speaking too freely about our ambivalences, as Sedgwick (2005, p1) once pointed out, can come across as disturbing, such as when a *gynaecologist shares fantasies about their patients*. We are sometimes too close for comfort. To many of us, this conveys risks for 'compartimentalised isolation', which feeds into the childhood fantasies of being responsible, special and at the same time ultimately alone. Kottler muses over the risks:

> *Maybe [this compartmentalised isolation] contributes to therapists' feelings of specialness and sainthood: we suffer in silence so that others may be released from their pain. We also may become secretive, mysterious, aloof, and evasive when we are not at work, while we continue to be authentic, transparent, and genuine with our clients.*
>
> (2011, p117)

Skovholt and Trotter-Mathison refer to the importance of having someone who understands where we are coming from. We need the *universality of experience effect* to maintain a sense of professional growth and vitality:

> *When we can talk to our colleagues openly and honestly about our work, then the 'universality of experience effect,' a curative factor in groups (Yalom and Leszcz, 2005), can be a powerful force for our own professional vitality.*
>
> (2011, p182)

Orlinsky and Ronnestad (2005, p187) also emphasise the importance of *collegial networks*. Therapists are more likely to experience a healing involvement with their clients, if they can access *peer group interactions of various sorts*. These groups need to, as Orlinsky and Ronnestad (2005, p187) put it, be *small enough to facilitate and encourage active involvement . . . yet large enough to ensure varied stimulation and input*. The concept of personal development groups is usually associated with training. A personal development group is, as Rose (2008, p5) puts it, *a place where students can genuinely learn about themselves and others*. A reflective writing group (see Chapter 5, page 92) is an example of a personal development group and a collegial network at both the training and post-training stage.

Reflective practice is a dialogical process where old meanings are reconstructed through an engagement in oppositional perspectives. Discussions and feedback are important aspects in reflective practice and reflexive awareness. *Effective reflective practice and reflexivity meet*, as Bolton (2005, p4) puts it, *the paradoxical need both to tell and retell our stories in order to feel secure enough to critically examine our actions for the sake of an increased understanding of ourselves and our practice.*

REFLECTION POINT

- Who would you consider suitable for a personal development group?
- What would you like to explore further? What niggles or perhaps seriously bothers you with regard to your practice?
- Would reflective writing work for you? Do you find it easier to express yourself through painting, clay or other 'creative' means? Or would perhaps a normal peer support format based on discussions work best?

VENTING AND CREATING

Writing can be a powerful experience on many levels. It has an important 'venting' effect, as Skovholt and Trotter-Mathison put it:

> [E]xpressive writing, specifically expressing feelings and thoughts about an emotionally impactful experience, can change a person's mental and physical health . . . It is called venting, a wonderfully descriptive term for the process by which people use words and nonverbal communication to let go of distressing emotions.

(2011, p184)

Writing can help us both to access and consider events and experiences more easily than everyday speech. Writing brings, as Smith (1991) puts it, a 'relative permanence' to our meaning-making processes. It allows us to linger with and return to the way we construct and understand events and experiences. Writing 'freezes' as Bolton (2005) suggests, moments of our thinking and helps us view our thought processes as on a film. Smith (1991) suggests a model with three stages of writing:

- **prewriting**, with scribbling, free association and the uninterrupted writing that you tried in Chapter 1;
- **writing**, with a more conscious effort to 'story' our experiences, sometimes approached in the form of creative writing; followed by
- **rewriting**, with a focus on themes and constructs that emerge in the text.

In reflective writing groups, both 'uninterrupted' and 'creative' writing (i.e aspects of prewriting and writing stages) are equally as important as the reflective rewriting phase. As in Sherna's account earlier (see Chapter 5, page 100), creative writing is an important part of the way we access and express our 'storying'. We can often reflect more openly when we are creative, asserts Bolton:

> If we had asked people to talk about their values in abstract terms, we would have received responses. By asking them to tell [write] stories about important experiences we were able to see something of how values reveal themselves in a complex, varied and shifting way in practice.
>
> (2005, p5)

As suggested, some might prefer other forms of creative outlet, such as art or working with clay etc. However, it is often found that writing suits more people than we normally tend to think. There is a common misperception that only some people can write.

WRITING FOR THE HELL OF IT CAN BE HEAVEN

As Cameron puts it, *writing for the hell of it can be heaven*. Cameron refers to stages when the *writing writes through the writer*, rather than the other way around:

> *When we 'forget ourselves', it is easy to write. We are not standing there, stiff as soldiers, our entire ego shimmied into every capital 'I'. When we forget ourselves, we then let go of being good and settle into just being a writer, we begin to have the experience of writing through us. When we are just the vehicle, the storyteller and not the point of the story, we often write very well – we certainly write more easily.*
>
> (1998, p11)

Winter et al. (1999) assert that the role of the creative, artistic imagination has been regrettably neglected in the course of professional education. They suggest that largely analytical forms of writing are too limited to understand what is really going on for us and our constructions. In a similar vein, Dorothea Brande refers to *the two persons of the writer*:

- *the unconscious must flow freely and richly, bringing at demand all the treasures of memory, incidents, scenes, intimations of character and relationships which it has stored away in its depths;*
- *the conscious mind must control, combine, and discriminate between the materials without hampering the unconscious flow. The unconscious will provide the writer with 'types' of all kinds, typical scenes, typical emotional responses.*

> (1934/1996, p44)

There is *the prosaic, everyday, practical person*, which Brande (1934/1996, p44) refers to as the conscious side of us. But it is, asserts Brande, *the unconscious, in the long run, which dictates the form of the story*. Rico writes about the *creative tension* between these two sides of the writer:

> *Most teachers of writing, certainly all investigators of the creative process, tend to agree that there are at least two distinctively different aspects of any creative act that sometimes come into conflict: the productive, generative, or 'unconscious' phase; and the highly conscious, critical phase, which edits, refines, and revises . . .*
>
> (2000, p3)

Rico continues:

> *Clearly, to great writers, philosophers, and psychologists such two-sidedness is nothing new. Over centuries, they have made distinctions between*

> *artistic/critical, unconscious/conscious, imagination/analysis, inspiration/*
> *perspiration, intuition/reason, restraint/passion, to name a few.*
>
> (2000, p75)

Further on in this chapter, you will be encouraged to compose your own ACCTT SMART story (see Chapter 2). Below is an example from my own attempt to write about the 'connecting and making sense' stage in the reflective writing group, which resulted in the book about therapists' motivations. This section is an example of an experience where the pen seems to take over, and you end up feeling as if the composition has taken a direction of its own. The section begins sensibly but plummets, literally, into deeper waters.

Case study 9.1

I have told [my therapist] about the eerie feeling I have had in my stomach . . . I try to comfort myself by talking about our painter at home.

'His dog just died. He's an army man, but when he told me about his dog he began to cry.'

'I think it is that they recognise something in you . . . something about your loss.'

When I hear my therapist saying 'your loss' something shifts inside of me, breaks down and I hear myself sobbing. I sound like a wounded animal.

The simple word 'loss', uttered with reference to me by a woman who I feel is on 'my side', works like a key to what Miller (1997, p20) would call my 'inner prison'. This kind of prison is secured, guarded by ourselves to keep 'intense emotional world of early childhood' at bay. An escape, addresses Miller, involves giving up what has constituted ourselves since as long as we can bear to remember. Breaking free involves confronting the 'mourning aroused by our parents' failure to fulfil our primary needs'. A fugitive will have to face 'the reality that s/he perhaps never was loved as a child for what s/he was but was instead needed and exploited for his or her achievements. . .'

[The word 'loss' in therapy opened up a flood gate]. I immerse myself in memories shared by my 'mad dad' and me. I use this expression in the fondest possible way, because it brings me as close as I can get to how it really was between us. For good and for bad my father invited me into his mist; I had a free pass and moved in and out of 'his' world as naturally as a child moves between parents in different countries or continents. In his mist there existed much pain, disappointments and agony. But there was also the Boogie Woogie which he played on the piano and the African dancing we performed on outings, be it in the forest, in shops, at the nursery when he picked me up at the end of the day or at grandma's during a too formal dinner. There was, above all, the endless jumping in waves. For hours and hours, until I became too self-conscious to do so, did we play together in the Baltic Sea. The latter captures perhaps my fondest memories of my father. We came to life in the water. My father would toss me up in the air again and again and again until I stopped asking to be

> *tossed any more. He would jump with me through the waves until I told him that I had 'run out of jumps'. In spite of seven years in total of personal therapy, these memories still make me want to weep and need to stop, sit and stay with the loss.*
>
> *Gone. My father is gone.*

COMMENT

This kind of writing triggered many discussions in our reflective writing group about links between strong emotions and professional interests. We discussed how my own particular strong interest in reflection and reflexivity resonates with experiences of trying to reconcile a 'normal' world with the 'misty' world(s) of my father during his illness.

SIDESTEPPING REASON

Freud valued methods that sidestepped 'reason', in order to access thoughts and feelings beyond our immediate, everyday awareness. Dreams were, in Freud's terms, the *royal road to knowledge of the unconscious activities of the mind* (1900/1976, p177). Freud also suggested that 'unwanted thoughts', or thoughts we normally try to avoid, surface through creative means such as painting or writing. Free writing worked as a valuable transmitter for bringing thoughts into our awareness.

Freud refers to Friedrich Schiller, a poet and philosopher who suggested that creativity causes reason to *relax its watch upon the gates*:

> *Where there is a creative mind, reason . . . relaxes its watch upon the gates. [Creativity helps] ideas rush in pell-mell, and only then does [reason] look them through and examine them in mass . . . Reason cannot form any opinion . . . unless it retains the thought long enough to look at it in connection with others . . . Looked at in isolation, a thought may seem very trivial or very fantastic; but it may be made important by another thought that comes after it, and in conjunction with other thoughts.*
> (Schiller, cited in Freud, 1900/1976, p177)

Freud used the creative means of writing himself to allow ideas to surface in the sense that Schiller proposed. Freud wrote that *it is by no means difficult . . . I myself can [relax] completely, by the help of writing down my ideas as they occur to me* (1900/1976, p177).

RELATIVE PERMANENCE

Smith (1991, p16) focuses on writing's capacity to help us in gaining access to knowledge that we otherwise *cannot explore directly*. Compared to, for instance, speaking, there is a 'relative permanence' in writing, so that we can stand back and examine our memories and experiences, which sometimes may have been stored outside our own awareness. It helps us *find out what we know, what we think*, asserts Smith (1991, p16).

In a similar vein, Carter and Gradin (2001, p5) refer to writing as an action and a means of imposing order on our stream of consciousness: *finding, ordering, and articulating ideas are activities that interrupt inertia, imposing order or the chaos that is our stream of consciousness.*

Hunt and Sampson (2006) capture Freud's thinking about accessing 'unwanted' thought through writing. They also pick up what the neurosciences propose in terms of our memories and experiences being outside our own awareness, but that this does not mean that they do not affect us in our daily lives. In fact, a large part of our decision making appears to be based on 'out of awareness' processes. Hunt and Sampson (2006, p178) refer to writing as a means of understanding self as part of a 'filtering process'. Everything that comes from outside is *inevitably filtered through our individual conscious and unconscious processes*. They continue:

> *If it is the case, as suggested by current thinking in the cognitive and neurosciences, that most of our processes are unconscious . . . then the filtering is going to be crucial to the way we work and re-work ideas into a final product.*
> (2006, p178)

As suggested earlier, the problem is that many often think that there are certain skills required for creative writing. Letting go of this perception usually becomes the first step in reflective writing groups; relaxing and having fun is an important part of this kind of writing.

ACTIVITY 9.1

In this activity you are invited to put everything else to one side and either write or draw/paint for five minutes about whatever comes into your head.

Below are three alternative prompts, to get you started.

* Focus on something 'small' in your immediate surroundings, such as dust on a lampshade or a shadow in the corner of the room.

- Focus on a feeling – perhaps cold feet, a wound on your finger or maybe a noise from outside.
- Write for five minutes starting with the sentence: 'He reached out his hand, and when it almost touched . . .'.

COMMENT

The third exercise is usually a fun place to start in reflective writing groups; it always leads to many different stories. Some write about passionate, romantic incidents, others have their children or their pets at the forefront, and some are thinking of gardening or visits to the doctors. There is no right or wrong here, only an opportunity to prove your inner critical voice wrong if it says that you cannot write.

CHALLENGING OLD UNDERSTANDINGS

Personal development emphasises change and ongoing growth, yet the emotional aspect of new learning is sometimes underestimated. Recognising new aspects of ourselves invariably brings a level of loss and confusion when certain ways of coping need to be challenged or reconsidered. Roffey-Barentsen and Malthouse remind us about how deep seated reflective learning can be, in terms of how it often challenges who we 'are':

> [W]hen reflecting, you will encounter change . . . you will have lost an element that made up a part of what you were.
>
> (2009, p20)

Rigid frameworks have served the purpose of defence. The therapist's ability to help may come from always having played the role of a helper, sometimes even to one's own parents.

Aveline highlights the importance of not demolishing outgrown coping strategies unless or until we have found better strategies to replace them with:

> People do not develop in the way they do by chance. A person's defences, however inappropriate and out of date they are now, were needed ways of coping with difficult situations in the past and should not be forced to yield, except as new strengths develop.
>
> (1997, p111)

TANGIBLE CONSTRUCTIONS

Just as writing or drawing can help us to open up, they can also, as described earlier, allow us to 'freeze', as Bolton (2005) suggests, moments of our thinking and help us view our thought processes as on a film. There is, as suggested earlier, a 'relative permanence' to our meaning-making processes, which allows us to analyse the way we construct and understand experiences. The following section is likely to be best suited for writing alone. Reflective writing in the context of personal and professional development involves, as suggested, the opportunity to loop back on to events with an interest in, for instance, potential blind spots and biases. We have looked at how research lends us valuable opportunities for exploring our practice from new angles. An essential part of any type of reflective learning is an awareness of the transformative value of prior experiences. It is illustrated in these two different accounts.

Case study 9.2

Below are two different accounts of being a good listener.

1. Telling it 'as it was':

   I have always been a good listener. I used to be the sensible listener in my family, and when I went to university, I discovered that other people also liked to come to me with their problems. It was easy, I found, to empathise with people; everyone says how good I am with understanding them. I know how hard it is to find someone who listens – people get impatient, they're often selfish. You hope that they're going to say 'thanks for listening, and how are you?' Well, people just don't do that. I find the world a cold and hard place, where not many people care. I don't want to live in a world where nobody listens; I decided to make a difference and have stuck to being someone who really cared; you have to start somewhere. I still catch colds easily and spend a lot of time in bed. I love tucking myself in under my thick duvet, with Ben & Jerry's ice cream, which always helps my throat.

2. Telling it with critical incidents and learning experiences in mind:

I have always been a good listener. When I left home for university, I repeated the pattern that I knew in terms of relating to others as a listener. I was often ill and turned regularly to my GP for physical symptoms, which again was a familiar pattern for me. I was at first stunned when my GP eventually suggested counselling for my 'problems'. I had never considered myself as someone with problems before. Although it momentarily turned my world upside down, this event prompted me to explore what the listener role meant to me. I began to explore in therapy how listening worked as a shield; I felt valued and was at the same time protected from having to look inward. My bouts of illness had been an attempt to be seen and heard. To rediscover a sense of self became a challenging and life-altering experience for me. I now work with clients with eating problems as their presented problems, and my own previous attempts to somatise symptoms help me now to respect the power of defence mechanisms and coping strategies; they are usually there for a reason and can be very powerful to shift.

REFLECTION POINT

Look at the differences between the two accounts of being a good listener, with the ACCTT points in mind (see Chapter 2, section entitled "ACCTT SMART in more detail", pages 32–6). To what extent can any of the following aspects be identified in either of the stories?

* Acknowledging/noticing a problem.
* Considering/making sense of it.
* Connecting/making meaning of the problem.
* Transforming into theory/working with meaning.
* Transforming new insights and awareness into practice.

ACTIVITY 9.2

Return to the third-person perspective on the 'person in the doorway' in Activity 1.1 (page 8).

* Write a story about the person in the doorway. Write whatever springs to mind, without thinking too much. You may already have some notes from before, and Brande's questions remain as triggers for your character:

> What do you look like, standing there? How do you walk? What, if you knew nothing about yourself, could be gathered of you, your character, your background, your purpose just there at just that minute? If there are people in the room whom you must greet, how do you greet them? How do your attitudes to them vary? Do you give any overt sign that you are fonder of one, or more aware of one, than the rest?

To describe oneself and one's everyday practice is sometimes more difficult than it sounds. The more familiar something is, the harder it can be to adopt a third-person perspective and describe it as an outsider; yet it is often this particular process that brings implicit, taken-for-granted assumption into awareness. The following writing exercise revolves around restructuring your own knowledge with a new theme in mind.

ACTIVITY 9.3

Reflection, as Moon (2004, p82) puts it, can be described as a *process of re-organising knowledge and emotional orientations in order to achieve further insight.*

- Rewrite the story from Activity 9.2 with the ACCTT themes, listed in the 'Reflection point' above, in mind.

DEFINING MOMENTS

The ACCTT SMART model has already been introduced as a means to conceptualise, discuss and act upon the personal, theoretical and cultural beliefs of the therapist. Acknowledging, connecting and transforming are examples of 'phases' that may help us to travel from simply noticing a problem to putting it into context and eventually reaching some kind of transformation. Reflective learning usually implies that this process of reorganisation has a specific purpose. We are, as suggested, re-storying events with a particular interest and focus in mind. In this section, you will be invited to reflect on your practice with 'defining moments' in mind. 'Defining moment' is a concept borrowed from Skovholt and Trotter-Mathison (2011) to explain powerful events that, in some way, have impacted on or shaped your professional identity.

> ## ACTIVITY 9.4
>
> If possible, divide into pairs and exchange experiences about powerful events that in some way have impacted on your sense of professional identity. Revisit Case studies 2.2 and 2.3, with Andy and Janet (see pages 24–5 and 26–7), and decide on:
>
> - a problem situation with a client;
> - how you approached the problem, with an example of using:
>   - your modality; and
>   - yourself as a person, to deal with the situation.

Below are some reflections to bear in mind, when considering your 'defining moment' in the context of an ACCTT SMART process.

- Acknowledging a problem is, of course, something that can happen in many ways. Remember the common scenario of a 'depleting cycle' if we try to push problems with our clients to one side. Fight or flight quickly escalates into stressful involvements. How do you 'listen' to yourself? Do you pay attention to dreams; keep an eye on eating or drinking patterns; listen out for signals from your family members; take note of your supervisor?
- Considering the situation in terms of 'sitting with', or 'staying with' the sensation can be appropriate at this stage. How would you describe your support system for this stage of the process? Do you have a 'critical friend' who is prepared to see where you are coming from, and at the same time help with bringing new and different perspectives?
- Connecting this 'multistructural' level can happen through discussions and your own reading and thinking. How can you frame your problem with regard to your own personal history? How can you take the experiences forward and begin to connect or anchor the incident to theories and different ways of looking at the problem?
- Transforming on a 'relational' level – how does your problem relate to, or 'fit' in with, your theory or modality? This is a stage when an overall context, with a new sense of significance of the parts in relation to the whole, is emerging.
- Transforming on an extended abstract level – how does the explanation offered within your 'espoused' theory compare with other ways of explaining? This stage is about putting the problem into a broader perspective, where you transfer principles and ideas underlying the specific instance into other contexts. This can, as suggested in Chapter 2, involve comparing psychotherapy with other mental health approaches, such as psychology and psychiatry, or

considering the role of the therapist with socio-economic, cultural and/or gender-related interests in mind.

As we have seen above, The ACCTT SMART model comprises five outcomes and levels of reflective learning. The SMART aspects can be linked to the learning phases at any ACCTT stage, as a means of keeping track on coping strategies and potential reflections, and in the development of action plans. You are invited to translate your action plan into a SMART format.

- Specific =
- Measurable =
- Achievable =
- Relevant/realistic =
- Time-bound =

ACTIVITY 9.5

- How would you formulate your own SMART plan?
- Compare also with your ideas arising in Chapter 1.
- To what extent have you taken your own interests into account? Do you feel that you have made a plan that contributes to your own job satisfaction?
- If not, perhaps you would like to consider the reasons for that, and explore what you might need for the future in order to achieve a comfortable balance between your own and your clients' needs?

The purpose of this book has been to explore personal development in terms of a deliberate attempt to review, plan and take responsibility for our own learning. All training involves changes, but it has been suggested in this book that therapy training involves particularly deep changes. Trainee therapists are, as Folkes-Skinner et al. (2010, p19) put it, *required to not only change their thinking and to develop new skills, but also adapt aspects of their personality.* An essential part of the training is *the task of learning how to creatively and effectively use oneself in the treatment process* (Klein et al., 2011, p297).

The boundaries between the personal and the professional are inevitably fluid, and much of the training revolves around understanding the ambiguous question: What makes a 'helping' relationship therapeutic? An essential quality of a therapist is to be able to feel what others feel. Trotter-Mathison et al. (2010) alert us, however, to the 'lay helper' tendency to care too much. It is easy to project our own wishes and needs on to the other, and offer advice on the basis of what we would have done or perhaps wish we could do, for ourselves. Therapy assumes a different stance towards the helping process; clients are not expected to come with the aim of copying the therapists' problem solutions. Our job is not to offer moulds based on our own way of dealing with issues; neither is it to impose ready-made fixes. Much of our work relies on the ability to understand the experiences of others. This involves, as suggested earlier, developing abilities for 'phenomenological' understanding' – that is, an ability to tune into the experience as it appears at the time to the client. As Klein et al. put it:

> The phenomenological experience of those who present themselves for treatment needs to be accurately understood if therapy is to have any chance to succeed.
>
> (2011, p19)

GENUINE CURIOSITY

Together with the ability to empathise and feel *with* the other, the very basis for therapeutic mastery is an inbuilt, genuine curiosity. If we do not want to see things from new and different angles, therapy is probably not the right job for us. Typical for people with an interest in working as therapists is rather, as Klein et al. (2011, p273) suggest, an almost *relentless quest for knowledge*. This urge to 'find out' is usually noted early in life, and will become what O'Leary (2011) reminds us is an inevitable streak in therapists – namely, psychological-mindedness. There are many components of psychological-mindedness. O'Leary (2011, p32) asserts that it typically involves *a delight in putting things together in new and interesting ways, a kind of puzzle solving* on different levels.

FINDING A BALANCE AND A FLOW

Being a listener with a voice involves sometimes listening inwardly. Solitude can be an essential place of 'hearing'. In her book, *Time to be Alone*, Tudor-Sandahl quotes Tillich, who writes:

> Language has created the word lonely to express the pain of being alone and the word solitude to express the glory of it.
>
> (cited in Tudor-Sandahl, 2004, p19)

As a single child from Sweden, with an interest in writing, solitude has always been a good friend of mine. To me, breaking out of this protected place has sometimes been important. To others, social involvement comes more easily. For all of us, the balance between listening and being heard, between receiving and giving, is likely to be important both for our own and our clients' well-being.

Family life and close, intimate relationships are fundamental components in the therapist's life; so much of our time revolves around restoring our clients' faith in close relationship and it is essential that we give our family and ourselves the right to enjoy the ultimate pleasure of love and closeness at this level.

To my mind, Mihaly Csikszentmihalyi (1990, p4) captures the balance between all these crucial components with his classic concept of 'flow'. He suggests that the best moments usually occur if a person's body or mind is stretched to its limits. He refers to a level of alertness, a sense of feeling alive and deciding to invest in this pull; it is applicable within all areas of life. To me, the playful child springs to mind. It is what can happen when we allow ourselves to become absorbed by something, and put other less significant matters to one side. Csikszentmihalyi (1990, p4) uses the concept of flow to describe a particular satisfaction in a state where *the person's body or mind is stretched to its limits in a voluntary effort to accomplish something . . . worthwhile.* Flow involves being totally absorbed in an activity, with an alert, unselfconscious and effortless control. Orlinsky and Ronnestad (2005, p44) revive the meaning of the concept. They use the term 'flow' to describe what therapists experience as job satisfaction and as healing involvement:

> [Flow results from involvement with our work which] closely matches [the therapist's] skills and demands that they be exercised fully, and at times stretched to new levels. [Flow] is one of intense absorption, finely calibrated responsiveness, and keenly felt satisfaction, generally accompanied by a withdrawal of awareness from extraneous situational cues and a diminution of reflective self-consciousness.

> (2005, p44)

ACTIVITY 9.6

- How does the earlier idea of a *delight in putting things together in new and interesting ways, a kind of puzzle solving* (O'Leary, 2011, p32) resonate with you and your approach to the world?
- Are you reserving time for your family, friends and other close relationships?
- Do you get time for yourself? How do you fit in solitude?
- Are your curiosity and your need for inspiration being met?
- Do you associate your work with 'flow'?

In Chapter 3, and Activity 3.1, you were encouraged to consider how you look after yourself. Please return to your writing about the imaginary therapist who would breach guidelines with regard to herself. Consider your imaginary therapist, with your own interests in mind again.

REFLECTION POINT

- What might you need in terms of emotional, educational and professional support to experience flow and 'healing involvement', rather than 'stressful' involvement?

CHAPTER SUMMARY

- This chapter has focused on how to connect with colleagues and combat the risk of 'compartmentalised isolation'.
- We have looked at personal development groups with a special focus on having fun and using creative outlets such as painting or writing.
- The idea of reflective writing has been explored in more depth, as a means of connecting with 'the other side' of ourselves.
- We looked at the value of your own close relationships, solitude and 'flow' – the concept that captures the balance of feeling comfortable and stretched or inspired.

References

Adams, M (2008) Abandonment: enactments from the patient's sadism and the therapist's collusion, in Mann, D and Cunningham, V (eds) *The Past in the Present: Therapy enactment and the return of trauma*. London: Routledge.

Agazarian, Y (2000) *Autobiography of a Theory*. London: Jessica Kingsley.

Alvesson, M and Skoldeberg, K (2000) *Reflexive Methodology*. London: Sage.

Argyris, C and Schön, D (1974) *Theory in Practice: Increasing professional effectiveness*. San Francisco, CA: Jossey-Bass.

Atherton, JS (2009) *Learning and Teaching: SOLO taxonomy*. Available online at www.learningandteaching.info/learning/solo.htm (accessed 30 April 2012).

Aveline, M (1997) Assessing for optimal therapeutic intervention, in Palmer, S and McMahon, G (eds) *Client Assessment*. London: Sage.

Bager-Charleson, S (2010a) *Reflective Practice in Counselling and Psychotherapy*. Exeter: Learning Matters.

Bager-Charleson, S (2010b) *Why Therapists Choose to Become Therapists*. London: Karnac.

Baradon, T. (2003) Psychotherapeutic work with parents and children, in Green, V (ed.) *Emotional Development in Psychoanalysis, Attachment Theory and Neuroscience: Creating connections*. London and New York: Routledge.

Barkham, M, Hardy, G and Mellor-Clark, J (2010) *Developing and Delivering Practice-based Evidence: A guide for psychological therapies*. Chichester: Wiley-Blackwell.

Beck, AT, Rush, J, Shaw, B and Emery, G (1987) *Cognitive Therapy of Depression*. New York: Guilford Press.

Biggs, J and Collis, K (1982) *Evaluating the Quality of Learning: The SOLO taxonomy*. New York: Academy Press.

Bike, DH, Norcross, JC and Schatz, DM (2009) Process and outcomes of psychotherapists' personal therapy: replication and extension 20 years later. *Psychotherapy: Theory, Research, Practice and Training*, 46(1): 19–31.

Bion, W (1962) *Learning from Experience*. London: Karnac.

Bolton, G (2005) *Reflective Practice: Writing and professional development*. London: Sage.

Bolton, G, Field, V and Thomson, K (2006) *Writing Works*. London: Jessica Kingsley.

Bowlby, J (1983) *Attachment and Loss*, Vol. 1 (2nd edn). New York: Basic Books.

Brande, D (1934/1996) *Becoming a Writer*. London: Macmillan.

British Association for Counselling and Psychotherapy (BACP) (2010) *Ethical Framework for Good Practice in Counselling and Psychotherapy*. Lutterworth: BACP.

British Association for Counselling and Psychotherapy (BACP) (2012) *CPD Directory*. Available online at www.bacp.co.uk/cpd (accessed 24 April 2012).

Buber, M. (1947) *Between Man & Man*. Glasgow: The Fontana Library.

Cameron, J (1998) *The Right to Write: An invitation and initiation into the writing life*. London: Pan Macmillan.

Cardinal, D, Hayward, J and Jones, G (2005) *Epistemology: The theory of knowledge*. London: Hodder Murray.

Carroll, M and Gilbert, M (2005) *On Being a Supervisee*. London: Vulkani.

Carter, D and Gradin, S (2001) *Writing as Reflective Action: A reader*. New York: Longman Pearson.

Cashdan, S (1988) *Object Relation Therapy: Using the relationship*. Ontario: Penguin.

Chasen, B (1996) Death of a psychoanalyst's child, in Gerson, B (ed.) *The Therapist as a Person*. Hillsdale, NJ: Analytic Press.

Chenail, RJ (1994) Qualitative research and clinical work: 'private-ization' and 'public-ation'. *The Qualitative Report*, 2(1). Available online at www.nova.edu/ssss/QR/BackIssues/QR2-1/private.html (accessed 30 April 2012).

Clarkson, P (1995) *The Therapeutic Relationship*. London: Whurr.

Connor, J (2011) Where lunatics prosper. *Therapy Today*, 22(8): 8–11.

Costa, B (2002) Psychodrama across cultures. *British Psychodrama and Sociodrama Journal*, 17: 37–47.

Costley, C, Elliott, G and Gibbs, P (2011) *Doing Work Based Research: Approach to enquiry for insider-researchers*. London: Sage.

Critchley, M (2010) Pam's story, in Bager-Charleson, S (ed.) *Why Therapists Choose to Become Therapists*. London: Karnac.

Crossley, M (2000) *Introducing Narrative Psychology: Self, trauma and the construction of meaning*. Buckingham: Open University Press.

Csikszentmihalyi, M (1990) *Flow: The psychology of optimal experience*. New York: Harper & Row.

Dallos, R and Miell, D (1996) *Social Interaction and Personal Relationships*. London: Sage.

Damasio, A (1999) *The Feeling of What Happens*. London: Vintage.

Daniels, M (2011) The use of role play as a therapeutic tool in clinical practice: what do sexual offenders experience when role reversing with their victims in Her Majesty's Prison Service Core Sex Offender Treatment Programme? Dissertation, Metanoia/Middlesex University, London.

Department of Health (2004) *Ten Essential Shared Capabilities: A framework for the whole of the mental health work force*. London: HMSO.

Despenser, S (2007) Risk assessment: the personal safety of the counsellor. *Therapy Today* (March): 12–16.

du Plock, S (2010) The vulnerable researcher, in Bager-Charleson, S (ed.) *Reflective Practice in Counselling and Psychotherapy*. Exeter: Learning Matters.

Eleftheriadou, Z (1994) *Transcultural Counselling*. London: Central Books.

Eleftheriadou, Z (2010) *Psychotherapy and Culture*. London: Karnac.

Faulkner, W (1951) *Requiem for a Nun*. New York: Random House.

Fitzpatrick, M, Kovalak, A and Weaver, A (2010) How trainees develop an initial theory of practice: a process model of tentative identifications. *Counselling & Psychotherapy Research*, 10(2): 93–103.

Folkes-Skinner, J, Elliott, R and Wheeler, S (2010) 'A baptism of fire': a qualitative investigation of a trainee counsellor's experience at the start of training. *Counselling & Psychotherapy Research*, 10(2): 83–92.

Fook, J (2002) *Social Work: Critical theory and practice*. London: Sage.

Foucault, M (1984) The birth of the asylum, in *Madness and Civilisation* (1961), in Rabinow (ed.) *The Foucault Reader: The introduction to Foucault's thoughts*. London: Penguin.

Frankl, V (1959) *Man's Search for Meaning*. New York: Washington Square Press.

Frawley-O'Dea, M and Sarnat, J (2001) *The Supervisory Relationship*. New York and London: Guilford Press.

Freud, S (1900/1976) *The Interpretation of Dreams*. Strachey, J. (ed. and trans.). London: The Pelican Freud Library, Vol. 4.

Freud, S (1959) *An Outline of Psycho-Analysis*. London: The Hogarth Press.

Freudenberger, H (1980) *Burn Out*. London: Arrow Books.

Friedman, M (1999) *The Worlds of Existentialism: A critical reader*. New York: Humanity Books.

Gans, JS (2011) The role of clinical experience in the making of a psychotherapist, in Klein, R, Bernard, H and Schermer, V (eds) *On Becoming a Psychotherapist: The personal and professional journey*. Oxford: Oxford University Press.

Gardner, H (1999) *Intelligence Reframed*. New York: Basic Books.

Gardner, H (2006) *Changing Minds: The art and science of changing our own and other people's minds*. Boston, MA: Harvard Business School Press.

Gay, P (1995) (ed.) *The Freud Reader*. London: Vintage.

Geller, JD, Norcross, JC and Orlinsky, DE (eds) (2005) *The Psychotherapist's Own Psychotherapy*. New York: Oxford University Press.

Ghyara Chatterjee, S (2010) Shernas's story: cults, culture and context, in Bager-Charleson, S (ed.) *Why Therapists Choose to Become Therapists*. London: Karnac.

Gibbs, G (1988) *Learning by Doing: A guide to teaching and learning methods*. Oxford: Further Education Unit.

Giddens, A (1999) *Runaway World: How globalisation is reshaping our lives*. London: Profile Books.

Gilbert, M and Evans, K (2000) *Psychotherapy Supervision: An integrative rational approach to psychotherapy supervision.* Maidenhead: Open University Press.

Gilbert, P (2005) Compassion: Conceptualisations, research and use in psychotherapy. Hove: Routledge.

Gilbert, P and Leahy, R (2007) *The Therapeutic Relationship in the Cognitive Behavioral Psychotherapies.* Hove: Routledge.

Gold, JH and Nemiah, JC (eds) (1993) *Beyond Transference.* Washington DC: American Psychiatric Press.

Green, V (ed.) (2003) *Emotional Development in Psychoanalysis, Attachment Theory and Neuroscience.* London and New York: Routledge.

Guggenbuhl-Craig, A (1991) Quacks, charlatans and false prophets, in Zweig, C and Abrams, J (eds) *Meeting the Shadow.* New York: Penguin.

Guy, JD (1987) *The Personal Life of the Psychotherapist.* New York: John Wiley & Sons.

Gyler, L (2010) *The Gendered Unconscious: Can gender discourses subvert psychoanalysis?.* London and New York: Routledge.

Habermas (1986) *The Theory of Communicative Action*, vol. 2. Boston, MA: Beacon Press.

Harris, CL (2009) *Language and Emotion in the Bilingual Brain.* Boston University Department of Psychology. Available online at www.qpower point.com/ppt/the-bilingual-brain.html (accessed 28 April 2012).

Hawkins, P and Shohet, R (2005) *Supervision in the Helping Professions*, 3rd edition. Maidenhead: Open University Press.

Hinshelwood, RD (1997) Psychodynamic formulation in assessment for psychoanalytic psychotherapy, in Mace, C (ed.) *The Art and Science of Assessment in Psychotherapy.* London and New York: Routledge.

Hofmann, S and Weinberger, J (2007) *The Art and Science of Psychotherapy.* New York: Routledge.

Holmes, J and Lindley, R (1998) *The Values of Psychotherapy*, revised edition. London: Karnac.

Howard, S (2010) *Skills in Psychodynamic Counselling and Psychotherapy.* London: Sage.

Hunt, C and Sampson, F (2006) *Writing: Self and reflexivity.* London: Palgrave Macmillan.

Johns, H (2002) *Personal Development in Counsellor Training.* London: Sage.

Kandel, ER (2006) *In Search of Memory.* New York and London: Norton.

Klein, M (1986) *The Selected Melanie Klein.* New York: Free Press.

Klein, R, Bernard, H and Schermer, V (2011) *On Becoming a Psychotherapist: The personal and professional journey.* Oxford: Oxford University Press.

Knott, C and Scraggs, T (2008) *Reflective Practice in Social Work.* Exeter: Learning Matters.

Kohut, H (1977) *The Restoration of the Self.* New York: International Universities Press.

Kolb, DA (1984) *Experiential Learning: Experience as the source of learning and development.* Upper Saddle River, NJ: Prentice Hall.

Kottler, J (2011) *On Being a Therapist*, 4th revised edition. San Francisco, CA: Jossey-Bass.

Laungani, P (1999) Culture and identity: implications for counselling, in Palmer, S and Laungani, P (eds) *Counselling in a Multicultural Society*. London: Sage.

Lehmann, J. (2008) Telling stories, in White, S, Fook, J and Gardner, F (eds) *Critical Reflection in Health and Social Care*. Maidenhead: Open University Press.

Mann, D and Cunningham, V (eds) (2008) *The Past in the Present: Therapy enactment and the return of trauma*. London: Routledge.

McGrath, S (2010) Susan's story, in Bager-Charleson, S (ed.) *Why Therapists Choose to Become Therapists*. London: Karnac.

McLeod, J (1999) *Practitioner Research in Counselling*. London: Sage.

McLeod, J and Balamoutsou, S (2001) A method for qualitative narrative analysis of psychotherapy transcripts, in Frommer, J and Rennie, D (eds) *Qualitative Psychotherapy Research Methods and Methodology*. Lengerich: Pabst Science.

Mearns, D and Thorne, B (1999) *Person-Centred Counselling in Action*, 2nd edition. London: Sage.

Mehr, KE, Ladany, N and Caskie, GIL (2010) Trainee nondisclosure in supervision. *Counselling & Psychotherapy Research*, 10: 103–13.

Merleau-Ponty, M (1999) What is phenomenology?, in Friedman, M (ed.) *The Worlds of Existentialism: A critical reader*. New York: Humanity Press.

Miller, A (1997) *The Drama of the Gifted Child: The search for the true self*. Ward, R (trans.). New York: Perennial.

Milner, J and O'Byrne, P (2004) *Assessment in Counselling: Theory, process and decision making*. Basingstoke: Palgrave Macmillan.

Moon, J (2004) *A Handbook of Reflective and Experiential Learning*. London: Routledge.

Neuhaus, EC (2011) Becoming a cognitive-behavioral therapist: striving to integrate professional and personal development, in Klein, R, Bernard, HS and Schermer, V (eds) *On Becoming a Psychotherapist: The personal and professional journey*. Oxford and New York: Oxford University Press.

Norcross, JC, Strausser-Kirtland, D and Missar, CD (1988) The processes and outcomes of psychotherapists' personal treatment experiences. *Psychotherapy*, 25(1): 36–43.

O'Leary, J (2011) Growing up to be a good psychotherapist, or physician – know thyself!, in Klein, R, Bernard, HS and Schermer, V (eds) *On Becoming a Psychotherapist: The personal and professional journey*. Oxford and New York: Oxford University Press.

Ogden, TH (1997) *Reverie and Interpretation*. London: Karnac.

Ogunfowora, B and Drapeau, M (2008) A study of the relationship between personality traits and theoretical orientation preferences. *Counselling & Psychotherapy Research*, 8: 151–9.

Orlinsky, D (1994) Research-based knowledge as emergent foundation for clinical practice in psychotherapy, in Talley, PF, Strupp, H and Butler, S (eds) *Psychotherapy Research and Practice: Bridging the gap*. New York: Basic Books.

Orlinsky, D and Ronnestad, MH (2005) *How Psychotherapists Develop: A study of therapeutic work and professional growth*. Washington, DC: APA.

Page, S (1999) *The Shadow and the Counsellor*. London: Routledge.

Page, S and Wosket, V (2001) *Supervising the Counsellor: A cyclical model*, 2nd edition. London and New York: Routledge.

Parker, I. (1994) Qualitative research, in Banister, P, Burman, E, Parker, I, Taylor, M and Tindall, C (eds) *Qualitative Methods in Psychology: A research guide*. Buckingham: Open University Press.

Parker, I (2004) *Qualitative Psychology: Introducing radical research*. New York: Open University Press.

Parker, I (2007) *Revolution in Psychology*. London: Pluto Press.

Phillips, S (2011) Up close and personal: a consideration of the role of personal therapy in the development of psychotherapists, in Klein, R, Bernard, HS and Schermer, V (eds) *On Becoming a Psychotherapist: The personal and professional journey*. Oxford: Oxford University Press.

Pistrang, N and Barker, C (2010) Scientific, practical and personal dimensions in selecting qualitative methods, in Barkham, M, Hardy, G and Mellor-Clark, J (eds) *Developing and Delivering Practice-based Evidence: A guide for psychological therapies*. Chichester: Wiley-Blackwell.

Polkinghorne, D (1988) *Narrative Knowing and Human Science*. Albany, NY: State University of New York Press.

Pope, KS and Tabachnick, BG (1994) A national survey of psychologists' experiences, problems and beliefs. *Professional Psychology: Research and Practice*, 25: 247–58.

Proctor, B (1986) Supervision: a co-operative exercise in accountability, in Marken, M and Payne, E (eds) *Enabling and Ensuring: Supervision in practice*. Leicester: Penguin Books.

Quality Assurance Agency for Higher Education (QAA) (2004) *Progress Files for Higher Education*. Available online at www.qaa.ac.uk/crntwork/progfile HE/contents.htm (accessed 4 September 2011).

Racker, H (1982) *Transference and Countertransference*. London: Karnac.

Ragen, T (2009) *The Consulting Room and Beyond*. New York: Routledge.

Rice, CA (2011) The psychotherapist as 'wounded healer': a modern expression of an ancient tradition, in Klein, RH, Bernard, HS and Schermer, V (eds) *On Becoming a Psychotherapist: The personal and professional journey*. New York: Oxford University Press.

Rico, G. (2000) *Writing the Natural Way*. New York: Tarcher/Putnam.

Ricoeur, P (1970) *Freud and Philosophy: An essay of interpretation*. Savage, D (trans.). New Haven, CT, and London: Yale University.

Ricoeur, P (1981) *Hermeneutics and the Human Sciences*. Thomson, JB (trans.). Cambridge: Cambridge University Press.

Robson, C (2002) *Real World Research*, 2nd edition. Oxford: Blackwell.

Roffey-Barentsen, J and Malthouse, R (2009) *Reflective Practice in the Lifelong Learning Sector*. Exeter: Learning Matters.

Rogers, C (1951/1999) *Client-centred Therapy*. London: Constable.

Rogers, C (1961) *A Therapist's View of Psychotherapy*. London: Constable.

Rogers, C (1995) *A Way of Being*. New York: Houghton Mifflin.

Rose, C (2008) *The Personal Development Group: The student's guide*. London: Karnac.

Rosen, H and Kuehlwein, K (1996) *Constructing Realities: Meaning-making perspectives for psychotherapists*. San Francisco, CA: Jossey-Bass.

Rowan, J and Jacobs, M (2002) *The Therapist's Use of Self*. Buckingham: Open University Press.

Scaife, J (2010) *Supervising the Reflective Practitioner: An essential guide to theory and practice*. London and New York: Routledge.

Scaife, J, Inskipp, F, Proctor, B, Scaife, J and Walsh, S (2001) *Supervision in the Mental Health Professions: A practitioner's guide*. Hove: Routledge.

Schön, DA (1983) *The Reflective Practitioner: How professionals think in action*. New York: Basic Books.

Schön, DA and Rein, M (1994) *Frame Reflection: Toward the resolution of intractable policy controversies*. New York: Basic Books.

Schore, A (2003) The human unconscious: the development of the right brain and its role in early life, in Green, V (ed.) *Emotional Development in Psychoanalysis, Attachment Theory and Neuroscience: Creating connections*. London and New York: Routledge.

Schwartz, J. (2003) *Cassandra's Daughter: A history of psychoanalysis*. London: Karnac.

Sedgwick, D (2005) *The Wounded Healer: Countertransference from a Jungian perspective*. London: Routledge.

Skovholt, T and Trotter-Mathison, M (2011) *The Resilient Practitioner: Counseling and psychotherapy: Investigating practice from scientific, historical, and cultural perspectives*. New York and London: Routledge.

Smith, F (1991) *Writing and the Writer*, 2nd edition. Hove: Laurence Erlbaum.

Smith, JA, Flowers, P and Larkin, M (2009) *Interpretative Phenomenological Analysis*. London: Sage.

Solms, M and Turnbull, O (2002) *The Brain and the Inner World: An introduction to the neuroscience of subjective experiences*. London: Karnac.

Solms, M and Turnbull, O (2003) Memory, amnesia and intuition: a neuro-psychoanalytic perspective, in Green, V. (ed.) *Emotional Development in Psychoanalysis, Attachment Theory, and Neuroscience*. London and New York: Routledge.

Spencer, L (2006) Tutors' stories of personal development training: attempting to maximize learning potentials. *Counselling & Psychotherapy Research*, 6(2): 100–8.

Steele, R (1989) A critical hermenutics for psychology, in Packer, J and Addison, R (eds) *Entering the Circle*. Albany, NY: State University of New York Press.

Stern, DB (2010) *Partners in Thought*. London and New York: Routledge.

Stern, DN (1985) *The Interpersonal World of the Infant*. New York: Basic Books.

Stern, DN (1998) *The Interpersonal World of the Infant*, paperback edition. London: Karnac.

Strean, H (1993) *Resolving Counterresistances in Psychotherapy.* New York: Brunner/Matzel.

Strean, H (1998) Sometimes I feel like a dirty old man: the woman who tried to seduce me, in Rabinowitz, I (ed.) *Inside Therapy: Illuminating writings about therapists, patients and psychotherapy.* Albany, NY: New York University Press.

Stuart, C and Whitmore, E (2008) Using reflexivity in a research methods course: bridging the gap between research and practice, in White, S, Fook, J and Gardner, F (eds) *Critical Reflection in Health and Social Care.* Maidenhead: Open University Press.

Styron, W (1990) *Darkness Visible: A memoir of madness.* New York: Random House.

Sussman, MB (1992) *A Curious Calling: Unconscious motivations for practising psychotherapy.* Northvale, NJ, and London: Jason Aronson.

Symington, N (1986) *The Analytic Experience: Lectures from the Tavistock.* London: Free Association Books.

Taylor, C (2006) Practising reflexivity: narrative, reflection and the moral order, in White, S, Fook, J and Gardner, F (eds) *Critical Reflection in Health and Social Care.* Maidenhead: Open University Press.

Thomas, L (1995) Psychotherapy in the context of race and culture, in Fernando, S (ed.) *Mental Health in a Multi-ethnic Society: A multi-disciplinary handbook.* New York: Routledge.

Thorpe, F (2011) Working with Thalidomide. *The Independent Practitioner,* 1: 11–14.

Trotter-Mathison, M, Koch, J, Sanger, S and Skovholt, T (2010) *Voices From the Field: Defining moments in counselling and therapist development.* London and New York: Routledge.

Tudor-Sandahl, P (2004) *Det omöjliga yrket: om psykoterapi och psykoterapeuter.* Stockholm: Wahlström and Widstrand.

Van Deurzen, E (2002) *Existential Counselling and Psychotherapy in Practice.* London: Sage.

Webber, M (2008) *Evidence-based Policy and Practice in Mental Health Social Work.* Exeter: Learning Matters.

Wheeler, S and Elliott, R (2008) What do counselors and psychotherapists need to know about research? *Counselling & Psychotherapy Research,* 8(2): 133–5.

White, S, Fook, J and Gardner, F (2008) *Critical Reflection in Health and Social Care.* Maidenhead: Open University Press.

Whorf, B (1956) The role of language, in Carroll, JB (ed.) *Language, Thought, and Reality: Selected writings of Benjamin Lee Whorf,* Boston, MA: MIT Press.

Winnicott, DW (1947) *Hate in the Countertransference: Through pediatrics to psychanalysis.* London: Karnac.

Winnicott, DW (1963) From dependence towards independence in the development of the individual, in *The Maturational Process and the Facilitating Environment,* reprinted 1966. London: Karnac.

Winnicott, DW (1990) *The Maturational Processes and the Facilitating Environment.* London: Karnac.

Winter, R, Buck, A and Sobiechowska, P (1999) *Professional Experience and The Investigative Imagination; The ART of reflective writing.* London: Routledge.

Withers, M (2007) Assessment, in Hemmings, A and Field, R (eds) *Counselling and Psychotherapy in Contemporary Private Practice.* Hove: Routledge.

Wosket, V (2001) *The Therapeutic Use of Self: Counselling practice research and supervision.* London and New York: Routledge.

Yalom, I (1980) *Existential Psychotherapy.* New York: Basic Books.

Yalom, I (2002) *The Gift of Therapy.* London: Piatkus.

Youngson, S (2009) Personal development in clinical psychology: the context, in Hughes, J and Youngson, S (eds) *Personal Development and Clinical Psychology.* London and New York: Wiley-Blackwell.

Index

therapeutic framework, psychoanalysis
62–5
therapeutic mastery 58–60
therapeutic metanarratives 75–6
therapeutic relationships 3–4, 16
CBT approach 72–3
common factors 74–5
parallel processes 48
and stressful involvement 50–2
'therapist congruence' 71
therapist–client contact 72
therapy training 18, 39, 92
'evolution' phases 10–12
generic model for psychotherapy 75
personal therapy for therapists 54, 54–6
see also supervisory relationships
Thorne, Brian 70, 71
Thorpe, Francesca 98–9, 115–16
Tillich, Paul 161
transference 8–10, 30, 31, 61–2, 67–9
transformative learning 19, 23–6
ACCTT SMART 32–6, 111, 152–3,
157–60
double-/single-loop learning 25, 26–30,
90, 92
reflexivity 31–2, 39, 80, 86–7, 118, 149
socio-cultural perspective 30–1
see also reflective writing
transpersonal stance 88–9
Trotter-Mathison, Michelle 8–9, 10, 18,
148, 149
trust 54, 54–6
trustworthiness, hierarchy of 108
truth(s) 76–7, 87
Turnbull, Oliver 65, 65–6

U
unconditional positive regard 72
unconscious, the 65–6, 151, 153, 154
understanding 4
dialectic process of 79–80, 82–3
phenomenological 4–5, 59–60, 69–70,
79–80
see also empathy
universality of experience effect 148

V
validity, research 117, 118
'venting' effect, writing 149–50
Verstehen/Erklärung 79
vulnerability 54–6

W
warmth, person-centred therapy
70–1, 73
Weinberger, Joel 74
Wheeler, Sue 105
Winnicott, Donald 15, 25, 29, 48
Withers, Melanie 53
witnessing, therapy as 3, 77
Wosket, Val 47–8
writing 12, 44–5
case studies 113
creative 7, 150–5
as research 104–6
three stages of 150
'venting' effect 149–50
see also reflective writing

Y
Yalom, Irvin 69, 11

IN DEO VERITAS - CAPTAIN GENERAL

Wargaming the Age of Marlborough and the Great Northern War

Philip Garton

HELION &
COMPANY

Helion & Company Limited
Unit 8 Amherst Business Centre
Budbrooke Road
Warwick
CV34 5WE
England
Tel. 01926 499 619
Email: info@helion.co.uk
Website: www.helion.co.uk
Twitter: @helionbooks
Visit our blog: blog.helion.co.uk

Published by Helion & Company 2020
Designed and typeset by Mary Woolley, Battlefield Design (www.battlefield-design.co.uk)
Cover designed by Paul Hewitt, Battlefield Design (www.battlefield-design.co.uk)

Text © Philip Garton 2020
Map design by Philip Garton © Helion & Company 2020
All artwork © Helion & Company 2020
Front cover figure is a grenadier of the Savoy-Piedmont Infantry Regiment Guardie 1709 by artist Bruno Mugnai © Helion & Company 2020
Acknowledgements: Helion Wargames would like to thank all those gamers who contributed photographs of their collections.

ISBN 978-1-914059-38-4

For details of other military history titles published by Helion & Company Limited contact the above address or visit our website: http://www.helion.co.uk.

We always welcome receiving book proposals from prospective authors.

Contents

Chapter 1

Introduction

In Europe, the first two decades of the eighteenth century were characterised by almost constant warfare. In the West, many countries had been involved in the Nine Years' War, which ended in 1697. The peace didn't last long and by 1701 the same major powers had started to fight again in the War of the Spanish Succession. This war has several large battles featuring one of the most famous commanders of the time, John Churchill, the 1st Duke of Marlborough. Ultimately, despite their battlefield successes, Marlborough and his famous colleague Prince Eugene of Savoy, lost political influence and were replaced. Peace was achieved in 1713 but it didn't last for long and the first two decades of the eighteenth-century end with the war of the Quadruple Alliance (1718–20). Elsewhere, the Danes and Swedes, who had been fighting each other on and off in the previous century, opened the century by starting another war: The Great Northern War. This would last for the twenty years of this expansion. Despite its name, the fighting was not confined to the North. It covered a vast area from Finland in the North to Turkey in the south. In this last theatre, the Ottoman Empire simply continued its battles of the previous century, spanning conflicts with Russia, the Austrians and the Venetian Empire.

There should be no shortage of inspiration for players interested in this period.

Command

Perceived success in combat remained the main selection mechanism for commanders in most armies. There's nothing very different in these two decades from the previous century. Given the expansion of armies there were many political appointments but also a much wider pool of experienced commanders. On balance the current rule mechanisms are fine. As stated in the rules, if you have evidence for any particular commander's characteristics then please use it to inform his profile.

Changes over the period

Infantry combat was more linear at the end of the seventeenth century. The trend towards linear battle lines continued in the first two decades of the eighteenth centuryandcavalry would remain the decisive element in most battles.

The infantry component was still not very mobile. Most countries lacked agreed drill manuals to organise the processes for moving bodies of troops, and a fixed pace for marching (cadenced step) would not be in use for another couple of decades. The flintlock

musket would become dominant, although in the first few years of the century the matchlock was still commonly used. The biggest change was the shift from pike-armed to musket-armed troops. Bayonets were still in their infancy and this limited the firepower of the infantry. Combat remained a close-range business.

Most artillery was still too heavy to play a significant role but its effects were clear. Development focused on lighter guns to support the infantry. Despite its effects, some countries did not adopt the newer technology until much later.

Chapter 2

Army Composition

The High Command and army structure

During this period armies tended to be larger. When an army is over 20,000 men it should include at least one **Subordinate Commander**.

Infantry Wings

The **'Early Tercios'** have disappeared.

Brigades

The most common unit of the period was the formed infantry unit of between 900–1200 men. Frequently called a **'Brigade'**, each unit represents a grouping of regiments. These would typically be musket armed men. Some units may retain a pike armed component.

Companies

'Artillery'. The guns were still difficult to move effectively. Developments in gun carriage design didn't match the progress in the manufacture of the gun barrels. More importantly, the ranges that could be achieved and the weight of shot both increased over the period.

Most armies had **Field Artillery** (firing shot between 4–8lbs). For some armies **Infantry Guns** (firing shot of up to 4lbs) became an important tactical element.

There were a few set-piece battles where **Heavy Artillery** (firing over 8lb shot) was used.

A common ratio for artillery remained around 1 company (4–6 guns) per 8 infantry brigades (fractions rounded down). The gradual increase in artillery meant that some armies, although by no means all, might achieve a ratio of 1 company per 5 infantry brigades.

Cavalry Wings

Brigades

The earlier **'Double Brigades'** have disappeared.

The major unit is the **'Brigade'** of 400–600 men. It usually represents a grouping from a number of regiments. The debate between shooting and charging attacks is very much alive at this time.

Some countries organised their dragoon troops into regiments which were large enough to be considered as **'Brigades'** under these rules. The purpose was to increase the amount of cavalry available and their previous role, as mounted infantry, became secondary. The limitations of lower-quality horses and equipment tended to continue and so many of these units should be rated as Raw. These large dragoon units may deploy as two single 'company' bases but may not recombine during a battle.

Companies

'Commanded Muskets' (infantry detachments in cavalry wings) have disappeared.

Chapter 3

Basing

Many players may wish to use the 80mm wide bases that they already have from other rulesets. This doesn't present any problem as these rules are not written to be dependent on a 4mm difference (6mtrs in scale terms). Indeed, many of the playtesters' bases had edges that are not perfectly square, and often had basing material over their edges. The main aim of the rules is to get an enjoyable experience, without the need for micro-measurement.

Chapter 4

Troop Quality

As in the previous century, it's difficult to gain accurate information about the state of a unit before a battle, and performance on the day could be varied. As with the Commanders' Characteristics you should consider the historical performance as a guide to the ratings that you use.

Raw – This reflects the state of many regiments during the period. Regiments that are newly raised, lack organisation (perhaps garrison troops), or affected by disease/exhaustion are generally, but not always, raw.

Trained – Regiments with a core of experienced soldiers, and been in existence for some time may be called Trained.

Veteran – A unit that has been in the field for three years or more, and not destroyed at some point, could be Veteran. A unit formed from selected elite companies should be considered Veteran.

There are no changes to the following chapters:

Chapter 5 The Battlefield	Chapter 6 Deployment
Chapter 7 Events	Chapter 8 Disorder
Chapter 9 Sequence of Play	Chapter 10 Orders
Chapter 13 Retreats	Chapter 14 Impetuous Pursuit

Chapter numbers in the above table refer to those used in the rulebook *In Deo Veritas*

Chapter 5

Movement

Deploying artillery

Deploying Field Artillery takes a full move without moving and the unit may fire in the immediately following combat phase. Limbering Field Artillery before moving takes a half move.

Chapter 6

Combat

The main changes in the Combat Table reflect the removal of the Tercios and Double Brigades.

The only other change is to add a line for musket-armed infantry brigades. There may be a few pikemen in these units but their impact is minimal. By the end of the period all armies had moved over to musket-armed brigades.

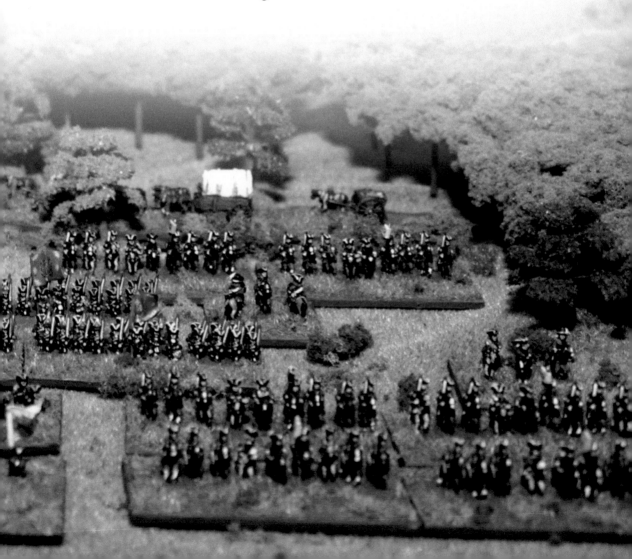

	Range	Shooting	Melee
Infantry detachments, dismounted dragoons	3 ins	1	1
Irregular infantry	3 ins	1	2
'Rabble' infantry and March Columns	-	-	1
Infantry brigades (pike armed)	3 ins	2#	2*
Infantry brigades (musket armed)	3 ins	3#	2
Cavalry brigades	2 ins	1	3
Dragoon company (mounted)	2 ins	1	1
Irregular cavalry	2 ins	1	1
Infantry guns (up to 4lb shot)	8 ins	1	-
Field Artillery (4–8lb shot)	16 ins	1	-
Heavy Artillery (over 8lb shot)	30 ins	1	-

Chapter 7

Cohesion

Shameful Conduct

Given the steady improvement in the quality of generalship over the first two decades of the eighteenth century this is now an Optional rule.

The Battle of Luzzara, 15th August 1702

After several months of defeat the French army in Italy was given a new commander. Appointed in June 1702, Vendôme set out to seize the initiative for the Imperial forces. By the end of July he had captured Guastalla and turned north to cut the Imperial army's supply line. He stopped near to the town of Luzzara, which is close to the River Po. The Imperial commander, Eugene of Savoy, reacted to the challenge and, taking as many of his troops as possible, he quickly marched to block the French.

To the west of Luzzara, there were several raised banks to prevent the river from flooding the countryside. A major road passed from Eugene's base in Mantua to Guastalla. This road sat on top of one of the embankments and it would form an important feature on the battlefield. Eugene planned to use the bank to cover his attack on the French in their camp south of Luzzara. His plan was to force his way through his opponents and to cut them from their supply bases across the Po.

Arriving in position on the 15th August, Eugene organised his attack in two columns: the left wing under Commercy, the right under Starhemberg. The Imperialists approached the French camp. Unfortunately, they were discovered about midday. Vendôme called in his troops and moved north to confront his enemy. The French had no immediate plan and would deploy on the battlefield as they arrived. Eugene sent out a reconnaissance and saw that the French had reacted more quickly than he expected. He set out to reorganise his attack

to focus his main effort on his right. This took time. Time which Vendôme used to get more units into position.

Despite this problem, Eugene was committed. If the French could concentrate their forces they outnumbered his army, and there were 10,000 more enemy troops on the other side of the Po. They would be across the river by tomorrow. It was attack now or retreat. Eugene chose to attack.

His changes to the deployment of his forces meant that he did not move off until 5:00 p.m. Time was running short so Eugene urged his columns to attack all along the line. His right wing almost isolated the French wing facing it but the French line managed to hold. In the centre and on the left, Eugene's troops attacked, were repulsed, and attacked again. Vendôme had to commit his troops as they arrived. The casualties mounted on both sides as the fighting continued past 9:00 p.m. The gathering night and sheer fatigue eventually brought the battle to a close.

Casualties on both sides were heavy. An average of some sources gives the French at 4,000 dead and wounded; the Imperial army lost slightly fewer at 2,500 but Eugene was less able to replace his losses. In effect, the overall result was a bloody draw although, in line with the practice of the times, both sides claimed it as a victory. They both dug lines of entrenchments and settled down to watch each other. Vendôme eventually moved from these lines in September.

Total engaged	No. of Brigades	Horse	Foot	Guns
French	26	8,000	16,000	24
Imperialist	27	7,000	13,000	35

A note on the numbers engaged

A German source says that Eugene had around 11,000 infantry and 9,000 cavalry, a total of about 20,000 men. He left 1,000 cavalry to cover the camp at Sailetto. There were also 1,200 unmounted cavalrymen in the camp, so it's likely that several of Eugene's cavalry units were understrength. According to the source, 'The infantry battalions [38] numbered little more than 300 men on average, the Squadrons [80] just over 100 horses.' Far from the hypothetical figure given by multiplying the number of battalions/squadrons by their organisational strength!

Similarly, the figure of French forces varies depending on whether the author has used a list for Vendôme's army as available on the day of battle. An earlier list from June shows 60 battalions, and doesn't include Savoyard or Spanish allied troops, but one source for the latter shows just 41, including his allies. The cavalry has 102 squadrons in the former but only 83 in the latter. At an average of 90 men to a squadron and 300 to a battalion, there's considerable potential for debate about the actual strengths engaged. Assuming the French were similarly understrength (38 v 41 bns and 80 v 83 sqdns) then the actual numbers engaged could have been closer than some sources suggest. This would help to explain the duration of the battle.

The French reserve of 4 battalions and 8 squadrons did not participate in the battle.

Objectives:

- The primary Imperialist aim is to break through to Guastalla. To achieve this, they must exit at least 4 brigades off the table to the South. This would be a major victory.

- Their secondary aim is to break the Will of the French army and force it to retreat, which would be a minor victory.

- The primary French aim is to stop the Imperialist force exiting to the south. Fewer than 2 Imperialist brigades exiting would be a major victory. If 5 or more brigades exit then it would be a major defeat.

- A secondary aim is to break the Will of the Imperialist army and force it to retreat. This would also be a major victory.

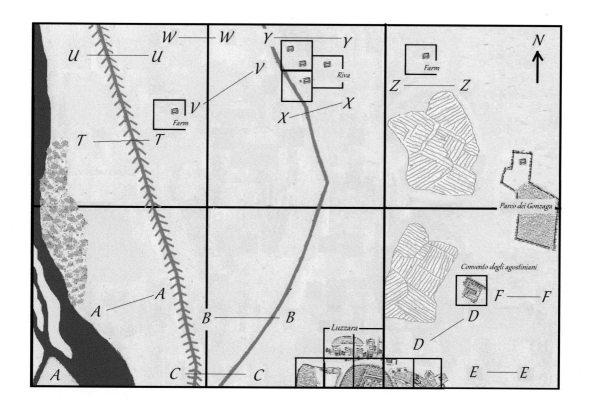

Game time Start at 6:00 p.m.   **Game length** 12 turns

Some notes on the terrain:

- Buildings – Luzzara, Riva, the convent and the two farms are all buildings.

- Enclosures – the area of the Parco dei Gonzaga is a walled enclosure.

- Difficult ground – the two areas on the eastern side represent areas of cultivated fields with ditches and vines so are considered difficult ground.

- The westernmost road is on a significant embankment – it counts as a linear obstacle but it also blocks any Line of Sight passing through it. Units on top of the road would be visible to either side.

Imperialist Army: Prinz Eugen of Savoy

Right Column – Starhemberg					
First Wing		**Second Wing**		**Third Wing**	
Guttenstein		**Trautmansdorff**		**Vaudemont**	
Grenadiers (Right)	T	Solari IR	T	Vaudemont CR	T
Nigrelli IR	T	G. Starhemberg IR	T	Neuburg CR	T
Infantry guns	T	Liechtenstein IR	T	Corbelli CR	T
Savoyen DR	T	*Infantry guns*	T	Alt Darmstadt CR	T
		Artillery	T	Commercy CR	T
		Herbeville DR	T		

Left Column – Commercy					
First Wing		Second Wing		Third Wing	
Liechtenstein		Haxthausen		Serenyi	
Grenadiers (Left)	T	Kriechbaum IR	T	Taafe CR	T
Bagni IR	T	Gehlen IR	T	Palffy CR	T
Infantry guns	T	Prins Carl (Danes)	T	Lothringen CR	T
Serenyi DR	T	Jung Daun IR	T	Vaubonne DR	T
		Infantry guns	T		
		Artillery	T		
		Trautmansdorff DR	T		
		Visconti			
		Guttenstein IR	T		
		Heberstein IR	T		
		Dronningen (Danes)	T		
		Infantry guns			

Optional rule:

The Imperial dragoon units (DR) were large by comparison to many other regiments. For example, the Savoyen regiment mustered around 600 men around the time of the battle.

In this battle there are reports of Imperialist dragoons fighting on foot. To reflect this, the Imperial dragoon regiments (DR) may dismount as 2 company-sized units. The dismounted units may not reform as a brigade during the battle.

Deploys:

Guttenstein   T – T   Trautmansdorf   U – U   Vaudemont   V – V
Visconti   W – W
Liechtenstein   X – X   Haxthausen   Y – Y   Serenyi   Z – Z

French Army: Duc de Vendôme

Left column infantry – Albergotti			
Langallerie		**Médavy**	
Piedmont IR	V	Saulx IR	T
La Marine IR	T	Lyonnais IR	T
La Rocque (Savoy)	T	Auvergne IR	T
Dillon IR	V	D'Aguilar (Spanish)	
Artillery	T	*Artillery (Spanish)*	T

Left column cavalry – de Créquy			
Bezons		**de Mongon**	
Montpeyroux	T	Rennepont	V
Sully	T	Gendarmerie	V
Carabiniers	T	D'Este (Spanish)	T
Monroy (Spanish) DR	T	*Dauphin DR*	T
Sennecterre DR	T	*Lautrec DR*	T

Deploys:

Langallerie A – A   Médavy B – B   Bezons C – C
De Mongon enters following Bezons any turn after Turn 1.
One field artillery company deploys on the island A.

Right column infantry – Vaubecourt			
de Murcey		**Sezanne**	
Perche	T	Anjou	T
Vaisseaux	T	Palavicini (Savoy)	T
Albemarle	T	Ile de France	T
Artillery	T	*Artillery*	T

Right column cavalry – de Revel			
de Roussy		**Barbessieres**	
Bordage	T	Broglio	T
D'Ourches	T	Choiseul	T
Vaudeuil	T	De Las Torres (Spanish)	T
D'Estrades DR	T	*S.A.R. (Savoy) DR*	T
Languedoc DR	T	*Genovese (Savoy) DR*	T

Deploys:

**Murcey D – D   Sezanne E – E   De Roussy F – F
Barbessieres enters on the south edge of the
battlefield, east of Luzzara any turn after Turn 2.**

The Battle of Speyerbach (Spire), 15th November 1703

In November 1703 two allied forces were heading to break the French siege of Landau. On the morning of the 15th the two commanders, the Erbprinz of Hesse-Kassel and the Graf of Nassau-Weilburg, met in Speyer and celebrated the Emperor's Name Day. They argued about command of the arrangements and the order of battle for the coming attack. Partly due to this lack of agreement the Allied camp was disorganised. Additionally, not all of their forces had arrived.

Aware of the opportunity to attack the dispersed allies the French commander, Marshal Tallard, had called in his outlying troops and by 8:00 a.m. his army was marching toward Speyer. It completed its deployment without interference and advanced toward the Allied camp. It was almost noon when the allied commanders in Speyer finally realised the French were attacking. They still lacked an agreed order of battle and this added to the chaos. As fighting commenced, Vehlen wanted to prevent the envelopment of his wing and moved to his left. Bourscheidt's infantry could not move as quickly and gaps were created in the front line.

On their right the French were successful. Their infantry drove Vehlen's cavalry back. The cavalry lost its cohesion and fled. The

French infantry then attacked the Palatine infantry. Exposed by the flight of the cavalry this also fled. A major part of the allied army had ceased to resist. The French then moved to envelop the Hessians.

Initially, there was good news for the Erbprinz. The Hessian cavalry won the fight against its French opponents and Pracontal was killed. The French infantry, however, pushed on into the Hessian foot. This was a bitter contest and caused significant casualties. The Hessian Grenadiers and several other regiments suffered over 50% casualties. It was during this period The French sustained many of their casualties. The Erbprinz dismounted to fight with his troops but his cause was lost.

The battle ended about 4:00 p.m. Covered by the remaining Hessian cavalry, the Hessian troops started their retreat toward the bridges over the Speyerbach. Tallard was content that the threat to his siege of Landau had been destroyed. He did not hinder the Hessian withdrawal or pursue the fleeing Palatinate troops.

There are estimates that indicate the Hessen-Kassel army lost about 2,500 men killed, wounded or taken prisoner. Nassau-Weilburg's army lost about 4,000 killed or wounded and about 2,000 taken prisoner. French losses were estimated to be as many as 4,000 killed or wounded.

The most immediate result of the battle was that the Alliance lost its supply train and artillery. Worse was to come. After hearing the result of the battle, the defenders of Landau capitulated at 5:00 p.m. Tallard's victory was complete.

Total engaged	No. of Brigades	Horse	Foot	Guns
Allied	25	5,500	18,000	10
French	23	8,500	15,000	15

Objectives:

- The Allies' primary aim is to break the Will of the French army and force it to retreat. This would be a major victory.

- The primary French aim is to break the Will of the Allied army and force it to retreat. This would be a major victory.

- A secondary aim is to stop the Allies exiting to the south. Fewer than 3 brigades exiting would be a minor victory. If 8 or more brigades exit then it would be a major defeat.

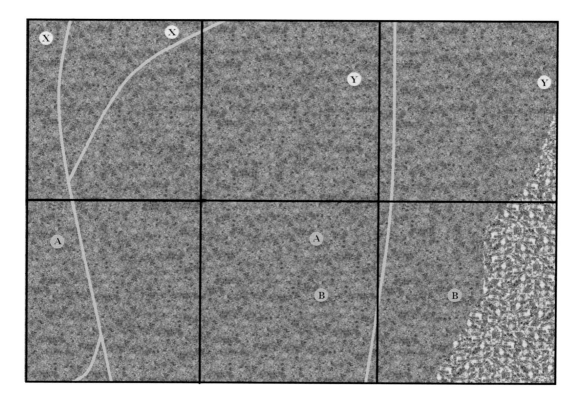

Game time Start at 12:00 p.m.   **Game length**   16 turns

Allied Army: No overall commander

Erbprinz von Hessen-Kassel							
Right cavalry		**Left infantry**		**Reserve**			
Spiegel		Hessen-Homburg		Schulenburg			
Bde Leib	T	Grenadiere IR	V	Stuckradt IR	T		
Bde Goden	T	Leib IR	V	Schenck IR	T		
Erbprinz DR	T	Anhalt-Bernberg IR	T	Tielemann IR	T		
Haremberg DR	T	Charles IR	T	*Hesse-Homburg DR*	T		
Schmettau DR	T	Erbprinz IR	T	*Schulenburg DR*	T		
Stubenvoll DR	T	Prinz Wilhelm IR	T				
		Wartensleben IR	T				
		Artillery	T				

Graf von Nassau Weilburg – arrives on turn 2							
Left cavalry		**Right infantry**		**Reserve**			
Vehlen		Bourscheidt		Aubach			
Bde Darmstadt	T	Leib & Grenadiere IRs	V	Darmstadt IR	T		
Bde Frankenberg	T	Lybeck IR	T	Isselbach IR	T		
Bde Hochkirch	T	Rehbinder IR	T	Barbo IR	T		
Bde Leib	T	Saxe-Meiningen IR	T	N. Weilburg IR	T		
Venningen DR	T	*Artillery*	T	Bde Lecheraine (cav)	T		
Wittgenstein DR	T			*Leiningen DR*	T		

Deploys: Hessen-Kassel X – X, Reserve enters on Turn 2 behind the front rank.

Nassau-Weilburg Y – Y, Reserve enters on Turn 3 behind the front rank.

French Army: Marechal de Tallard

First Line – Deploys A – A			
Left Cavalry		Right Cavalry	
Pracontal		Locmaria	
Bde Forsat	T	Bde d'Humieres	V
Bde Puiguion	T	Bde Vertilly	V
Bde Silly	T	Bde La Valliere	T
Flavacourt DR	T	*Col.-General DR*	T
Le Roi DR	T	*La Reine DR*	T
Mestre de Camp DR	T	*Rohan DR*	T

Centre Infantry			
Surville		Clerembault	
Croy IR	T	Navarre IR	V
Le Roi IR	T	La Marche IR	T
Orleans IR	T	Royal IR	T
Surbeck IR	T	Sillery IR	T
Artillery	T	*Artillery*	T

Second Line – Deploys B – B					
Left Cavalry		Centre Infantry		Right Cavalry	
Grammont		**Hornes**		**St. Maurice**	
Bde Chepy	T	Robecque IR	T	Bde d'Asfeld	T
Bde Fraula	T	Grenada IR	T	Bde du Chatelet	T
		Brie IR	T	Bde Gaetano	T
		St. Second IR	T		
Artillery		T			

The Battle of Helsingborg, 28th February 1710

In November 1709, with the main Swedish army shattered by defeat at Poltava in July, a Danish force under General Reventlow was landed unopposed in the Swedish province of Scania. The main Danish objective was to capture the Swedish naval base at Karlskrona. In order to offer any resistance troops had to be gathered in from a variety of depots. The Swedish commander, General Stenbock retreated, trading space for time. Several of his regiments were rapidly constituted and they were exclusively armed with muskets; not equipped with the usual third of the men armed with pikes.

By January 1710, the Danes were ready to advance on their main target. Stenbock was preparing his counter-attack. His target was Helsingborg, the key to the Danish supply lines. Reventlow, saw the threat and turned to meet the Swedes, but he was taken ill and command passed to General Rantzau. Rantzau hurried back to Helsingborg with his force of 10,000 infantry and 4,000 horse. He deployed the army in a defensive, blocking line on a north–south axis.

On the morning of 28th February Stenbock marched south towards Helsingborg. A thick fog lay over the two armies. When it lifted Rantzau saw that the Swedish army was deploying on his left and he sent troops to reinforce that flank. Around midday, Rantzau's artillery on the Ringstorp heights started firing on the advancing Swedes. Rantzau was expecting the Swedish attack to fall on his weaker left flank and shifted his right toward the east. Stenbock also turned his army east towards the Danish right flank. The Danes saw this as an attempt to encircle their exposed flank, and to prevent this they marched further east. This opened

up gaps in the line that couldn't be filled. At the eastern end of the line the Danes were initially successful, the Swedes were repelled and the opposing Swedish commander, Burenskjöld, was captured.

The Swedes slowly forced the Danes backwards. Rantzau joined in the fighting but he was seriously wounded. It has been said that a rumour developed on the Danish east flank that the Swedes were attacking from behind. For whatever reason, the entire flank collapsed, with the troops retreating back to Helsingborg. Rantzau's loss from the field was also felt in the centre of the Danish line. These remaining Danes had great difficulties resisting the Swedish assault and, seeing the collapse of their eastern flank, the centre also started to buckle.

At this point in the battle, the Swedes attacked the gap that had formed between the Danish centre and the western flank. In the centre, the elite regiments of the Guards and the Grenadier Korps tried to resist the Swedish advance to allow the other forces to pull back in good order. They caused serious casualties amongst the attacking Swedes but their efforts were in vain. They were in danger of being surrounded as the Swedish cavalry pursued the fugitives on both left and right. The situation was increasingly untenable for the Danes. The senior commander remaining, Major-General Valentin von Eickstedt, ordered a general retreat and the Danes fled into Helsingborg, bringing the battle to an end.

The Danish army was crippled by the engagement. It lost 1,500 men killed, 3,500 men wounded and 2,700 men captured. It was trapped within the walls of Helsingborg. The Swedes were camped outside and Stenbock invited the Danes to capitulate. His offer was rejected. The Swedes lacked the control of the sea needed for a traditional siege. So, Stenbock settled down to bombard the city.

By 5th March the remains of the Danish army had taken to their ships and left Scania, never to return.

Total engaged	No. of Brigades	Horse	Foot	Guns
Swedish	20	5,000	11,000	30
Danish	16	3,500	12,500	30

Objectives:

- The Swedish army's primary aim is to break the Will of the Danish army and force it to retreat. This would be a major victory.

- The primary Danish aim is to break the Will of the Swedish army and force it to retreat. This would be a major victory.

- A secondary aim is to stop the Swedish force exiting to the south. No brigades exiting would be a minor victory. If 5 or more brigades exit then it would be a major defeat.

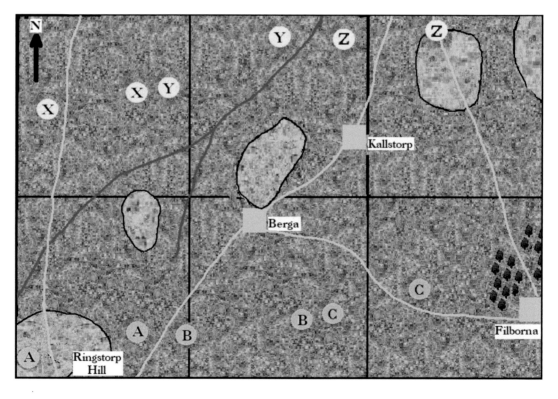

Game time Start at 11:00 a.m.   **Game length** 15 turns

Swedish Army: General Stenbock

First line							
Left cavalry		**Centre infantry**		**Right cavalry**			
Buhrenskjöld		**Taube**		**Meyerfeldt**			
Västgöta CR	T	Jönköping IR *	T	Ankedrottingen CR	V		
Östgöta CR	T	Kronoberg IR	T	Livregiment CR	V		
Västgöta 3M CR	T	Saxon IR *	T	Småland CR	T		
		Infantry Guns	T	Uppland 5M CR	T		
		Infantry Guns					

Lewenhaupt		Palmquist		
Skanska 3M CR	T	Älvsborg IR *	T	
Småland CR	T	Småland 5M IR *	T	
Gyllenstierna DR	T	Uppland 5M IR *	T	
		Infantry Guns	T	
		Infantry Guns	T	

Second line	
Von der Noth	
Kalmar IR	T
Östgötland IR	T
Sodermanland IR *	T
Uppland IR	T
Västmanland IR	T
Infantry Guns	T

* Units marked with an asterisk have a 'traditional' (1/3rd) allocation of pikes. All other infantry units are musket armed.

Deploys: Right   X – X,   Centre Y – Y,   Left   Z – Z
Von der Noth enters on Turn 1 behind the Centre.

Danish Army: General Rantzau

First line					
Left cavalry		**Centre infantry**		**Right cavalry**	
Devitz		**Eichstedt**		**Rodstein**	
1st Fynske CR	T	Dronningen's IR	V	Livgarden til Hest CR	V
1st Jyske CR	T	Grenadiere Corps	V	1st Sjaellandske CR	T
Bulow DR	T	Livgarde til Fods IR	V	Prins Christian's IR	T
Bulow DR	T	Fynske IR	T	*Livregiment DR*	T
Field Artillery	T	Jyske IR	T	*Livregiment DR*	T
Field Artillery	T	*Infantry Guns*	T	*Sjaellandske DR*	T
		Infantry Guns	T		

Second line			
Sprengel		**Hessen**	
Leepel IR	T	Prins v. Hessen IR	T
Mariner IR	T	Lollandske IR	T
Sjaellandske DR	T	East Sjaellandske IR	T
		West Sjaellandske IR	T
		Infantry Guns	T

Deploys: Right A – A, Centre B – B, Left C – C

The second line enters on Turn 1 behind the respective first lines.

The Battle of Francavilla, 20th June 1719

The War of the Spanish Succession ended in 1713 with the Peace of Utrecht. Spain resented the outcome, having lost many of her overseas territories. In 1717 this pressure broke into open conflict. In August, Spanish forces recaptured Sardinia virtually unopposed. This success was followed up in 1718 by a landing of 30,000 men on Sicily. The invasion was initially successful, but in August 1718 the Spanish navy was defeated. The Spanish army in Sicily was now isolated from its base.

In contrast, its Imperial opponents received reinforcements from Italy. In May 1719, under the command of the Earl of Mercy, an army of 24,000 men set out to attack the Spanish army besieging Melazzo. The Spanish commander, the Marquis de Lede, was forced to abandon his siege. The Imperialists pursued and a battle became inevitable.

De Lede deployed his army skilfully. He chose a site near the town of Francavilla that was protected by a river, and centred on a heavily built Capuchin convent. The convent was built on a hill that dominated the flood plain through which the Imperialists would approach. On this major feature the Spanish deployed 4 battalions of Guards and a few light guns. Behind this major feature was the town of Francavilla and a dry stream bed, along this line the Spanish entrenched 5 infantry battalions. The end of the line was guarded by 6 cavalry squadrons. To the right of the convent, the Spanish deployed 17 infantry battalions and 12 squadrons of dragoons entrenchments alongside the river.

The Imperial army approached in three columns. The first of these descended from the hills opposite the Spanish line and waited for the other columns to launch their attacks. The aim was to pin the Spanish main body in its entrenchments. The second column marched along the road to Melazzo in its divisions, one after another, to attack the convent hill. This attack was to be combined with the attack of the third column approaching through the high ground to the north. This third column was to climb over the ridge and attack downhill towards the convent.

This flanking attack disorganised the defending Spanish. The second column now joined in, forcing the Spanish back. There was heavy fighting during which the Imperialist commander, Mercy, was wounded and had to leave the field.

On the Spanish left, Seckendorff attacked the trench defending the town of Francavilla three times, but was repulsed at every attempt. On the Spanish right, the Imperialist main body finally launched itself in a frontal attack. The Spanish behind their entrenchments successfully resisted. Although fighting continued it was fairly clear that there would be no decisive outcome.

The battle finally ended around 8:00 p.m., when the Imperialist army began to withdraw. The Spanish army stayed in its entrenchments and did not pursue. Lacking artillery, which had already been sent back, and cavalry, de Lede had little choice but to continue his own withdrawal. The Imperialists recovered and moved on to besiege Messina. Without command of the sea to ensure supplies, that city surrendered in October. The lack of supplies was critical and by May 1720 de Lede had signed an armistice. What remained of his army was evacuated later that year.

As with many battles of the period there are no accurate records for the losses of either side. Some partisan sources indicate the Austrians suffered 6,000 casualties (dead and wounded) and the Spanish fewer than 1,000. By contrast an Austrian source states Mercy's loss as 850 dead and 2,400 wounded. The truth is undoubtedly somewhere between.

Total engaged	No. of Brigades	Horse	Foot	Guns
Spanish	16	2,500	15,500	4
Imperialist	19	3,000	17,000	12

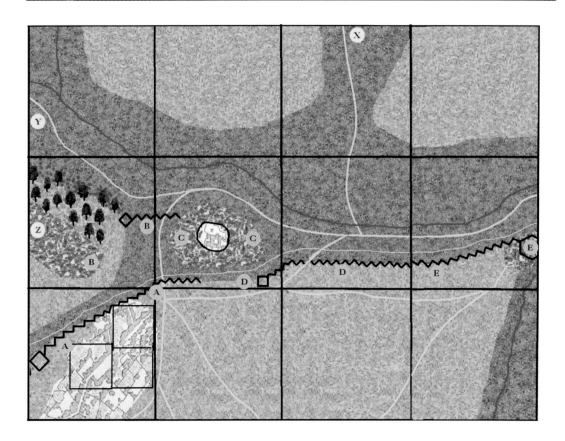

The table for this battle is 4' x 3'. Each square is 1' x 1'.

Game time Start at 4:00 p.m.   **Game length**   12 turns

Some notes on the terrain:

- Buildings – Francavilla, and the convent are buildings.

- Difficult ground – the area to the south of Francavilla represents cultivated fields. The area around the convent was cultivated with ditches and vines. The area to the eastern edge was rocky ground. The area on the western edge was an outcrop overlooking the Alcantara river.

- Streams – the stream in front of the entrenchments is dry and does not affect movement or combat. Its purpose is purely visual.

- Fortifications – the zig-zag black lines show the Spanish entrenchments (Fortifications p.27).

Objectives:

- The Imperialists' aim is to break the Will of the Spanish army and force it to retreat. This would be a major victory.

- The only Spanish aim is to stop the Imperialists breaking the will of the Spanish army.

<u>Spanish Army</u>: Marquis de Lede

Left rear		Left pickets		Centre left	
Almendariz		**Tenqueur**		**Marquis de Villadarias**	
Castile IR	T	Cantabria IR	T	Spanish Guards IR	V
Guadalajara IR	T	*Borgona IR*	T	Spanish Guards IR	V
Farnese CR	T	*Hainault IR*	T	Walloon Guards IR	V
Flandres CR	T	*Utrecht IR*	T	Walloon Guards IR	V
		*Combined elite cav coys **	V	*Infantry Guns*	T

Centre right		Reserve		Right	
Carvajal		D'Huart		Araziel	
Ultonia IR	V	*Edinburgh DR*	T	Cordoba IR	T
Asturias IR	T	*Frisia DR*	T	Milan IR	T
Saboya IR	T	*Batavia DR*	T	Lombardia IR	T
Aragon IR	T	*Lusitania DR*	T		

* *The combined elite cavalry companies are treated as a sub-unit of veteran dragoons.*

Deploys:

Left rear A – A, Left pickets B – B, Centre left C – C

Centre right D – D, Right E – E

Reserve behind Centre Wings (may deploy dismounted)

Imperialist Army: Graf von Mercy

First column		Second column		Third column	
Wallis		**Zum Jungen**		**Seckendorff**	
G. Starhemberg IR	T	Ansbach IR	T	Alt-Wallis IR	V
Holstein IR	T	Wetzel IR	T	Alt-Württemberg IR	V
Loffelholz IR	T	O'Dwyer IR	T	Hesse-Kassel IR	T
Traun IR	T	Konigsegg IR	T	M. Starhemberg IR	T
Converged Grenadiers	V	Converged Grenadiers	V	Converged Grenadiers	V
Field Artillery	T			*Ebergenyi HR*	T
Field Artillery	T				

Eck	
Hannover CR	T
Portugal CR	T
Ansbach DR	T
Tighe DR	T

Deploys:

On Turn 1 – Wallis enters deployed at X.

On Turn 2 – Zum-Jungen enters at Y in road column. Eck follows this column.

On Turn 3 – Seckendorff enters deployed within 6" of Z.

Optional arrival –

On Turn 2 – dice for Seckendorff's arrival. He must score 1 or 2 to enter. If he scores 3–6 dice again on Turn 3 – he arrives on 1–3. If he fails again, he arrives automatically on Turn 4.